AFT

ANTONY LOEWENSTEIN is an independent journalist, author, filmmaker and co-founder of Declassified Australia. He has written for *The Guardian, New York Times* and *New York Review of Books*. He is the author of the bestselling book, *The Palestine Laboratory: How Israel Exports the Technology of Occupation Around the World*, which won the 2023 Walkley Book Award. His other books include *Pills, Powder and Smoke, Disaster Capitalism* and *My Israel Question*. He was based in East Jerusalem between 2016 and 2020.

AHMED MOOR is a Palestinian American writer and activist. He received a Masters in Public Policy from Harvard as well as a Soros Fellowship, and has written for the *Washington Post, Los Angeles Times, London Review of Books, Guardian* and Al Jazeera English. He is the founder and was formerly the CEO of an emerging markets lender based in Amman, Jordan. He now resides in Philadelphia where he is an elected Committee Person in the Democratic Party.

"Nothing will change until we are capable of imagining a radically different future. By bringing together many of the clearest and most ethical thinkers about the Israeli–Palestinian conflict, this book gives us the intellectual tools we need to do just that. Courageous and exciting." Naomi Klein

"This book is nothing if not thought-provoking, in the best sense of the phrase ... *After Zionism* is an uncompromising book which boldly relinquishes nationalism in favour of human rights as an organising paradigm ... these essays point the way to a possibly rewarding and perhaps inevitable new direction for the Palestinian struggle." *Ceasefire Magazine*

'Important and timely ... a significant contribution to the literature on the one-state/two-state debate.' *Electronic Intifada*

"*After Zionism* is rich in history and context, pointing to many failures in the past or attempts at two-state solutions that form a convincing argument for its abandonment."
Middle East Monitor

"*After Zionism* provides a stimulating and much needed critique of the present reality in the Holy Land."
Washington Report on Middle Eastern Affairs

'At a time when Israeli society has shifted increasingly to the right and narrowed the acceptable limits of conversation, this volume offers valuable contributions to a debate that should be front and center, yet is confined to ever-smaller margins.' *Publishers Weekly*

"Timely and readable .... New thinking is needed to climb out of the stultifying box erected by years of meaningless 'peace' negotiations ... This book will hopefully spark a broader debate." *Jordan Times*

After Zionism

ONE STATE FOR ISRAEL AND PALESTINE

Edited by
Antony Loewenstein and Ahmed Moor

SAQI

To our parents,
and the Palestinians and Israelis who deserve better

SAQI BOOKS
Gable House, 18-24 Turnham Green Terrace
London W4 1QP
www.saqibooks.com

First published in 2013 by Saqi Books
This edition published 2024

ISBN 978-0-86356-941-8
eISBN 978-0-86356-739-1

A full CIP record for this book is available from the British Library.

Printed and bound by Clays Ltd, Elcograf, S.p.A

MIX
Paper | Supporting
responsible forestry
FSC® C018072
FSC
www.fsc.org

Contents

Preface to the New Edition

We write this as bombs continue to fall on Gaza, obliterating families and hopes. Achieving true equality and justice for all Israelis and Palestinians is now more urgent than ever. This book presents a realistic alternative to the two-state fiction presented in the White House and the opinion pages of Western media. Clinging onto failed myths about two separate states is a grave disservice to the millions of people in the Middle East who deserve hope that a democratic nation for all is possible.

Some will accuse one-state advocates as unrealistic, dangerous dreamers at a time when Israelis and Palestinians are at war. But it's precisely because we're in this precarious moment that we believe discussing one-state options is so crucial.

The ideology of separatism favoured by the Israeli state – caging millions of Palestinians behind high walls, underground barriers and mass surveillance and under the constant watch of military drones – has failed. It is only through cooperation, sharing resources and addressing historical and present grievances that peace can be achieved.

Ten years ago, when we first published this collection, we believed that the prospects for a two-state outcome to the Israel/Palestine conflict had expired. The basic idea, separation of two people in a small place, a country the size of New Jersey, was a non-starter. In 2009, more than 500,000 Jewish settlers occupied the West Bank and East Jerusalem. Today, that number stands at roughly 750,000 people – a 40 percent increase in just fourteen years. Practically, their presence is an effective coagulant to the Apartheid status quo. There can be no Palestinian state when Jewish Israelis occupy Palestinians, and when Israeli law – which is paramount in the land of Israel/ Palestine – extends to Israeli Jews wherever they may live.

While predictions of the future are always fraught and unreliable, it seems reasonable to say that the number of Israeli settlers will continue to grow out of all proportion to natural population growth. In other words, Israel will continue to transfer large numbers of civilians into occupied territory, unopposed by a divided world.

Numbers comprised one pillar of our argument against the two-state paradigm, but the main force of the discussion was moral. As liberals we do not believe that ethnic, religious states are defensible as such. We conceive of political spaces in which voluntary participation is the basic principle underlying citizenship, in which people, in all their individual diversity, are the only currency that counts. An ethno-religious state, Israel, and an ethnic state, Palestine, do not conform to our view of what a liberal democratic state should be.

So, ten years later we find that our arguments continue to resonate for all the same reasons. Yet much has happened in the intervening period to underline the urgency of the need for change in Israel/Palestine.

During the Obama administration, Washington's once obsessive focus on the Middle East began to shift as US policy strategically redirected towards China and its ambitious foreign policy. This continued during the Trump administration, but with a new dimension: an effort to "normalise" relations between Israel and the autocratic Arab regimes in the Middle East, which began in 2016.

The Biden administration that came to power in 2021 quickly extended the Trump era "Abraham Accords" – the grandiose name ascribed to the series of economic and security arrangements brokered by the United States, linking a handful of anti-democratic regimes in the region to one another and Israel. Yet the effort to sideline the Palestinians has proven disastrous, as was witnessed on 7 October 2023 when the Palestinian group Hamas killed about 1,200 Israeli civilians and soldiers, and in Israel's subsequent genocide in Gaza where at the time of writing, more than 20,000 Palestinians have been killed.

And still, despite everything, the two-state outcome has persisted among policymakers, a zombie whose grotesque aspect has only grown with the number of dead in Israel/Palestine. Less than two weeks after the horrific Hamas attack on Israel, US President Joe Biden was in Tel Aviv rehashing old talking points. "We must keep pursuing peace", he said. "We must keep pursuing a path so that Israel and the Palestinian people can both live safely, in security, in dignity and in peace. For me, that means a two-state solution."

As if on cue, the European Union Foreign Policy Chief, Josep Borrell, reiterated the same message soon after. "The solution can only be political, centred on two states," he tweeted. Other Western governments followed suit, speaking as if the Oslo Peace Accords from the early 1990s were a fresh document full of potential, capable of bringing an enduring peace between Israelis and Palestinians.

Seemingly, the White House and its Western allies had missed the rapid expansion of Israeli settlements across the West Bank and East Jerusalem in the last decade and the sharp turn to the far-right of the Israeli public and political establishment. Today, arguments for the forcible transfer of Palestinians into neighbouring states, a repeat of the *Nakba*, have entered the Israeli mainstream.

Eager not to be outdone, *New York Times* columnist Thomas Friedman was desperate to join in on the two-state bandwagon.[1] In late November 2023, he was writing about the need to "revamp" the corrupt Palestinian Authority to enliven the prospects of the two-state solution because it is the "keystone for creating a stable foundation for the normalisation of relations between Israel and Saudi Arabia and the wider Arab Muslim world." Friedman acknowledged that two-state advocates, presumably including him, are looking tired and increasingly irrelevant. "These two-staters right now are on the defensive in both communities in their struggle with the one-staters", he wrote. "Therefore, it is in the highest interest of the United States and all moderates to bring back the two-state alternative."

We regard the renewed talk of a two-state outcome as a cynical diversion. It's the "solution" stated ad nauseam when there is no interest in resolving the century-old conflict between Israelis and Palestinians. It's the "solution" for fewer Israelis and Palestinians than ever before.

Unsurprisingly, the lack of any progress towards peace in the Middle East has negatively impacted the views of Israelis and Palestinians towards the two-state solution. In one Gallup poll, before 7 October, only around one in four Palestinians in East Jerusalem, the West Bank and Gaza supported the idea of a two-state solution.[2]

Backing for two-states has plummeted in the last decade. In 2012, 59 percent of Palestinians had endorsed it.

This collapse was particularly acute for young Palestinians with only one in six between the ages of fifteen and twenty-five support- ing it. As 69 percent of the population in the Occupied Territories is under twenty-nine years of age, disillusionment with the two-state solution will only grow. Unsurprisingly, the majority of Palestinians polled had no faith in US President Biden bringing peace either.

Israeli Jews were equally pessimistic about the two-state solution, although their lives were comparatively privileged compared to Palestinians living under occupation. According to a Pew poll released in September 2023, just 35 percent of Israelis thought it was possible "for Israel and an independent Palestinian state to coexist peacefully."[3] This percentage had dropped 15 points since 2013. Arab Israelis were especially despondent, far more than Jewish Israelis, concerning the likelihood of a two-state solution.

Yet it doesn't follow that Israeli Jews will come around to a single shared state with equal rights for everyone. Indeed, people with privileges have rarely yielded them without some external pressure.

Ten years since the first publication of *After Zionism*, the need to explain and promote the necessity of the one-state solution has never been more vital. How do we put a stop to endless war and Apartheid? What will it take to achieve justice in Israel/Palestine? How do we secure the future? How do we move beyond Zionism – and what comes after Jewish nationalism?

This collection seeks to grapple with those questions. We are grateful to each writer who has contributed to this book. We are privileged to share their company and have learned much from each of them over the years.

The events of 7 October 2023 and since have shaken us profoundly. Hamas's ruthless incursion into Israel and slaughter of Israeli civilians were horrific. But this did not happen in a vacuum. Gaza has been an Israeli laboratory for close to twenty years, blockaded and surrounded by electronic fences, drones and surveillance equipment. The majority of Gazans are unable to move freely outside the territory to work, study, live or receive medical care. Hamas may have sought to turn the world's attention to the plight of the Palestinians, when the world had largely turned away – but their methods were indefensible.

The Israeli retaliation has been devastating. Vast swathes of Gaza are uninhabitable, rendered apocalyptic by relentless Israeli bombing and a merciless ground invasion. Most horrifyingly, Israel has killed more than 7,000 children.

Palestinians are the primary losers in this war between an extremist Israeli government led by Prime Minister Benjamin Netanyahu and a Hamas leadership that faces annihilation in Gaza.

The genocidal rhetoric and actions of the Israeli government are having a profound impact on how Americans, Jews and Palestinians view the conflict. The Netanyahu regime has proud and unrepentant homophobes, racists and bigots in its cabinet, spewing bile on a daily basis against Palestinians.

But this is about so much more than one man, Netanyahu, and if he continues as leader. The far-right fringe has entered the Israeli mainstream, normalising the exterminationist mindset. For too many Israelis, Palestinians are second-class citizens simply because they're not Jewish. Israeli settler-led pogroms, ubiquitous violence against Palestinian civilians and constant house demolitions in the West Bank are all clear signs that Israeli ultranationalists are in charge. These realities have existed for decades, but never on such a disturbing scale.

When we first published this book, the reality of the Israeli occupation was clear to anybody who cared to look. But now, a decade later, there's been a sea-change in how much of the world views the conflict. Today, every leading Israeli and Palestinian human rights group, along with Human Rights Watch and Amnesty International, have concluded that Israel is committing the crime of Apartheid in the Occupied Territories.

This language, of Israeli Apartheid, has entered the mainstream. That is why in March 2023, more than six months before the Hamas attacks, a Gallup poll found for the first time that a majority of American Democrats had more sympathy for Palestinians than Israelis.[4] Eventually and inevitably, endless occupation will incur a political price in the nation that sustains it the most, the United States.

The ubiquity of social media, allowing Palestinians to show

the reality of rampaging Israeli soldiers and settlers, often acting in coordination with one another, has undeniably impacted this global awakening. Don't look away, these Palestinians are telling us: this is the face of Israeli fascism, and it's backed and defended by almost every Western government.

One encouraging sign – and few exist in the current period – is the surge in public Jewish support for Palestinian rights. US-based groups such as Jewish Voice for Peace and If Not Now? dispense with the once-held fears of speaking out against a Jewish establishment that prioritises Jewish lives and narratives. These Jews back equal rights for all citizens in Israel and Palestine, and eschew Zionism as a militant nationalist movement that cannot provide safety and justice for Jews and Palestinians.

This volume's co-editor Ahmed Moor was born in Rafah, in the southern Gaza Strip. Like so many others, he has lost family members to the Israeli onslaught since 7 October 2023, deliberate war crimes by the occupying army. The reality of Israel's war on Palestinians has caused him to question his own conclusion about the possibility of a single state shared by Palestinians and Israelis; the prospect of living alongside Israeli Jews who participated in the genocide is anathema.

Yet, other societies have dealt in atrocity, and from them we draw inspiration. The Truth and Reconciliation Commission of South Africa is illustrative in this regard. The principles of restorative justice, which seeks to repair the harm done to victims as a first principle, hold, no matter how seemingly unforgivable the crime. The only hope for the living – those who survive the genocide and carry forth their cultural memory and real trauma – is to process what's been done to them. There will be no recovering the tens of thousands of dead in Gaza, but honouring their memory must mean a future for all the children who survive. This is why we carry on this work.

There is also the question of what Israel's genocide in Gaza means for Palestinians and Israelis in the diaspora. In the United States, which is the singular contributor to the seventy-five-year conflict, the Democratic party's embrace of Israel after the events of 7 October was expected. More surprising was the near total failure of the foreign policy establishment in managing the genocide and its consequences.

President Biden in particular demonstrated a total lack of empathy for the Palestinians. By embracing Israel, he demonstrated his unsuitability for the job of the Presidency – he failed to meet the needs of a youthful electorate whose demands for justice flow easily from George Floyd, the African American man murdered by a white police officer in Minneapolis in May 2020, to Gaza.

There is an argument that the president is a figurehead – that his advisors, a suite of informed and thoughtful foreign policy staff, steer the ship of state. But that argument necessarily relies on the balance of the evidence for its coherence. Secretary of State Antony Blinken demonstrated his own lack of judgement when he greeted Benjamin Netanyahu not as the US Secretary of State, but rather as a Jewish man on a personal mission in one of his visits to Israel in October 2023. His lack of restraint resulted in creating greater distance between the United States and its Arab allies and Turkey.

Meanwhile, Jake Sullivan, the president's National Security Advisor, chose to publish an essay in *Foreign Affairs* in the week before 7 October designed to demonstrate his command of international strategy. The profound wrongness of a central claim – in so many words, that the Palestinians had been pacified – was made larger by Sullivan's towering ambition. These failures by the President's policy staff, and by the president himself, make their claims of a two-state outcome's desirability even more suspect. Ambition cannot stand in for talent or ability, and slogans and "security arrangements" cannot stand in for justice. It has become clear that the American policy apparatus does not know what to do, nor do the people crafting policy know what they're doing. The impact of the 7 October attacks and their aftermath will be felt in many arenas, perhaps even in the organisation of the American policy establishment.

Nor are Arab states striving to drive a just outcome to this conflict. The total impotence of Arab leaders, almost all of whom rely on American support in one form or another, means that they are effectively non-entities when it comes to effecting change. Morally, many of them are deeply compromised, holding their own people in stasis through broad, forceful repression.

And so, we return to our theme – one state for two peoples,

rooted in justice and in the principles of international humanitarian law. We call for informed analysts and non-specialists alike to begin to continue the effort of discussing and exploring the contours of a single state. Are we talking about a federation of Israel/Palestine, or a consociational democracy – one that prizes community rights above all? The answers to those questions remain for us to grapple with and to answer to the best of our ability.

Equally challenging is the effort to develop a theory of change. How do we go from today – an entrenched Apartheid where Ashkenazi Israeli Jews rest at the top, maintaining a firm hold on the political and economic life of Israel/Palestine, while Palestinians from Gaza, the West Bank and inside Israel, many of them refugees, lay prone, exposed at the bottom of the societal totem?

We believe that the Boycott, Divestment and Sanctions movement will continue to carry the force of our argument – the force of justice – forward. And that the emerging global coalition of labour and justice workers, particularly Black Lives Matter activists in the United States, will help carry the work beyond its traditional limits among Palestinians, Arabs, Muslims and anti- or post-Zionist Jews. We cannot talk of hope emerging from the wreckage of Gaza, only a renewed commitment to work for a just future, for everyone.

Antony Loewenstein and Ahmed Moor
December 2023

Introduction

Antony Loewenstein and Ahmed Moor

The Middle East has changed in profound ways in recent years. The succession of popular uprisings (intifadas), Israeli military operations in the West Bank and Gaza, as well as changes in the political landscape, such as the so-called "Abraham Accords", have affected everyone in the most conflicted part of our world. However, some institutions remain, from the most right-wing government in Israel's short history, to the ineffectual and crippled Palestinian Authority.

The Al-Aqsa Intifada marked the end of the 1990s and the Oslo Process before it bled into the twenty-first century, bringing with it widespread cultural and political change for both Palestinians and Israelis. In Israel, society shifted drastically to the Right as the Left disintegrated, and the occupation became more deeply entrenched. The transformation found broad expression in a new consensus: that the Palestinians must be shut out and forgotten. The status quo became permanent.

The settlers in Israel have always had an outsized impact on their society. This partly has to do with the way in which majorities are cobbled together in the Israeli Knesset, but it is also because of deliberate Israeli government policy. Virtually every Palestinian has witnessed the accelerated rate of land theft and growth of illegal settlements in the Gaza Strip and the West Bank on a first-hand basis. The conquest of Palestinian land typically occurs in the presence of an army patrol, acting on official orders, protecting state machinery; there is never anything rogue about what the settlers do.

Until 2005, Jewish fundamentalists in the West Bank and Gaza – who form the ideological core of the settler movement – were contented by the arrangement. It was only when former Israeli Prime Minister Ariel Sharon decided to extract roughly 8,000 of them from the Gaza Strip that the arrangement ceased to be comfortable. It did not matter to the settlers that Sharon was working to buttress their interests by placing the "peace process" in "formaldehyde".[1] All that was relevant was that the state had exhibited a willingness to defy the settler community.

Sharon succeeded. The "peace process" was frozen at the most senior levels of the American government. It was during that period that the second intifada faded from Israeli consciousness and a reasonable standard of security returned to Tel Aviv.

During the past twenty-five years, the average Israeli has become less liberal, less "progressive" and more right-wing, a fact reflected by the election of Benjamin Netanyahu in 2009 and then his startling return to power at the end of 2022, after a series of deadlocked elections. It was a notable failure of the mainstream Left in Israel that the ongoing colonisation continued unopposed – a factor that contributed to the Left's ultimate dissipation. The general apathy and right-wing malice directed at Palestinians worked to further empower the settlers who had learned the lessons of 2005 well. They worked successfully to place their representatives in high posts in the cabinet and infused the army with their numbers. Today, any move to evict large numbers of settlers from the West Bank would likely be met by mass insubordination. While the takeover of Israel by the settler minority was perhaps unforeseen by Ariel Sharon and David Ben-Gurion, the permanence of the settlement project was not.

Among the Palestinians, the second intifada's renewed focus on armed resistance and suicide bombings resulted in political isolation and the diminishment of Palestinian society. The violence provided Israel with an opportunity to distract from the fact that its colonisation of the West Bank was proceeding apace. The occupation was endorsed, funded, defended and built with Israeli and foreign money. Tragically, since the Oslo period, the international community has also funded the Palestinian Authority, a body designed to manage the occupation for Israel. It is an arrangement that suits the Zionist state well.

The tragedy deepened for the Palestinians when the man who embodied the struggle – the international symbol of their aspirations – was besieged in his compound by the Israelis for more than two years. Yasser Arafat was deprived of his dignity right up until the weeks preceding his death. His humiliation was something that many Palestinians felt acutely, both at a symbolic level and in their own lives.

Subsequent years brought political divisions between them. The fissure that existed between Fatah and Hamas under Arafat burst into armed conflict after his death. The violence worsened after Hamas won parliamentary elections in 2006. The following year saw the Islamic movement pre-empt a Fatah coup, and with that the Palestinian political body split along geographical lines. Fatah held the West Bank with Israeli and American help, while Hamas continued to govern the Gaza Strip, first with Iranian and Syrian help, then with aid from Qatar, as the Palestinians distanced themselves from the civil war in Syria. Hamas controlled the Strip with an iron fist until its unprecedented attack on 7 October 2023, after which Israel aimed to eradicate its presence entirely from Gaza.

By 2007 it became clearer than ever that any talk of a two-state solution was empty though this hasn't stopped its advocates in the US, European Union and beyond from continuing to push it at every opportunity. The combined effect of a ravenous colonisation project in the West Bank and deep internal Palestinian divisions both highlighted the reality. At the same time, Palestinian calls for equal rights were gaining in strength; and the Boycott, Divestment and Sanctions (BDS) movement appeared to provide an opening for a different kind of resistance to the occupation. BDS has now gone global at universities, businesses and in public debate.

Outside Israel and Palestine, global discussion about the conflict began to shift. Although the mainstream media still sympathised with the Zionist narrative, it wasn't so uncommon to hear the occasional call for the one-state solution and Palestinian Right of Return. Social media and citizen reporting from the West Bank and Gaza offered the world on-the-ground insights that made it impossible to deny the daily harsh reality for Palestinians.

We – Antony Loewenstein and Ahmed Moor – first began discussing this anthology in the autumn of 2010. Adam Horowitz and Phil Weiss, the editors of the Mondoweiss website, introduced us at a time when so much in Israel and Palestine was changing and connections between people on different continents were quickly deepening thanks to the

Internet. Indeed, that is as true today as it was thirteen years ago.

Ahmed is a Palestinian-American who witnessed the disastrous effects of the Israeli occupation firsthand. Antony is an Australian Jew who was brought up expecting to believe in Zionism and the Israeli state, but by his late teens started to question its legitimacy. We come together on this book not because we agree on everything – we don't – but because of a shared belief that Jews and Palestinians are destined to live and work together, whatever our differences in background, ideals and daily life. We are connected by a desire for justice for our peoples.

To us, it seemed that the conversation about the end of the Oslo process and what may come afterwards was widespread. New sources of web information like Electronic Intifada, Mondoweiss and dissenting Israeli and Palestinian bloggers and tweeters were forcing a fresh openness in the discussion of the facts in Israel/Palestine. More and more people seemed to recognise that the obstacles to the emergence of a Palestinian state were deep, enduring and growing. Despite that, most mainstream media coverage in America and elsewhere continued to talk about a "peace process", supposedly generous offers by Israel and America to the Palestinian leadership, and ongoing "terrorism" by Palestinians in Gaza and the West Bank. The Barack Obama administration, despite liberal hopes of "Yes, We Can", became little better than a handmaiden to Israeli demands. Washington's position changed little during the Trump and Biden eras, entrenching Israeli control over all of Palestine.

We are frustrated with the largely myopic journalism that appears from the West. Palestinians are often portrayed as savages, terrorists or just faceless people. Israelis are the peace-seeking, aggrieved party. Neither stereotype is even remotely true, and the web has cracked this illusion. New and younger voices – such as Palestinian bloggers in Gaza, anti-Zionist Israelis, western peace activists and non-violent Palestinian leaders in the West Bank – are being heard online. They deserve wider coverage.

The decision to compile the essays in this collection was a natural one. These are the conversations that are pertinent today and the issues they raise will continue to be relevant for years to come. There is a diversity of issues and views represented, but in requesting the essays, we asked all of our contributors to keep the one-state solution in mind as they wrote.

The writers are from a wide variety of backgrounds: some from the academic establishment, while others are new media reporters in the West Bank. Some are Jewish, some are Muslim. Palestinians, Israelis and the Diaspora are all represented here. We wanted diversity, not conformity. We don't agree with everything that appears in the book, but we believe in having the debate. Moving from the discussion over how to achieve the unjust two-state solution – something that still occupies the minds in the White House, much of the corporate media and elements of the Palestinian and Zionist lobbies – to another, more equitable outcome is the challenge we seek to address.

After Zionism is a series of steps along that road, with the necessary twists, turns and contradictions at a time when facts on the ground are finally bringing a realisation that the one-state solution is the best way forward.

The idea that Palestinians and Israelis can share a single country is not a new one, but it was buried and forgotten for a long time. As the two-state outcome has faded from the minds of people who know the region, many are beginning to revisit the idea. In America and elsewhere in the West, the one-state solution is no longer a fringe discussion being conducted at the margins of the political debate.

We are both long-time advocates for a single state solution, but not all the contributors to this book have always agreed. So, part of this process has been about chronicling recent history – what happened, what changed, why can't we go back to Oslo? A strong emphasis on human rights is a common current throughout this book, but that doesn't necessarily translate into a common vision. We feel, however, that a wide range of the historical and moral debate is presented within these pages – and that these discussions necessarily inform our view of the future.

After Zionism isn't a position statement. It is a collection of essays that challenge much of the accepted status quo for the last decades. If the two-state solution will never happen, surely it's time to try something different, something more just? The obstacles to achieving justice are huge and the critics and cynics are many. But what is the alternative?

In our minds, the one-state solution's time has surely come.

ONE

Presence, Memory and Denial

Ahmed Moor

I remember the fall of 2003 clearly. I'd just commenced my freshman year at the University of Pennsylvania and like many seventeen-year-olds, I was glad at being newly independent.

The school had undertaken a programme to socialise incoming students. It consisted mostly of ice-cream parties, which did a lot to create a low-stress, adjustment-mode environment. It was after one of these events that I met another freshman in my class. Our conversation carried on normally until the young woman I was speaking with asked: "Where are you from?"

"Palestine," I said.

She looked at me for a moment before replying, "There's no such thing."

The politics of denial is the politics of occlusion and erasure, of negative spaces and dark holes. It is a manic, hysterical and angry politics. It is sometimes the politics of atrocity.

For several weeks in early 2012, members of the Republican presidential line-up tripped, lurched, and tumbled over one another in the frenzied competition to announce their deep love for Israel. Governor Rick Perry of Texas promised that the small Mediterranean state would be the first country he visited as president. Former Massachusetts Governor Mitt Romney insisted that he would confront Iran head on – to spare the Israelis the burden of doing so themselves. And as comedian Jon Stewart humorously pointed out, only Israel could cause Congresswoman Michelle Bachman to boast proudly of her time spent as a labourer on a socialist commune – a kibbutz.

The grim slide from comedy to anguished absurdity accelerated when former Speaker of the House Newt Gingrich sought to

mark himself apart. In an interview with a small Jewish cable television network, he made the blandly genocidal statement that the
Palestinians were an "invented people".[1] It was an assertion he felt
comfortable repeating days later when he evoked Ronald Reagan – a
mythical, folklorish figure among Republicans – to underline his "historical" claim. Gingrich's mendacious statement was not a historical
or an anthropological one. It was politics – one with a long history
in Palestine.

Zionism, the nineteenth-century European movement to colonise Palestine, has always struggled with an inconveniently inhabited
Holy Land. In the minds of Theodor Herzl and David Ben Gurion,
the indigenous people – the Palestinians – were a direct obstacle to
the redemption of an allegedly effete, bookish European Jew. Labour
Zionism – the unlikely admixture of Marxist labour principles and
ethnic nationalism – emphasised the role of the land in the Jewish
man's "redemption". In a practical sense, this meant that the new
Jewish immigrants to Palestine would be charged with tilling the
fields, picking the fruit, drawing the water – becoming native.

This preoccupation with sunburned brows and rugged silhouettes
marked Zionism apart from other nineteenth-century colonialisms.
In Palestine, the idealised Jewish man would learn that he had no use
for indigenous labour, only the land upon which it toiled. Zionism's
horizontal latticework – the Yishuv or early Jewish settler community – sought to project a positive vision of a natural world forced
to yield to Jewish brawn. The invention of the New Jewish man, the
Israeli, required the negation of the Palestinian. That was partly to
entice European Jews into emigrating from their countries; indigenous resistance to immigration would have diminished the allure of
the Holy Land.

But the erasure of the indigenous Arabs was also ideological. The
foundational mythology told by Jewish storytellers about their heroes
took form in a wild, untamed and unconquered landscape; an unpeo-
pled landscape. It was written in long, flowery script that bloomed
on clean, unspotted parchment. Harangued across the ages, the time
had come for the Jewish people to forge their destiny in their spiritual
foundry. The uncomplicated story of return and exile was successfully
distilled into the facile language of mass politics. Today, most of us

are familiar with Zionism's most hackneyed rhetorical lozenge – that Palestine was a "land without a people for a people without a land".

Of course, the land was peopled. And it was peopled by the indigenous Palestinian Arabs. They were the ones who built the port cities of Haifa and Jaffa and cultivated the citrus and olive groves. They were the ones who, with undeniably real minds and bodies, issued the most forceful moral rejoinder to a vision of a Jewish-only society in Palestine. "We are here," they said.

But not for ever, as it turned out. The early Zionists had adeptly accumulated arms and political support in western capitals in preparation for the moment they knew would arrive. Plan Dalet was carried out with more success than could have been predicted: by the end of the war in 1948 most of Palestine had been successfully emptied of its Palestinian inhabitants. More than five hundred villages, where roughly 700,000 people had lived, were summarily razed; the erasure climaxed in an epic act of ethnic cleansing.

They were forgotten. Or rather, the founders of the state of Israel tried to forget them. In their minds and books, the state of Israel was heroic – God's manifest will and his people's benedictory return. The opportunistic Arabs who had arrived for material gain with the first Aliya had been vanquished. They fled at their leaders' behests, or otherwise ceased to be. Israel was a trial-borne miracle.

The Palestinians did not forget, however. Their families learned to inhabit the dark peripheral spaces – the preserve of refugees. But they did not grow comfortable there. In their hearts they nurtured the memory of a place that they owned, fields that they tilled, weddings and births and funerals. Their thoughts burned with the late knowledge of their history; they had been exiled. Zionism had destroyed their towns and villages, but it hadn't destroyed them.

Their young people collected themselves and began to fight. They fought for a life worth living, for home, for recognition. They fought in the alleyways of their refugee camps and in the streets of their conquered places. They fought with their words, their songs and their literature.

The memory of them – who they were, where they are from and who they are today – gradually began to shake the scales from the eyes of peoples around the world. In the East, they recognised the

Palestinians' worn faces and calloused soles; they were alike. In the West too, they were recognisable. Their fierceness was unfriendly and their righteousness threatening. They were the indigenous people clamouring for a reckoning – the barbarians at the gate.

That was in the 1960s and 1970s, when Golda Meir felt comfortable denying their existence entirely. "There is no such thing as a Palestinian people ... It is not as if we came and threw them out and took their country. They didn't exist," she said.[2]

The intervening decades saw the world change. The East grew, asserting itself and its own historical experience. The West grew too. Contrition over a past blackened by imperialism and colonialism became widespread, and recognition of indigenous peoples' right to independent life and self-determination developed similarly. But the Palestinians stayed the same – and so did their Zionist adversaries.

Today, just as one hundred years ago, the denial of the existence of the Palestinian people is widespread amongst Zionists. Its superficial form has changed – instead of the Palestinians, it is Palestine that does not exist (the "Palestinians" can call themselves whatever they like). But the thrust is the same. The idea and the words used to produce the denial carry an emotional charge, a pugilistic readiness to fight over the "right of the Jewish people" to colonise and occupy all of Palestine. All the while, the denial wraps Israel in a plastic, impermeable sheath. The Palestinians did not exist – there was no one to dispossess. Palestine does not exist – wrongdoing cannot be perpetrated in a void.

Nor could the great historical extirpation of the Palestinians be consigned to 1948 or 1967. The cleansing of Zionist memories has been a high-maintenance and a continuous undertaking which has required diligence and an entire society's energies. The cost of a single crack in the facade is too high. To stop denying the existence of the Palestinians would signify a readiness to confront the state's original sin – the ethnic cleansing of Palestine. Israel would be de-sanctified and the cries, pleas, muffled shouts, and roars of a million refugee voices would burst forth in a deluge: "We are coming home!"

Zionism cannot withstand the decibel level. That has been true all along.

Israeli inculcators weaved their mythologies so tightly that the Palestinians ceased to exist, not only in history, but in the present as well. It is this manufactured non-existence of the Palestinians that has enabled generations of Jewish Israelis to steal and settle land in the Occupied Territories. It is that same dehumanisation that has enabled their larcenous governments to encourage their often violent activities. Today, the cataracts have grown so thick that when young Israelis move to colonise the West Bank, they do not see fellow humans. Standing in their way are the dehumanised, unchosen Arabs with inferior rights, or none at all. These are the memories they have been taught.

The process of purging memory has a strangely prophetic quality. The forgotten, erased, obviated, occluded, denied, clouded, wiped, blanked and stricken reaches its tentacular form into our present. Palestine existed, but it's been colonised out of existence.

The transition from memory and imagination to reality can be an abrupt one. The unacknowledged truth is that Palestine/Israel is already one country. A visitor from another country will struggle to isolate one from the other. Artificial-looking Israeli settlements penetrate deeply and violently into the West Bank, cantonising the territory. Jewish-only roads snake heavily there; the sieve that strains Palestinian lives. All the while, Israeli pipes swiftly draw water from Palestinian aquifers beneath Gaza and the West Bank. The country is a unified one, but Apartheid's ugly scrawl mars its surface.

This is a basic truth that Rick Santorum – another Republican politician – inadvertently bungled into when he said that: "All the people that live in the West Bank are Israelis. They are not Palestinians. There is no Palestinian. This is Israeli land."[3] Santorum sought to deny the existence of the Palestinians – to erase them. But he mangled the lie and unintentionally claimed Israeli citizenship for the two-and-a-half million Palestinians who reside in the West Bank. In essence, his words were a tidy summation of the spiral history of Zionism: there are no Palestinians, and Israel is an Apartheid state which disenfranchises half its citizens. The Palestinians have been unremembered, yet there they remain.

Memory and Reality

My family lived in the West Bank at the height of the Oslo process in the mid- to late 1990s. Even at that time, I remember thinking that the settlements around us were immovable; they were fortresses that rested heavily on a now spoiled landscape.

My father wanted to show us as much of the country as he could, so we took weekend trips to different sites in the West Bank. Jerusalem and Israel were closed to us. I remember winding drives from one valley to the next and the oppressive sense that we were being locked in. Even at that time, the road system in the West Bank was segregated. For me, that was an early hint of how things were supposed to develop.

It was around that time that I began to think that the discussions and handshakes being broadcast into every occupied home were a sham. Our lives were getting more difficult almost on a daily basis. Yet the news anchors insisted that Jericho was now free, Ramallah was nearly there, and that Jerusalem would come next.

The second intifada started in the summer of 2000 and my family left Palestine. It was probably in 2002 or 2003 that I realised that there would never be a viable Palestinian state. That awareness didn't bother me very much because the knowledge that anything Palestinian would be truncated and crippled by an immensely more powerful Israel had developed by that time. So it didn't make sense to mourn a non-state where non-self-determination would take place.

That was also around when Tony Judt published his essay "Israel: The Alternative" in the *New York Review of Books*.[4] The essay had a tremendous impact on me. I wasn't aware that the Palestine Liberation Organization (PLO) and others had called for a binational state decades earlier. All I saw was an alternative, one that could provide justice for the refugees and everyone else. The Palestinians had a way out, a path to freedom. The years that followed saw the violence in the Occupied Territories and Israel explode. When the intifada was stamped underfoot and snuffed out, Palestinians were left with nothing to do but count the dead. It was a very dark period, morally and spiritually, for many of us. We had resisted the erasure, the deliberate forgetting, and we had forced the Israelis to acknowledge our existence. But at what cost?

I travelled back to Palestine for the first time in a decade in December 2010. Everything I remembered was still there – kind of. The world had changed; mobile phones were ubiquitous, USAID money had transformed Ramallah into something that looked relatively prosperous, and some of the cars were newer. There was even a Mövenpick. But the starkest changes were most obvious and irreversible. The settlements had taken over and much of the bucolic landscape had simply stopped existing. I'd known it had happened, but I was still deeply saddened to see it.

I also knew about the Wall. But confronting it turned out to be more difficult that I had imagined. My old neighbourhood of Al-Ram had been ruined and partially de-peopled by the Wall which was built through the heart of the town. It weighed heavily on Palestinians; tons of vertical concrete can do that. In Bethlehem, too, I was stricken, both by its size and by the brazen offence it offered to anyone who chose to visit the holy sites there. I once believed that the world's Christians would speak up in the face of desecration, but I was wrong.

That trip was an important one for me. I saw at first hand for the first time in a decade that Palestine was gone – there was nothing left. The two-state outcome was dead. I had borne witness to the fact.

The Presence of Morality

The second intifada succeeded in reasserting the existence of the Palestinians but it failed in almost every other way. For many Palestinians the exclamatory statement was a costly one to make. Thousands of them were killed by Israel, which also lost more than a thousand civilians to Palestinian violence. By the end of 2004 the Palestinians were worn, tired and dispirited. But the basic dilemma remained: how to resist oppression and Apartheid, and how to do it in a way that did not diminish their moral claims?

The answer came through the Boycott, Divestment and Sanctions (BDS) movement. Palestinian civil society united in 2005 to issue a near-unanimous call for non-violent resistance to Israel. The movement recaptured and highlighted the moral core of the Palestinian claim and broadcast it widely to the world.

Modelled on the South African call, which helped to bring about an end to Apartheid in that country, the BDS movement has seen an increase in effectiveness with every passing year. That has been particularly true on the cultural boycott front, which is the most important for effecting change. Some Israelis have begun to acknowledge the offensiveness of their Apartheid regime, but only after popular musicians like Coldplay began to refuse to play in Tel Aviv. The key here is that the Israeli occupation will continue to be maintained so long as the majority of people in that country can continue to ignore it. The BDS movement makes it harder to ignore Apartheid.

It is important to remember that BDS is not an outlook, an article of faith or a panacea. Nor will it likely be a tool for *economically* undermining the occupation; moneyed interests run too deep. Besides helping awaken the Israelis to the suffering they cause, BDS is a tool with which the Palestinians can highlight their moral claims to a receptive international audience. That is especially true for people who may not feel completely authoritative when talking about a just solution to the "complicated" Palestinian–Israeli conflict. BDS helps to simplify and distil the Palestinian message because the call is fundamentally about upholding human rights and ending the occupation. In that context, many people around the world can speak with power about the necessity of ending Apartheid.

But BDS is not enough.

For some Palestinians, the call for an end to occupation and Apartheid has accompanied a positive vision for the future. Working to overcome the barriers to self-determination has also meant transitioning from one definition of what being a Palestinian means to another conception entirely. It has meant abandoning the struggle for a Palestinian state and adopting the struggle for equal rights in its place.

It is easy to recognise the necessity of ending the occupation, particularly when Palestinians effectively communicate the urgency and durability of their cause. It has been more than sixty years since the first refugees settled into their tented encampments – the original refugee camps. And for all those years their basic rights were never upheld – not by the Egyptians, the Jordanians, the Israelis, the Syrians, the Lebanese, or anyone else.

The message broadcast by the Palestine Liberation Organization (PLO) for all those years was one of national self-determination. The theme dominated the discourse of the developing world throughout the twentieth century, so it was no surprise that the Palestinians also adopted it. But the focus on national rights failed to convey the urgency of the plight of the refugees and the humanitarian dimension of their struggle to people around the world. For many, the Palestine problem was fundamentally about creating a state for a stateless people. Therefore, any solution for the refugees could only come through the creation of a state; a political solution for a humanitarian problem.

The call for a one-state solution eliminates all of the confusion around the right of the Palestinians to live free, unmolested lives with full dignity. The Palestinian–Israeli conflict is no longer inaccessible to the layperson because it is about rights and Apartheid and ethnic privilege. One does not need to know the history of a century-long struggle to understand that something is deeply wrong with the reality today and to stake a position on that basis. It is now enough to know that there are roads in the West Bank that are restricted to some people because they possess certain unalterable traits.

It is also meaningful that the equal rights message resonates in the American context. That is important because of the outsized role the American taxpayer plays in maintaining the occupation. Europeans can understand what occupation is because it was something they experienced during World War II and its aftermath. In the post-colonial world, life in the context of European settler-colonialism is similarly easy to remember. But the American experience carries no recognisable historical parallels to the Palestinian situation when it is framed as a quest for a state. The American revolutionary period is a distant memory that bears little resemblance to the twentieth-century occupation experience. That's not true about the equal rights struggle, however. Rosa Parks and Martin Luther King are alive in the national spirit of the United States – and they are the best-fit for understanding what is really happening in Israel/Palestine.

The question of how to arrive at equal rights in Israel/Palestine is an open one, with which many of us are currently engaged. It is an urgent question, and I suspect that the answer lies partly in the BDS movement. But a full discussion of how to get there and what the single state will look like is beyond the range of this essay. For now, it is enough to say that many people of good will around the globe and in Israel/Palestine are currently grappling with how to achieve the most just and moral outcome for everyone in the country.

At the same time, their adversaries are working to preserve Jewish privilege in Israel and the Occupied Territories. Despite the efforts of increasing numbers of activists and others, much of the American political establishment, the Israeli establishment, and the Palestinian establishment (who are mainly affiliated with the Palestinian Authority) are working to produce the Bantustan option – a series of non-contiguous Palestinian cantons in the West Bank governed by a corrupt elite subset of society.

It is very likely that before the one-state solution is fully developed, the Bantustan option will be established in the West Bank. But the Palestinian struggle will continue despite that. This is a crucial point that people invested in the "peace process" may not understand or may choose to ignore: any outcome that does not provide the Palestinians with their inalienable rights and address their legitimate grievances is only a variation of the status quo. And the status quo is untenable. The refugees must see their Right of Return upheld. They cannot be unremembered or disappeared. Their full rights must be honoured for the conflict to end.

TWO

The State of Denial: The *Nakba* in the Israeli Zionist Landscape

Ilan Pappe

For the Israelis the year of 1948 is *annus mirabilis*. In that year the Jewish national movement, Zionism, claimed it fulfilled an ancient dream of returning to a homeland after two thousand years of exile. It is a chapter in history that broadcasts not only triumph or realisation of dreams; it also carries associations with moral purity and absolute justice. This is why anything that happened in that year is wedded with the most basic values of the present Israeli society. Hence, the military conduct of the Jewish soldiers on the battlefield in 1948 became a model for generations to come, and the leadership's statesmanship in those years is still a paragon for future political elites. The leaders are described as people devoted to the Zionist ideals, men who disregarded their private interests and good for the sake of the common cause. It is a sacred year, revered in more than one way as the formative source of all that is good in the Jewish society of Israel. This poetic description of the year is to be found not just in official governmental publications but also in the work of academics.[1]

From another perspective this was an *annus horribilis*. The *Nakba* was the worst chapter in the history of Jewish abuses. In that year, Jews did in Palestine what Jews had not done anywhere else in the previous two thousand years. Even if one puts aside the historical debate about why what happened in 1948 happened, no one seems to question the enormity of the tragedy that befell the indigenous population of Palestine as a result of the emergence and success of the Zionist movement. Jews expelled, massacred, destroyed and raped in that year, and generally behaved like all the other colonialist movements operating in the Middle East and Africa since the beginning of the nineteenth century.

23

In normal circumstances, as Edward Said recommended in his seminal *Culture and Imperialism*, the painful dialogue with the past should enable a given society to digest both the most evil and the most glorious moments of a nation's history and moment of birth.[2]

But this could not work in a case where moral self-image is considered to be the principal asset in the battle over public opinion, and hence the best means of surviving in a hostile environment. The way out for the Jewish society in the newly founded state was to erase the unpleasant chapters of the past from the collective memory and leave the gratifying ones intact. It was a conscious mechanism put in place and motion in order to solve an impossible tension between two contradictory messages coming from the past.

Because so many of the people who live in Israel lived through 1948 this was not an easy task. The year 1948 is not a distant memory, and the crimes are still visible in the landscape for the present generation to behold and understand. Above all, there are still living victims who are there to tell their story and when they are gone, their descendants – who have heard the tales of the 1948 horrors – are most likely going to represent their point of view for generations to come. There are people in Israel who know exactly what they did, and there are even more who know what others have done.

Even more important in a way is the fact that the crime continues. Israel has pursued a policy of ethnic cleansing in other means ever since 1948 and continues to execute such policies as these words are written. The treatment of the Palestinian minority that remained after the 1948 ethnic cleansing is a first chapter in this trajectory. They suffered an actual policy of expulsion up to the mid-1950s and were then submitted to a ruthless military rule that made life quite unbearable for many until the abolishment of that rule in 1967.[3]

The successful Israeli fragmentation of the Palestinian existence caused one huge concern for the Israelis. There were many Palestinian "problems" to deal with and each required a different treatment. Yet, however one reviews the policies towards the various Palestinian existences – as citizens in Israel, as occupied in the West Bank, ghettoised in the Gaza Strip, or exiled as refugees elsewhere – all these policies rest on an ideological infrastructure that can be defined as ethnic cleansing. The military rule over the Palestinians in Israel until

1966 and the spatial policies and comprehensive legal, economic and cultural discrimination ever after are the manifestation of that policy towards the Palestinians in Israel. Not allowing repatriation for the refugees is another; and the actual expulsion, enclavement and Bantustanisation of the Occupied Territories is the third.

But one probably needs a particular ethical point of view in order to associate past crime with present policies. Far more obvious as an "original sin" of the state was the crime of 1948. Yet the Israeli authorities still succeeded in eliminating these deeds totally from society's collective memory while struggling rigorously against anyone trying to shed light on these repulsive chapters of history, both in and outside Israel. Even a cursory look at Israeli textbooks, curricula, media and political discourse will indicate that this chapter in Jewish history – the chapter of expulsion, colonisation, massacres, rape, and the burning of villages – is totally absent. It is replaced by chapters of heroism, glorious campaigns, and amazing tales of moral courage and military competence unheard of in any other histories of popular liberation in the twentieth century.

It would be therefore useful to begin this essay with a short reference to the denied chapters of the history of 1948. Some of these chapters are also currently missing from the Palestinian collective memory. The double amnesia stems of course from two very different ways of dealing with the past: the Jewish Israelis are unwilling to acknowledge or be accountable for what happened in 1948, whereas the Palestinians, as a community of victims, have little inclination to revisit the traumas of the past. For this reason, on both sides, popular memory and the more professional representation of the past were unable or unwilling to draw a clear picture of the 1948 events.

The Erased Chapters of Evil

The diplomatic manoeuvres and military campaigns of the 1948 war are well engraved in the Israeli Jewish historiography. What is missing is the ethnic cleansing carried out by the Jews in 1948. As a result of that campaign, five hundred Palestinian villages and eleven urban neighbourhoods were destroyed, 700,000 Palestinians were expelled and several thousands were massacred.[4] Even today it is hard to find in Israel a succinct and available summary on the planning, execution and repercussions of these tragic results.

One of the major blocs preventing liberal Zionists from opening up towards a sympathetic view towards the *Nakba* is their assertion that the Palestinians in a way deserved what they got for refusing to accept the 1947 partition resolution. In November 1947 the United Nations offered to partition Palestine into a Jewish and an Arab state as the best solution to the conflict. The scheme was very problematic from its inception for three major reasons.

Firstly, it was presented to the two warring parties not as a basis for negotiation but as a fait accompli, although the Palestinian total rejection of the principles underpinning the plan was well known to the UN. The alternative course, as offered by few UN member states, and later recognised by the American State Department as the best option, was to begin in 1948 negotiations for several years under the auspices of the UN. The scheme offered by the UN, on the other hand, faithfully represented the Zionist strategy and policy. Imposing the will of one side, through the agencies of the UN, could not have been a recipe for peace, but for war. The Palestinian side regarded the Zionist movement as the Algerians regarded the French colonialists. As it was unthinkable for the Algerians to agree to share their land with the French settlers, so was it unacceptable for the Palestinians to divide Palestine with the Zionist movement. The cases were different, even the Palestinians recognised it, and thus a longer period of negotiations was needed, but not granted.

Secondly, the Jewish minority (660,000 out of two million people) was offered the larger part of the land (56 percent). Thus the imposed partition was to begin with an unfair proposal.

Thirdly, because of the demographic distributions of the two communities – the Palestinians and the Jews – the 56 percent offered to the Jews as a state included an equal number of Jews and Palestinians. All the Zionist leaders, from left to right, concurred on the need to maintain a considerable Jewish majority in Palestine; in fact, the absence of such a solid majority was regarded as the demise of Zionism. Even a cursory knowledge of Zionist ideology and strategy should have clarified to the UN peace architects that such a demographic reality would lead to the cleansing of the local population altogether from the future Jewish state.[5]

On 10 March 1948, the *Hagana*, the main Jewish underground in Palestine, issued a military blueprint preparing the community for the expected British evacuation of Palestine, scheduled for 15 May 1948. The total Arab and Palestinian rejection of the UN resolution led the Jewish leadership to declare it dead for all intents and purposes. In May 1947, the Jewish Agency had already drawn a map which included most of Palestine, apart from the West Bank of today, which was granted to the Transjordanians, as a Jewish state. A plan was devised on that day, in March 1948, to take over these parts, constituting 80 percent of Palestine. The plan was called Plan D (plans A, B and C had been similar blueprints in the past formulating Zionist strategy *vis-à-vis* an unfolding and changing reality). Plan D (or *Dalet* in Hebrew) instructed the Jewish forces to cleanse the Palestinian areas falling under their control. The *Hagana* had several brigades at its disposal and each one of them received a list of villages it had to occupy and destroy. Most of the villages were destined to be destroyed: only in very exceptional cases were the forces ordered to leave them intact.[6]

From December 1947 well into the 1950s, the ethnic cleansing operation continued. Villages were surrounded from three flanks and the fourth one was left open to flight and evacuation. In some cases it did not work, and many villagers remained in their houses – these were the places where massacres took place. This was the principal strategy for Judaising Palestine.

The ethnic cleansing took place in three stages. The first one was from December 1947 until the end of the summer of 1948 when the coastal and inner plains were destroyed and their populations evicted by force. The second one took place in the autumn and winter of 1948 and included the Galilee and the Naqab (Negev).

By the winter of 1949 the guns were silenced in the land of Palestine. The second phase of the war ended and with it the second stage of the cleansing was terminated, but the expulsion continued long after the winds of war subsided. The third phase was to extend beyond the war until 1954 when dozens of additional villages were destroyed and villagers expelled. Out of about 900,000 Palestinians living in the territories designated by the UN as a Jewish state, only 100,000 remained on or nearby their land and houses. Those who remained became the Palestinian minority in Israel. The rest were expelled, or fled under the threat of expulsion, or were massacred. [7]

The countryside landscape, the rural heart of Palestine, with its one thousand colourful and picturesque villages was ruined. Half of the villages were erased from the face of the earth, demolished by Israeli bulldozers. The government turned many of them into cultivated land or else built new Jewish settlements on their ruins. A committee for naming granted the new settlements Hebrewised versions of the original Arab names – thus Lubya become Lavi and Safuria was turned into Zipori. David Ben Gurion, the first prime minister of Israel, explained that this was done as part of an attempt to prevent future claims to these villages. It was also an act supported by Israeli archaeologists, who had authorised the names not as a takeover of a title but rather as poetic justice which returned "ancient Israel" to its old map.[8] They salvaged geographical names from the Bible and attached them to the destroyed villages.

Urban Palestine was torn apart and crushed in a similar way. The Palestinian neighbourhoods in mixed town were wrecked apart from a few quarters left empty, waiting to be populated later by incoming Jewish immigrants from Arab countries.[9]

The Palestinian refugees spent the winter of 1948 in tent camps provided to them by voluntary agencies; most of these locations would become their permanent residence. The tents were replaced by clay huts that became the familiar feature of Palestinian existence in the Middle East. The only hope for these refugees, at the time, was the one offered by UN resolution 194 (11 December 1948), which promised them quick return to their homes. This was one of many international pledges made by the global community to the Palestinians that remains unfulfilled to this day.

The catastrophe that befell the Palestinians would be remembered in the collective Palestinian national memory as the *Nakba* – the disaster, kindling the fire that would restore the Palestinians as a national movement. Its self-image would be of an indigenous population led by a guerrilla movement wishing to turn the clock backwards with very little success. The Israelis' collective memory would depict the war as an act of a national liberation movement fighting both British colonialism and Arab hostility and winning against all odds. The Israeli Jewish loss of 1 percent of the population clouded the joy of achieving independence, but not the will and determination to Judaise Palestine and turn it into the future haven for world Jewry.

Israel turned out to be the most dangerous place for Jews to be living in the second half of the twentieth century. Most preferred to live outside the country, and quite a few did not identify in general with the Jewish project in Palestine and did not wish to be associated with its dire consequences there. But a vociferous minority of Jews in the United States continued to give the impression that world Jewry condoned the events of 1948. The illusion that the majority of the Jews legitimised whatever Israel had done in 1948 and thereafter has dangerously complicated the relationship of Jewish minorities in the western world with the rest of society; particularly in places where public opinion since 1987 has become increasingly hostile towards Israel's policies in Palestine.[10]

The Academy and the *Nakba*

Until very recently, the Israeli Zionist representation of the 1948 war dominated the academic world, and probably because of that the more general public's recollection of the *Nakba* as well.[11] It meant that the 1948 events were described as an overall war between two armies. Such an assumption calls for the expertise of military historians, who can analyse the military strategy and tactics of both sides. Actions and atrocities are part of the theatre of war, where things are judged, on a moral basis, very differently from the way they would be treated in a non-combat situation. For instance, it is within this context that the death of civilians during a battle is accepted as an integral part of the battlefield; an action deemed necessary as part of the overall attempt to win a war (although of course even within war there are exceptional atrocities which are not accepted and are treated as illegitimate in the military historiography).

Such a view also entails the concept of parity in questions of moral responsibility for the unfolding events on the ground, including in our case the massive expulsion of an indigenous population. From very early on, the academic representation of this question in Israel was an attempt to argue that the Israeli explanation of what had happened in 1948 was "academic" and "objective". In the early stages, the Israelis were depicted only as victims of Arab aggression. Later on, a more "balanced" view was offered – that there were two armies involved in the war.

The Palestinian *Nakba* narrative, which claimed that there were not two equally equipped armies, but rather an expeller and expelled, an offender and its victims, was seen as sheer propaganda.

This was the view not only in Israel. Until the 1990s, it was also the accepted view in western academia, and of course in the media and political establishments. The erosion of this external support for the Zionist narrative of 1948 and in particular to the more "sober" one had the potential to raise questions at least in Israeli academia about the 1948 catastrophe. Whereas it did lead to the emergence of the "new history", seen from the vantage point of the twenty-first century, it did not in any significant way impact on the mainstream and consensual Israeli point of view.[12]

But as I have tried to show elsewhere, the missing parts of this chapter in history can only be truthfully approached if the events that unfolded after May 1948 in Israel and Palestine are reviewed from within the paradigm of ethnic cleansing and not only as part of military history.[13] Historiographically, this means that the deeds were part of domestic policies implemented by a regime *vis-à-vis* civilians. In many cases, the ethnic cleansing took place within the designated UN Jewish state, which means that these operations were conducted by a regime against its own citizens.

A Palestinian resident of the village Tantura has described this new reality better than any historian. His village was situated thirty kilometres south of Haifa, on the coast. According to UN resolution 181 – the partition resolution – the village became part of the Jewish state on 15 May 1948. On 23 May, this person, like many others, found himself in a prison camp in Um Khaled (thirty kilometres to the south of his village); after sitting there for a year and half, he was expelled to the West Bank. "'I became prisoner of war instead of a citizen, a few days after my new state occupied me." He was a young boy – not an "enemy soldier" at the time. He was luckier than others of his age, who were massacred in that village.[14]

This was not a battlefield between two armies, it was a civilian space invaded by military troops. Ethnic ideology, settlement policy and demographic strategy were the decisive factors here, not military plans.

Massacres, whether premeditated or not, are an integral, and not exceptional, part of the ethnic cleansing act, although history has taught us that in most cases expulsion was a preferred means to killing. The evidence for historians of the regime committing ethnic cleansing blear a clear picture, since the aim of the regime from the very beginning was to obscure its intentions and this is manifested in the language of orders and the post-event reports. This is why even in hindsight, the evidence of victims and victimisers are so vital. The act of reconstruction is achieved mainly through the bridging between the collective and personal memories of victim and victimiser alike.

The ethnic cleansing paradigm explains why expulsions and not massacres are the essence of such crimes. As with the Balkan wars in the 1990s, sporadic massacres that occurred during the ethnic-cleansing process were motivated more by revenge than by any clear-cut scheme. But the plan to create new ethnic realities was assisted by these massacres no less than by systematic expulsion.

The Jewish operation in 1948 fits the definitions of ethnic cleansing offered in the UN reports on the Balkan wars of the 1990s. The UN council for human rights linked the wish to impose ethnic rule on a mixed area – the making of Greater Serbia – with acts of expulsion and other violent means. The reports define acts of ethnic cleansing as including separation of men from women, detention of men, explosion of houses and repopulating with another ethnic group later on. This was precisely the repertoire of the Jewish soldiers in the 1948 war.

The criminality of this act is the major obstacle to a fully Jewish Israeli engagement with its effect. However, neither the question of acknowledgement nor the question of accountability can be resolved without recognition of the nature of what happened.

Nakba Memory in the Public Eye

The story of the ethnic cleansing is denied in and by Israel. The reason that the mechanism of denial is so forceful in Israel and among its ardent supporters in the West is that the view offered here exposes much deeper questions. The most important of these is the relevance of Zionist ideology in general to the crimes committed in 1948. As others have shown, the massive expulsion was indeed the inevitable outcome of a strategy dating back to the late nineteenth century.[15] This ideology of transfer emerged the moment the leaders of the Zionist movement realised that a Jewish state in Palestine could not materialise as long as the indigenous people of Palestine remained on the land. The presence of a local society and culture had been known to the early Zionists even before the first settlers set foot on the land. Theodore Herzl, the founding father of Zionism, predicted that his dream of a Jewish homeland in Palestine would necessitate expulsion of the indigenous population, as did the leaders of the Second Aliya, a kind of a Zionist Mayflower generation.[16] The rank and file of the first waves of Zionist colonisation were brought up on the notion, later embedded into the educational system of the young state, that the local native population was an obstacle to both the survival of the Jewish state and its ability to thrive.

The Zionist movement employed two means for changing the local reality in Palestine and imposing the Zionist interpretation on it: the dispossession of the indigenous population from the land and its re-population with newcomers, that is, expulsion and settlement. The colonisation effort was pushed forward by a movement that had not yet won regional or international legitimacy and therefore had to buy land and create enclaves within the indigenous population. The British Empire was very helpful in bringing this scheme into reality. Yet from the very beginning of the Zionist strategy, the leaders of Zionism knew that settlement would be a very long and measured process, one which might not be sufficient to realise the revolutionary dreams of the movement and its desire to alter the realties on the ground and impose its own vision on the land's past, present and future. To achieve that, the movement needed to resort to more effective means.

Transfer and ethnic cleansing as means of Judaising Palestine had been closely associated in Zionist thought and practice with "historical opportunities"; namely appropriate circumstances such as an indifferent world or "revolutionary conditions" such as war. This link between purpose and timing was elucidated very clearly in a letter David Ben Gurion sent to his son Amos in 1937.[17] This notion re-appeared ever after in Ben Gurion's addresses to his MAPAI party members throughout the mandatory period, up until such an opportune moment arose – in 1948.[18]

This ideological infrastructure was solidified and strengthened as a result of the mild and even sympathetic reaction in the West to the crime of ethnic cleansing in 1948. The very thought and vision of a pure, exclusive, supremacist Jewish state were legalised internationally and these form a very important part in the way with which the 1948 *Nakba* is engaged in present-day Israel.

One group of people, the demographers, are those on the "Right". They envision the implementation of the plan within the borders of historical or mandatory Palestine – whether for strategic or ideological reasons. Hence they are looking for solutions that would not allow the demographic balance to undermine the vision. These can include a wish to expel the Palestinian–Israeli population, to enclave it in secure areas or to subject it to discriminatory policies that would either force the Palestinians to remain non-citizens, second-hand citizens, or to leave.

The geographers from the "Left" or the peace camp are thus called because they are not looking for ways of downsizing the population but rather are willing to downsize the territory which is Israel. In the name of "peace", they are willing to limit the territory under their control provided it is as clean of Palestinians as possible.

Both demographers and geographers are looking, as did Ben Gurion in 1937, for the opportune moment to finalise the Zionist project by completing what had in 1948. At the end of the twentieth century and the very beginning of our century, it was Ariel Sharon in particular that both fused and symbolised this consensual continuation of the project that commenced in 1948. Later on Kadima, the new party he formed, continued in the same vein until it lost power in 2009. Since then Israel has been ruled by the demographers and it is impossible to predict how their plan to retain the whole territory with as few Palestinians as possible will materialise.

Quite often Sharon likened himself to Ben Gurion; he was the one who was going to settle the Palestine question for once and for all. At the time, the media in the West was misled to believe that this was part of a reformed warmonger's newly adopted discourse of peace. In fact, Sharon was like Ben Gurion. He, too, sought a moment that would enable the further, if not complete, de-Arabisation of Palestine which had begun in 1882.

The Struggle Against *Nakba* Denial

Nakba denial in Israel and the West was helped by the overall negation of the Palestinians as a people (the notorious sentence by the Israeli Prime Minister Golda Meir in 1969 epitomised this attitude). Towards the end of the 1980s, as a result of the first *intifada*, the situation improved somewhat, with the humanisation of the Palestinians in the western media and, as a result, with their introduction into the field of Middle Eastern Studies as legitimate subject matter. Academically or publicly, in those years Palestinian affairs were still discussed within Israel only by academics who had been intelligence experts on the subject in the past, and who still had close ties with the security services and the Israel Defense Forces (IDF). Thus, this Israeli academic perspective erased the *Nakba* as a historical event, preventing local scholars and academics from challenging the overall denial and suppression of the catastrophe in the world outside the ivory tower.[19]

The mechanism of denial in Israel is very effective: it relies on indoctrination covering the citizen's life from the cradle to grave. It assures the state that its people do not get confused by facts and reality, or alternatively that they view reality in such a way that does not create any moral problems.

There were already visible cracks in the wall of denial in the 1980s. Even in Israel and the West, the wide exposure in the world media of Israeli war crimes ever since 1982 raised troubling questions about Israel's self-image of being the only democracy in the Middle East, or a community belonging to the world of human and civil rights and universal values.

It was the emergence of critical historiography in Israel in the early 1990s, known as the "new history", which re-located the *Nakba* at the centre of the academic and public debate about the conflict – legitimising the Palestinian narrative after it had been portrayed for years as sheer propaganda by western journalists, politicians and academicians.[20]

Simcha Flapan, Benny Morris, Avi Shlaim and I presented the challenge to the Zionist presentation of the 1948 war in Israeli society. Our work appeared in various areas of cultural production – in the media, academia and popular arts. It affected the discourse in both the US and Israel; but it never entered the political arena.

Public response to our findings in Israel moved between indifference and total rejection. It was only in the media and through the educational system that people hesitantly began taking a new look at the past. However, from above, the establishment did everything it could to quash these early buds of Israeli self-awareness and recognition of Israel's role in the Palestinian catastrophe, a recognition that would have helped Israelis to understand better the continued deadlock in the peace process.

Outside the academic world, in the West in general, and in the US and Israel in particular, this shift in academic perception had very little impact on the media and the political scene. In America and in Jewish Israel, terms such as "ethnic cleansing" and "expulsion" are still today totally alien to politicians, journalists and common people alike. The relevant chapters of the past that would justify categorically such definitions are either distorted in the recollection of people, or totally absent.

Introducing the terms to western public opinion is a crucial factor in assessing the possible impact of a *Nakba* awareness in Israel. In several European countries, new initiatives to relocate the refugees' history and future emerged in the 1990s; it is as yet too early to judge how much such efforts – taken by pro-Palestinian NGOs – will affect governments' policies. So far, from our vantage point of early 2012, there is no success at all in this respect. There were signs of movement in a similar direction in the United States, where in April 2000 the first ever American Right of Return conference was convened with the attendance of 1,000 representatives from all over the country. But so far their message has failed to reach Capitol Hill, the *New York Times* or the White House.

The events of 11 September 2001 have to date put an end to the new trend and revived old anti-Palestinian demagogues in America. In some respects, although it is still a little premature to judge, the second Israeli war against Lebanon in 2006, the attack on Gaza at the very end of 2008 and the attack on the Turkish flotilla in 2010 may have reorientated the trend once more. The current president at first seemed to be a harbinger of such a new trend, but soon retreated to the old line on the issue of refugees, return and the *Nakba* in general.

Nakba Denial and the Israel/Palestine Peace Process

Even before the U-turn in American public opinion after 11 September 2001, the movement of academic critique in Israel and the West and its fresh view on the 1948 ethnic cleansing was not a very impressive player on the local, regional or international stages. It did not in any way impact the Israel/Palestine peace agenda; and Palestine was the focus of such efforts at exactly the time when the fresh voices were heard. At the centre of these peace efforts were the Oslo Accords, which began rolling in September 1993. The concept behind this process was, as in all the previous peace endeavours in Palestine, a Zionist one.

Hence, the peace process of the 1990s, the Oslo Accords, was conducted according to the Israeli perception of peace – from which the *Nakba* was totally absent. The Oslo formula was created by Israeli thinkers from the Jewish peace camp, people who have played an important role in the Israeli public scene ever since 1967. They were institutionalised in an ex-parliamentary movement, "Peace Now", and had several parties on their side in the Israeli parliament. In all their previous discourses and plans, they had totally evaded the 1948 issue and sidelined the refugee questions. They did the same in 1993 – this time with the dire consequences of raising hopes of peace as they seemed to find a Palestinian partner for a concept of peace that buries 1948 and its victims.

It is noteworthy that the potential partners withdrew from the process twice at the last moment; ultimately, they could not betray the Palestinian Right of Return (nor is any leader empowered to do so, as the right is an individual one). The first was Yasser Arafat at the Camp David summit in the summer of 2000. He was later followed by Abu Mazen in the various, admittedly much less significant, attempts to reach a solution with the Israeli governments of Olmert and Netanyahu.

When the final moment came, and the Palestinians realised that on top of not witnessing a genuine Israeli withdrawal from the occupied West Bank and Gaza Strip, there was no solution offered for the refugee question, they rebelled in frustration. The climax of the Oslo negotiations – the Camp David summit meeting between then Israeli Prime Minister Ehud Barak and Arafat in the summer of 2000 – gave the false impression that it was offering the end of the conflict. Naïve Palestinian negotiators located the *Nakba* and Israel's responsibility for it at the top of the Palestinian list of demands, but this was rejected out of hand by the Israeli team, which succeeded in enforcing its point of view on the summit. To the Palestinian side's credit, we should say that at least for a while the catastrophe of 1948 was brought to the attention of a local, regional, and, to a certain extent, global audience. Nonetheless, the continued denial of the *Nakba* in the peace process is the main explanation for its failure and the subsequent second uprising in the Occupied Territories.

Not only in Israel but also in the United States, and even in Europe, it was necessary to remind those concerned with the Palestine question that this conflict entailed not only the future of the Occupied Territories, but also that of the Palestinian refugees who had been forced from their homes in 1948 (and indeed from the whole area that was once Palestine). The Israelis had earlier succeeded in sidelining the issue of the refugees' rights from the Oslo Accords, an aim helped by ill-managed Palestinian diplomacy and strategy.

The *Nakba* had been so efficiently kept off the agenda of the peace process that when it suddenly appeared on it, the Israelis felt as if a Pandora's box had been prised open in front of them. The worst fear of the Israeli negotiators was that there was a possibility that Israel's responsibility for the 1948 catastrophe would now become a negotiable issue; this "danger" was, accordingly, immediately confronted. In the Israeli media and parliament, the Knesset, a position was formulated: no Israeli negotiator would be allowed even to discuss the Right of Return of the Palestinian refugees to the homes they had occupied before 1948. The Knesset passed a law to this effect, and Ehud Barak made a public commitment to it on the stairs of the plane that was taking him to Camp David.²¹

The mechanism of denial therefore was crucial not only for defeating counter claims made by Palestinians in the peace process, but, more importantly, for disallowing any significant debate on the essence and moral foundations of Zionism.

The Struggle over *Nakba* Denial in the Twenty-First Century

When the twentieth century came to an end, it seemed that the struggle against *Nakba* denial in Israel had had a mixed impact on the society and its politics. The appearance of the "new history" and a far more concentrated political, cultural and academic effort to protect the *Nakba* memory by the Palestinians in general, and those within Israel in particular, did crack the wall of denial and repression that surrounds the *Nakba* in Israel. The new atmosphere has also been helped by a clarification of the Palestinian position on the refugees issue towards the end of the Oslo Peace Process. As a result, after more than fifty years of repression, it became more difficult for Israel to deny the expulsion and destruction of the Palestinians in 1948. However, this relative success has also brought with it three negative reactions, formulated after the outbreak of the Al-Aqsa intifada. The effect of these reactions is still felt today, and it characterises the state of the *Nakba* denial in Israel in this century.

The first reaction was from the Israeli political establishment, led by Ariel Sharon's two governments (2001 and 2003), through the Ministry of Education, to expunge the actual history of 1948 from the education system. It began systematically removing any textbook or school syllabus that referred to the *Nakba*, even marginally. Similar instructions were given to the public broadcasting authorities.²²

The second reaction was even more disturbing and encompassed wider sections of the public. Although a very considerable number of

Israeli politicians, journalists and academics ceased to deny what happened in 1948, they were nonetheless willing to justify it publicly, not only in retrospect but also as a prescription for the future. The idea of "transfer" entered Israeli political discourse openly for the first time, gaining legitimacy as the best means of dealing with the Palestinian "problem".[23]

Transfer was and is openly discussed as an option when the captains of the nation meet annually in one of Israel's most prestigious academic centres, the Centre for Interdisciplinary Studies in Herzliya. It was openly discussed in the early twenty-first century as a policy proposal in papers presented by senior Labour Party ministers to their government. It is openly advocated by university professors and media commentators, and very few now dare to condemn it. At the very end of the last century, the leader of the majority in the American House of Representatives openly endorsed it.[24]

There was a third reaction that followed in the footsteps of the renewed denial and worse disregard for the *Nakba*; this was the appearance of a neo-Zionist professional historiography of the war, some of it written by a former new historian. This U-turn was led by Benny Morris, formerly one of the most important new historians of the 1990s. Morris has not changed his narrative: Israel was still in his eyes a state that was built with the help of ethnic cleansing of the Palestinians. What he changed was his moral attitude towards that policy and crime. He justified it and did not even rule it out as a future policy.[25] This justification appears also in his latest book on 1948, aptly called *1948*: every means is justified in a war against a Jihadi attempt to destroy the state of Israel.[26]

Morris's retraction was typical to the whole professional historiography of the 1948 war in Israel in the twentieth century. As I have shown elsewhere, the pattern in the new century is very much the same.[27] The facts that the "New Historians" exposed about 1948, in particular those concerning the depopulation of the indigenous people of Palestine, are not doubted any more. What changed is the total acceptance of the moral validity of this policy. In many ways, the professional historiography in Israel once more regards 1948 as the miraculous pristine moment of the state's birth.

Conclusion

In 2012 a circle has thus been closed. Any doubts about the chances for a genuine political settlement in Israel and Palestine based on a two-state solution have been affirmed. We are now faced with the fact of an irreversible Jewish republic built all over historical Palestine. That means that the conflict which had two dimensions in the past – geographical and demographic – has now been reduced to an issue about demography: its politics, its morality and its future.

Because the conflict is no longer about territory but about content – or, to put it politically, about the nature of the regime and rights of people who live, used to live, or wish to live there – the *Nakba* has regained paramount importance. The way it is assessed will affect the nature of the future solution. Should it be acknowledged as a crime that still continues today, peace can only be achieved through a regime change throughout Palestine and Israel. Should it be depicted as an unfortunate, and closed, chapter of the collateral damage of a war, then it will have no bearing on the present balance of power. More specifically, in the former case, only the return of the refugees can close the chapter of the *Nakba* denial; in the latter, their rights will continue to be ignored, which will ensure that the conflict continues.

The realisation that this is the juncture that was reached by the beginning of the twenty-first century explains the state of the struggle over the *Nakba* memory in the last decade. The boundaries of this debate also reflect the ideological map of Israel, and to a certain extent that of the Palestinian polity. The Zionist position has never been clearer and more united on the issue of the *Nakba* (although the cleavages in society on other issues are still there: religion versus secularism, *Mizrachi* versus *Askhenazi* and the poor against the rich) and on the vision for the future in the relationship with the Palestinians.

Thus the struggle in this century is not just to protect the memory of the *Nakba* and confront its denial. In many ways, the *Nakba* did not end in 1948. It continued in different ways and is still in progress today. There are two ways in which the struggle over the memory of *Nakba* in Israel is carried out. The first is the struggle against the continued policies of dispossession which is beyond the scope of this essay. The second is a struggle against erasure and over memory. The principal means for preserving that memory is by visiting and maintaining destroyed villages and neighbourhoods.

Initially, visits were organised by the committee for internal displaced persons that represents the refugees inside Israel (namely those who lost their homes in 1948 but remained within the borders of the Jewish State). They were later coordinated with the Arab-Jewish NGOs such as *Zochrot* ("remembering" in Hebrew). The latter organisation still tries today to educate the Jewish public by indicating with physical signs where destroyed villages are located and by organising guided tours to these locations. Palestinian NGOs make a routine and steadfast effort for commemoration despite new legislation that tries to stop them. In films, theatres and plays, that memory is alive among Palestinians in Israel; it is more difficult to continue the dialogue with Jewish society on this question.

Nakba thus is no longer denied in Israel; on the contrary, it is alive in the minds, actions and discourse of the Palestinians in Israel. It is also alive when its memory is confronted so brutally by the Israeli authorities, as it has been ever since the beginning of this century. However, it is worthwhile to continue the struggle, even if the horrors have been expunged from the official educational system, the media and public discourse. There are those among the Jews of Israel that do not know the magnitude of what occurred, and knowledge must be the first step towards acknowledgement.

The struggle against Israeli *Nakba* denial is now the agenda of certain Palestinian groups inside and outside Israel. Since the fortieth anniversary of the *Nakba* in 1988, the Palestinian minority in Israel has associated its collective and individual memories of the catastrophe with the general Palestinian situation in a way that it never did previously. This association has been manifested through an array of symbolic gestures, such as memorial services on *Nakba* commemoration day, organised tours to deserted or formerly Palestinian villages in Israel, seminars on the past, and extensive interviews with *Nakba* survivors in the press.

Through its political leaders, NGOs and media, the Palestinian minority in Israel has been able to force the wider public to take notice of the *Nakba*. This re-emergence of the *Nakba* as a topic for public debate will also disable any future peace plans that will be built on the *Nakba* denial (the various plans and initiatives of 2003 were such attempts: the Road Map, the Ayalon-Nusseibah initiative and the Geneva agreements).[28]

When this article was written, another round in this struggle began, by no means the last one. The neo-Zionist government, in power since 2009, embarked on a series of racist and anti-Palestinian legislation; among them was what is called in the popular parlance "The *Nakba* Law". Its official name is the "The Budget Foundation Law". The law authorises the finance minister to reduce or eliminate all state funding to any institute that commemorates the *Nakba* or marks the Israeli day of independence as a day of mourning.[29] In addition, schools have been ordered by the new Ministry of Education to avoid any mention of the *Nakba* during Independence Day celebrations. Needless to say, this law is not abided by but it also has not been tested in court.

And maybe something is slipping through the walls of denials and erasure. The blog of the right-wing daily, *Marariv*, described the demolition of houses in the *Mizrachi* neighbourhood of Tel-Aviv, Kefar Shaem, as the "Social *Nakba*". Maybe this is a precursor for empathy which is the first step on the way to acknowledgement, accountability return – and closure.

THREE

Reconfiguring Palestine: A Way Forward?

Sara Roy

There is a new dynamism in Palestine. This can be seen in Mahmoud Abbas's Palestinian membership initiative at the UN (September 2011), Hamas's prisoner exchange with Israel (October 2011), Palestine's admission to UNESCO as a member state (October 2011), and the renewed, albeit difficult, unity talks between Fatah and Hamas. While the situation remains uncertain, to say the least, and the future impossible to predict, the political terrain is undeniably changing in a way not seen since the first Palestinian uprising in 1987. As a friend and highly respected analyst in Gaza told me, "Everything seems strange and seems possible at the same time."

Setting the Context for Change[1]

In the twenty years since the Middle East peace process began, Palestinians have had to confront an extremely adverse reality marked by continued loss and dispossession of land and other resources. This is seen most dramatically in the massive expansion of Israeli settlements and infrastructure and in the building of the separation barrier; in the territorial and demographic fragmentation, cantonisation and isolation; and in the economic fracture and decline. More than anything, these factors reflect the continued failure of the political process and the American-led negotiations, which largely define them. The fundamental problem is Israel's continuing and deepening occupation, which from its inception has been defined by different forms and different degrees of collective deprivation. Add to this the terrible failures of the Palestinian leadership and of the Arab states, which constitute nothing less than a betrayal of and disdain for the Palestinian people and their aspirations.

Twenty years of decline and loss have given rise to some new and unprecedented strategies and policies, both at the official level and at the level of civil society in Palestine, which should be understood not as a coup or revolution but as a transformational and evolutionary model. What follows is a brief examination of some key dynamics and changes.

Establishing A New Framework: The End of Negotiations as Defined by the US under Oslo

The failure of the US-led Oslo process and the illegitimacy of the Palestinian political system were powerfully underlined in January 2011 by the release of the Palestine Papers, which some observers regard as a critical turning point in Palestinian politics. These documents highlighted the bankruptcy of the negotiation process as it had existed since the Oslo period; characterised by open-ended negotiations with no terms of reference, allowing Israel to dramatically alter the facts on the ground; and in which the Palestinian leadership offered concessions that went well beyond the national consensus yet were rejected by Israel. During this period, Israel made it clear that its conditions for accepting a Palestinian state included: annexation of settlement blocs, fragmenting the Palestinian state; demilitarisation of the state; no Right of Return; no sovereignty over the Jordan Valley, which is nearly 30 percent of the West Bank; and no sovereignty over Jerusalem.

The Oslo negotiation model focused on *negotiable* rights – borders, land, water (issues of statehood) – before addressing *non-negotiable* rights – the right to work, travel, move, build a house, market goods, and plant a tree. These were largely ignored under the Oslo framework.[3] Oslo and the US did not treat Israel as an occupying power but rather ignored the illegality of settlements, displaying a clear disregard for human rights and international law.[4] Furthermore, negotiable rights such as land were gradually reframed and redefined in adverse ways as part of an interminable process, which, the analyst

Mouin Rabbani has argued, "effectively transformed the West Bank and Gaza Strip from occupied to disputed territories, and in which Israeli claims are considered as at least as valid as Palestinian rights."[5]

The post-2006 split between the West Bank and Gaza, eventually pitting Fatah and Hamas against each other, introduced other complications. First, if the notion of democracy is to be taken seriously, then the Hamas-led government is the legitimate government in Palestine; yet it is considered a terrorist entity and has been precluded from meaningful political engagement. As Prime Minister Netanyahu stated, "The Palestinian Authority [PA] has to choose between peace with Israel and peace with Hamas"[6] (while his predecessor Ehud Olmert argued that Israel could not negotiate with a Palestinian Authority that was divided). Second, the demonisation and rejection of Hamas as a viable political actor means that the negotiation process as defined by Oslo would not proceed should the two factions reconcile. In this way, political negotiations precluded inter-Palestinian reconciliation, indeed were actively positioned against it – which remains the case – further delegitimising the US-led Oslo negotiation model over time. Despite this, the US administration continued to embrace the same formula of direct bilateral negotiations – negotiations that under the leadership of Dennis Ross (who in November 2011 resigned his position as chief White House advisor on Middle East policy) have been and continue to be aimed at preventing the very two-state outcome they claim to be pursuing, which has proved such a failure for the last twenty years.

Furthermore, in calling for a resumption of the peace process based on US diplomacy and Israeli demands as a formula for negotiations as he did in a May 2011 speech, President Obama failed to break any new ground. Perhaps most important of all, he did not reflect in any measure the repressive reality on the ground for Palestinians, let alone offer any practical recommendations for addressing it. In fact, "the illegitimacy of Israel's repression of [Palestinian] basic human rights never enters Obama's lexicon";[7] nor does Israel's well-documented obstructionism of earlier negotiation efforts. This is particularly striking for another reason: by invoking a new peace process in terms that remain unchanged, the president is situating Israeli policy toward Palestinians and Palestinian nonviolent challenges to that policy *outside* the revolutionary changes taking place in the region. In effect, the US is saying that it will not hold Israel accountable to the standards demanded of other countries in the region, placing it in a category of exceptions that is otherwise reserved for Saudi Arabia and Bahrain.[8] The US made it clear that it would continue to protect and defend Israel's occupation and colonisation and reject Palestinian self-determination. This would consign Palestinians to a form of indefinite occupation, making it impossible for the political leadership in the West Bank to reengage Israel through the existing negotiation structure and be seen as legitimate.

Official Responses: UN Admission of A Palestinian State on 1967 Borders

The shift to non-negotiable rights in Palestinian strategic thinking is reflected in changing policies at the leadership level. A Palestinian official captured the bankruptcy of the political process for Palestinians. "We already have two states," he said, "Israel within 1967 borders, and a state of settlers with Palestinian cities on the periphery." Since the Oslo period Palestinian officialdom has sought international political legitimacy, which has only led to continued losses, greater disenfranchisement and deepening defeat.

Within this paradigm – and with direct US involvement – the Palestinian Authority (PA) did a great deal to delegitimise itself. As Adam Shatz powerfully observes in the *London Review of Books*:

> The PA ... uses the American-trained National Security Force to undermine efforts by Palestinians to challenge the occupation (Hamas, in Gaza, has cracked down on protest even more harshly). "They are the police of the occupation," Myassar Atyani, a leader of the PFLP, told me. "Their leadership is not Palestinian, it is Israeli. On 15 May – the day Palestinians commemorate their Nakba – more than a thousand Palestinians, mainly young men, marched to the Qalandia checkpoint between Ramallah and Jerusalem and clashed with Israeli soldiers; but when Atyani tried to lead a group of demonstrators to the Hawara checkpoint outside Nablus, PA

security forces stopped them. The road from Ramallah to Qalandia is in Area C, which is not controlled by the PA; the road from Nablus to Hawara is in Area A, which is. And protestors who have attempted to march to settlements along PA-controlled roads have also found themselves turned back. *It is an extraordinary arrangement: the security forces of a country under occupation are being subcontracted by third parties outside the region to prevent resistance to the occupying power, even as that power continues to grab more land.*[9] [emphasis mine]

Indeed, the occupation has long been comfortable if not profitable for the Israeli government, particularly with the separation and isolation of the West Bank and Gaza. Furthermore, the Oslo negotiation structure and its prolongation have been used for the last eighteen years to preclude the establishment of the Palestinian state, while the West Bank has steadily dissolved under the weight of continuous resource expropriations, settlement expansion, the Wall and territorial cantonisation.

America's virtually unqualified support for Israeli policies has weakened the US position among Palestinians over time. This support is characterised by: an insistence on the Oslo "peace process" framework of open-ended, bilateral negotiations, which defer final status issues to some indeterminate point; the argument that the Palestinian bid for statehood on 1967 borders is illegitimate while refusing to acknowledge Palestinian losses and despite a stated US commitment to a Palestinian state within those borders; and the unwillingness to accept a reconciliation agreement between Fatah and Hamas, shown by the insistence that there can be no Palestinian unity government unless Hamas agrees to renounce violence, recognise Israel as a Jewish state, and abide by previous agreements. This is irrespective of the fact that Israel itself has violated some of these conditions.

The February 2011 American veto of the UN Security Council (UNSC) resolution condemning Israeli settlements as illegal – a negation of its own official position and the only "no" vote cast – further underscored the futility of continuing to participate in a US-led process.[10] With this veto, the US strikingly demonstrated that it is unable and unwilling to deliver a just solution to the conflict, preferring instead to maintain its hegemony over the Israeli–Palestinian process and manage the conflict indefinitely with no accountability. The US veto was a defining event in official Palestinian thinking. One highly placed Palestinian official close to the leadership confided that while it remains a vital political actor, the US is increasingly regarded by the Palestinian leadership as "handicapped" and "impotent"; unwilling to implement its own policies, and unable to offer anything but a diplomatic dead end, let alone Palestinian liberation.

Consequently, the Palestinian leadership has decided to pursue an alternative, more assertive and proactive strategy informed by two key factors: an acceptance that the US will not meaningfully confront Israel, whose interests are paramount; and a change in strategy from acceding to US partisanship to challenging it.[11] This new strategy appeals to international institutions rather than to Israel and the US primarily as seen in an internal document presented to the Palestine Central Committee in March 2011:

> [Going to the UN] gets the establishment of the State of Palestine out of the box of negotiations, which Israel insists upon ... to the box of the Palestinian people['s] right to self-determination, which means that the birth of Palestine and bringing it back to the map of geography is something that comes in accordance with international law and resolutions of international legitimacy and the rights of peoples to self-determination ... Negotiations are [therefore] about the dates of withdrawal, security arrangements and guarantees ..."[12]

In effect, this new strategy aims to set "borders of a two-state solution along internationally recognised lines and determines the endgame for a political resolution of the conflict".[13] It seeks international *legal* legitimacy, an "internationalisation of the conflict as a legal matter"[14] that will establish a term of reference that will improve Palestine's bargaining position,[15] fostering a set of relations based on equality rather than domination and exclusion. The aim, to quote Dr Husam Zomlot, the deputy director of Fatah's Department of Foreign Relations, is to "legislate Palestine", "to give us the option of saying this is unlawful".[16] The crux of the bid is not to delegitimise Israel but to internationalise Palestine and the Israel/Palestine conflict as a legal (and not only as a political) matter.

Hence the PA's refusal to engage in the Oslo negotiations structure should be understood as a strategic decision to end the status quo and not an attempt to eliminate negotiations as a diplomatic tool, which Palestinians continue to support. However, it should also be understood that the Palestinian leadership is no longer willing to tolerate past approaches and is prepared – at least for the present – to bear costs and consequences that were unthinkable just a few years ago.

In this regard, says Zomlot, statehood is "a tactic, not a goal". The strategic objective is not one or two states but an end to occupation and the creation of an inclusive political system that encompasses Hamas. The objective is also:

> ... to ensure that the Right of Return is implemented, and to establish equal rights for the Palestinian citizens of Israel. Whether these objectives are achieved in one state, or two states, or a hundred states, doesn't matter to most Palestinians. We have options. The apocalyptic option is to dissolve the PA, but we can also withdraw security co-operation, or transform the PA into a resistance authority. What's happened in the last twenty years is not set in stone. It could be undone.[17]

There is a range of arguments – Israeli, American, European and Palestinian – for and against the UN initiative. While it is beyond the scope of this chapter to detail them,[18] there are certain facts that appear hard to dispute. One is that should a Palestinian state be admitted to the UN via the Security Council or General Assembly (GA), sovereignty would lie with the occupied not the occupier. While the GA cannot grant full membership to Palestine, it can upgrade its status from observer to non-member state or observer state, a status the Vatican currently holds and one that Switzerland, Germany and both Koreas previously held. Palestine would enjoy virtually all the rights of a full member, except voting rights. But as a state, Palestine would be able to join a range of international organisations and treaty groups such as the International Court of Justice and the International Criminal Court (where it could sue Israel for settlement building and crimes against humanity; Israel, similarly, could sue Palestine for violations), among various UN agencies.

In October 2011 the state of Palestine was admitted as a full member of UNESCO against US and Israeli objections. As the *New York Times* pointed out, "If a United Nations resolution defines Palestine as within the 1967 lines, that means 500,000 Israelis will be defined as occupiers in another country."[19] An Israeli army jeep driving through Ramallah or Hebron could become an international incident. Indeed, the entire discourse could change.

Palestinian officials are well aware of the problems surrounding their bid for UN membership, but view it as a necessary though insufficient step in the process of liberation. It will neither end the occupation nor create a viable state in the short term but rather create a new basis for negotiations, restoring the Palestine issue to a central position without violence and allow Palestine "to insist upon a relationship based on sovereign equality ... Moreover, Palestine's status will be formally recognised without Palestine having to make any concessions on settlements, the Right of Return, or Jerusalem etc."[20] Perhaps one question that should be asked regarding the debate is this: Will the status of Palestine as a state enhance or diminish Palestinians' ability to pursue a legal strategy? Legal parity would also suggest that the process of ending the occupation no longer depends solely on the United States; the fear of losing its monopoly over the process is a principal US concern.

Official Responses: Fatah–Hamas Reconciliation and the Agreement on Unity

Another critical dynamic reshaping the Palestinian political landscape is the stated commitment by Fatah and Hamas to Palestinian unity despite the formidable obstacles confronting them.[21] Palestinian fragmentation and disunity – a direct outcome of the Oslo negotiation framework – have played a critical role in strengthening the occupation. The pressure to preclude reconciliation was a cornerstone of US policy and the Oslo negotiation model.

There can be no doubt that the uprisings in the Middle East and popular pressure demanding unity as seen in the March 15 movement – a call for unity that goes beyond Fatah and Hamas – played a vital role in pushing both sides to an agreement to form an interim government.[22] Critically, the PA's continued failure to reach an agreement with Israel and most importantly, the US's failure to promote serious two-state negotiations, converged with internal popular pressure, compelling the parties to seize the initiative and compromise because "the alternatives were worse".[23] "The region will not reverse itself," said a Fatah official, "and this is a new and constant variable"[24] that greatly influenced political thinking regardless of US or other reactions. There can also be no doubt that for Abbas and the Ramallah PA, the removal of Mubarak was a loss of an important patron and source of support. Yet the Palestine Papers further revealed that Mubarak's Egypt was not an honest broker in earlier Fatah–Hamas talks but, to the contrary, "collaborated with Israel in trying to weaken and isolate Hamas".[25] Thus, it is also true that with the departure of Mubarak and his regime, Israel has lost a critical ally who helped secure a repressive status quo in the West Bank and Gaza.

The pressures on Hamas were similarly strong. For example, Hamas has come under enormous pressure from its population in Gaza for its economic and political failures including: the futility of armed resistance and the firing of rockets; the loss of 1,400 lives during Israel's 2008–9 assault; continued military attacks by Israel; the lack of economic improvement, change or reconstruction; the continued (intensified) closure and sealing of the borders; rising unemployment, now around 30–35 percent but having approached 50 percent at the beginning of 2011; unrelieved impoverishment, with approximately 70–80 percent of the population still dependent on some form of humanitarian assistance; and the lack of political legitimacy domestically and internationally. Hamas cannot continue to rule Gaza indefinitely under a state of constant closure nor does it appear to want to.[26]

Hamas's ambition goes beyond ruling an internationally isolated Gaza. The Arab revolutions taught Hamas that the potential for civil unrest in Gaza is very high. The party's achievements notwithstanding, the relationship between Hamas and the Gazan population is unstable. People are exhausted by their diminished environment, which is worsened by various Hamas policies, in particular the growing Islamisation of society. Hamas, in short, finds itself on the same course that made Fatah unpopular in 2005. Indeed, a Gazan friend argued that the alternative to Hamas is not necessarily Fatah or the PLO. Gazans, like Palestinian refugees elsewhere in the world, feel abandoned and forgotten. This is a potentially dangerous situation, not only for the government in Gaza but also for its counterpart in the West Bank.

The turmoil in Syria has also placed Hamas in a tenuous position. In fact, the Syrian regime demanded that Hamas take a position on the political situation in Syria. The international Muslim Brotherhood (MB) came out in support of the protestors while Hamas kept silent, which did not satisfy the Syrian government or its allies in Tehran.[27] Diplomats have cited Iran's unhappiness over Hamas's refusal to hold rallies in support of Assad, especially in Palestinian refugee camps in Syria, and there are reports that Iran has reduced if not ended its financial support for Hamas. Hamas also has been criticised for remaining silent when Syrian forces attacked those same camps. However, as the Qaddafi regime was falling in Libya, a series of articles appeared in the Palestinian daily, *Falastin*, which is close to Hamas, attacking Syrian President Assad, in effect clarifying Hamas's position. In one such article the following appeared: "The oppression will not last. Allah, who granted victory to the Egyptians, Tunisians and Libyans will [likewise] grant victory to the Syrians and Yeminis and any people that desires honour, freedom, and to get rid of a [tyrannical] ruler."[28] The split between Hamas and the Syrian leadership was completed when the Islamic organisation ended its political operations in Damascus in early 2012.

The Egyptian Muslim Brotherhood also played a vital role in pushing Hamas toward reconciliation. With their decision to form a political party and become part of the political system, the Egyptian MB argued that Hamas, as a branch of the MB, must do the same. The first step toward this end was to reconcile with Fatah and prepare for elections within the year. Hamas was told that it could no longer ignore changing developments in the region, meaning it must seek other, new alliances that would mitigate its dependency on Syria and Iran.[29]

Hamas has less to lose and more to gain from a reconciliation with Fatah. Its decision to do so reveals its support of the UN initiative despite its public criticisms and denunciations, which seem to focus in large part on the fact that Hamas was not consulted beforehand. This seems to be a vocal complaint from the external leadership, notably Khaled Meshal. Meshal has also stated that Hamas favours a Palestinian state on the territorial lines as they stood before the 1967 war, with East Jerusalem as its capital, and on the condition that all refugees be permitted to return to their homes in what is today Israel, all settlements be dismantled and no recognition be granted to Israel, a position prime minister Ismail Haniyeh has reiterated.[30]

Mohammed Awad, foreign minister of the Hamas government, said Abbas's speech at the UN contained "important positive points". Mousa Abu Marzouq, deputy head of the Hamas politburo, has given a guarded welcome to Abbas's stated commitment to unity talks and called for strategic dialogue on securing Palestinian statehood. These statements among others suggest that Hamas began to rethink its public position when it became apparent that Abbas's defiance had struck a nerve with ordinary Palestinians and enjoyed bipartisan support. Generally, writes the *New York Times*, "[Hamas's] leaders speak of full Palestinian sovereignty in the 1967 lines and a twenty-year truce without granting Israel recognition."[31]

Arguably, Hamas will emerge strengthened by a success at the UN, since it remains in firm control of Gaza and Gaza is a vital part of the Palestinian state. At present, there can be no viable state without Gaza and there can be no Gaza without engaging Hamas. The fact remains that given Hamas's longstanding opposition to the Oslo-defined negotiations (and its refusal to recognise Israel and renounce violence) – but not to negotiations as a diplomatic tool – and the low likelihood that Abbas will resume direct negotiations with Israel, it may be harder for Hamas to discredit or reject overtures from Abbas. Within a month of Abbas's UN appearance, Hamas had also gained politically by successfully negotiating a prisoner exchange with Israel in which over 1,000 Palestinian prisoners were released in exchange for the Israeli soldier Gilad Shalit (who had been in Hamas captivity for five years). The timing of the prisoner exchange allowed Hamas to score a concrete and highly popular political victory that clearly upstaged Abbas's UN bid (and likely was meant by Israel to punish Abbas for his defiance).

A critical factor for Hamas is Egypt. For now Egypt is no longer part of the problem, at least as it was under Mubarak. The political dynamics of Gaza changed after the Egyptian revolution. The interim military government opened the Rafah border crossing despite continuous and cumbersome problems, which are expected to improve after the upcoming Egyptian elections (although massive demonstrations in November 2011 against Egypt's increasingly authoritarian government could change this). Hamas classifies the government in Egypt as a friendly one; contacts between both governments take place on all levels and their relationship appears to be more and more direct. Security chiefs from Hamas and Egypt meet on a regular basis to deal with security breaches in Sinai (which are a growing and serious problem), tunnel smuggling and human trafficking. There are rumours in Gaza that Hamas has agreed to close some of the tunnels operating between Egypt and Gaza, keeping only the "necessary" ones open. There is some speculation that Hamas's improved relationship with Egypt may, as part of the reconciliation agreement with Fatah, be used by Abbas to support a new more comprehensive Palestinian approach to Cairo. Could Gaza become a bridge between Ramallah and Cairo?

A real unity agreement will also strengthen Hamas against the established extremist groups that are challenging Hamas's governance, other problems notwithstanding. Hamas is not the only political actor in Gaza, despite the fact that it is, unquestionably, the most powerful. Hamas faces real competition from more militant extremist groups, such as the Salafi-Jihadis, whose goal is not the liberation of Palestine but the defence of Islam against non-Muslim enemies; these also include Shi'ites and Palestinian secularists.[32] They do not see themselves as Palestinian but as part of a global movement that is al Qaeda-like, and they advocate a strict interpretation of Islamic law. Unlike Fatah and Hamas, they do not define the resistance in nationalist terms but in transnational terms.

The extremist challenge lies not in their numbers or military capacity, which to date remains limited, but in the constraints they impose on Hamas – and potentially on its future policies.[33] The Salafi-Jihadis have long accused Hamas of betraying Islam and of religious moderation; this is due to Hamas's willingness to engage Israel and the West politically and diplomatically (so far with little success, particularly with regard to ending the closure and the occupation), and to hold elections, and also to its failure to implement Sharia. This in turn has put pressure on Hamas for more militancy and Islamisation.

Changes in Civil Society Action

The shift in strategy from negotiable to non-negotiable rights can also be seen at the level of civil society. Even before the March 15 demonstrations in Gaza and the West Bank, which called for popular unity and the end of internal divisions, Palestinian civil society organisations had embraced a new strategy informing the popular struggle against occupation. This had as its core imperative the unity of people over the unity of land (the latter being a practical impossibility, at least in the near term). There is a growing consensus that as long as the Palestinian struggle for independence remains focused on land – which of course remains important – it cannot be won (particularly given the gross asymmetries in power between Israelis and Palestinians, and the latter's virtual abandonment by the US and other members of the international community).

According to this argument, Palestinians should not be fighting for a state *per se* but for their rights – human, political, economic, social and civil – within that future state; rights which others (Israelis and Americans among them) possess and which transcend borders. The assumption informing this strategy assumes that the occupation will remain in the short to medium term, even with the establishment of a Palestinian state. This strategy calls for people to organise around specific issues such as housing rights, human rights, anti-Wall (like the mobilisation of popular resistance committees in places like Nilin, Budros and Bilin protesting the confiscation of their farmland by settlers or by the Wall), or access to international markets; and attempting to forge linkages and alliances with Palestinians inside the West Bank and Gaza, with Palestinians and other groups regionally and internationally, and with Israeli groups who support the Palestinian struggle.[34] On 15 July 2011, for example, 2,500 people, the majority Israelis and internationals, marched with Palestinians from East

Jerusalem neighbourhoods and from inside Israel in East Jerusalem in support of the Palestinian bid for UN membership. Similarly, hundreds of Palestinians in Ramallah, Nablus and Gaza demonstrated in support of the hunger strike by Palestinian prisoners, which began on 27 September 2011. Another civil society movement has been organised around the UN statehood/membership initiative at the UN. It is known as the National Campaign – Palestine State #194, referring to Palestine as the 194th member of the General Assembly (and echoing UNR 194 regarding the Palestinian refugees). This campaign has mobilised supporters in both the West Bank and Gaza in the form of town hall meetings and other discussion forums.

The victories, when they do occur, are small and sometimes ephemeral, but they have enormous symbolic importance and mobilisational force.[35] This is clearly seen in the actions of six Palestinian activists who boarded a segregated bus in the West Bank meant only for Israeli settlers. Re-enacting the actions of the Freedom Riders of the 1960s civil rights movement in the US, the six Palestinians aimed to bring attention to the system of segregation that governs their lives in an act of non-violent civil disobedience.[36]

These changes point to another emerging and critical dimension of civil society activism: extending the strategy of non-violent mass mobilisation (a potential source of conflict or complementarity with the leadership) to include the revitalisation of a common national identity and "reunified body politic with representative mechanisms and political and intellectual pluralism"[37] that aims to incorporate all sectors of Palestinian society including Palestinians citizens of Israel and the refugee communities outside of Israel/Palestine. As one Palestinian activist explained:

> Our roof is the occupation and our floor, the political factions. In Gaza, nearly all political demands have been associated with one party or the other. If you demand elections you are accused of supporting Fatah and if you support ending Oslo you appear to be supporting Hamas. So, in order to maintain neutrality and establish a popular position, we have demanded an end to the division.[38]

Popular pressure, particularly among Palestinian youth, is building and being mobilised around demands that transcend borders and statehood, as seen in two key issues. The first is a renewed campaign around the refugee right of return, which has reasserted itself after years of absence during the Oslo period. This right is considered sacred by all Palestinians, not just Hamas; and any attempt by any Palestinian, official or otherwise, to renounce it (as the Palestine Papers revealed the PA was willing to do), especially before Israel has recognised it, is seen as treasonous. For many if not most Palestinians, the Right of Return does not amount to actual repatriation but a political acknowledgement of the crimes committed in 1948; it is also about reparations and the "restoration of their freedom of movement inside the entire country, regardless of whether it is called Israel or Palestine".[39]

Palestinians are publicly demanding "a right that is recognised under international law and by UN resolutions but has not been implemented for sixty-three years".[40] They also are calling for elections for the Palestinian National Council (which meets every two years to decide the direction of the PLO should take and to elect its executive committee) in order to "reconstruct a Palestinian national programme based upon a comprehensive resistance platform" that rejects the concentration of power in the Occupied Territories (meaning Fatah and Hamas) and is based on a one man, one vote system that includes all Palestinians inside and outside the territories. (This would clearly threaten the interests of the two factions.)[41] The aim is not only to "memorialise the past but also to demand a new future",[42] characterised by the absence of factionalism and incorporating the "entirety of Palestine before 1948".[43]

In this regard, the second demand concerns the position of the Arab citizens of Israel and their relationship to other Palestinians. When the second intifada broke out in 2000, thirteen were killed, all but one inside Israel. Disabused of their belief that they were protected as citizens of Israel, the Arab community became increasingly subject to discriminatory laws, land confiscations and home demolitions.[44] One of their most prominent political representatives, Azmi Bishara, was forced into exile in 2006 after being accused by Israel of aiding Hizbullah during the summer war. More recently, the Knesset passed the Budget Foundations Act, which punishes Arab cultural institutions that engage in activities commemorating the *Nakba*. Like the Palestinians under occupation, the Arab citizens of Israel are still part of the national conflict.

However, when the Arab citizens of Israel hear talk of territorial swaps – settlements in the West Bank in exchange for Arab lands inside Israel – they fear transfer into the West Bank with the accompanying loss of land, mobility, rights and citizenship. While they support the establishment of a Palestinian state they do not want to be sacrificed to it, nor do they wished to be marginalised even further by Israel's consolidation as a Jewish state. Consequently, Palestinians in Israel are beginning to mobilise (non-violently) around the same issues animating Palestinians in the West Bank and Gaza: human rights and equality.[45] This has enabled Israel's Arab citizenry to engage with Palestinians in the Occupied Territories and regionally in common cause – despite the very real differences that remain between them – around an emerging and coalescing political agenda.

This speaks to another critical strategic component that has taken root in Palestinian civil society: the adoption of peaceful non-violent resistance as the dominant Palestinian strategy for dealing with Israel going forward. This strategy, which has a long history among Palestinians, rejects continued accommodation to the status quo in favour of peaceful confrontation and has assumed a prominent role in the collective struggle.[46] This was further seen on Nakba Day when, in an unprecedented measure, thousands of unarmed Palestinians in the West Bank, Gaza, Jordan, Lebanon and Syria approached the border with Israel, a march that was coordinated by Facebook and Twitter activists. In the case of Syria, over one hundred actually crossed the border into the Druze town of Majdal Shams in the Golan, and one man made it all the way to his ancestral city of Jaffa, and "without so much as a sidearm, penetrated farther into the country than any army in a generation".[47]

Key Strategic Features of A Changing Political Paradigm

The new political paradigm described above, which continues to take shape, is characterised, at least in part, by two emerging strategic shifts: one internal and the other external.

Strategic shift: Internal

One important component of Palestine's changing political paradigm is an internal strategic shift in civil society-state relations, which is beginning to emerge despite the obstacles that continue to plague it.

A huge problem for Abbas is his continued lack of popular legitimacy inside the Occupied Territories and beyond. His constituency, like elsewhere in the region, is predominantly young and unemployed, and largely unmobilised. This mistrust of Abbas, the PA and politicians generally, verges on the ideological.

Throughout the Palestinian areas, Abbas's decision to seek UN recognition of a state is seen as a major policy shift – bypassing Israel, defying the US – which may lead to common ground, not only between Fatah and Hamas but between the Palestinian "state" and civil society. The attempt to re-internationalise the Palestinian struggle, statehood aside, wrest the negotiation process from US control and return it to international law and UN resolutions has considerable support among Palestinians.

Apparently, the need to "reconfigure internally", as one individual in the Fatah hierarchy put it, to reestablish legitimacy with his own people, is an issue Abbas now wants to address. This "reconfiguration" refers to a vision that is not limited to day-to-day issues of control and power but is longer term; inclusive of civil society, political factions including Hamas, and the Diaspora. This vision speaks to reciprocity and a willingness to respond to popular demands for greater accountability: ultimately, it speaks to redefining the social contract between Palestinians and their state. Over the last few years, there has been growing pressure from an increasingly active and organised civil society, pressure which gained momentum after regional eruptions and which played a crucial role in the Fatah–Hamas reconciliation agreement.

The leadership can no longer afford to ignore, or, even worse, obstruct or repress civil society actions as it has done. Popular opinion matters more in Palestine than it did in the past, as it does elsewhere in the region, and ignoring it carries relatively greater costs. The important point is that post-UN there may be a new space taking shape for common action that has not existed for a long time. And while such realignments may or may not take place, they are now an increasing part of the popular discourse when before they were not.

This raises another important point concerning Palestinian unity. Despite the many challenges that remain, a key feature of the Fatah–Hamas unity agreement is the return of Gaza to the conflict, to the struggle and to the Palestinian cause after five years of separation and isolation. The political re-engagement of Gaza and its repositioning back in the centre of the conflict is key to the reconstruction of a national movement and end to occupation. Arguably, if Gaza had remained politically engaged, Israeli policies in the West Bank would have been more difficult to implement; the Ramallah PA would also have had to rule differently.[48]

It is important to understand that people are truly fatigued and fragmented. They are also angry and frustrated. Israel's occupation "essentially dissolved the West Bank as a coherent entity"[49] and converted the Gaza Strip into an imprisoned enclave for 1.65 million people, a disconnection that extends to Palestinians beyond the territories. The majority of young Palestinians in the West Bank have never been to Gaza or Israel, and their counterparts have never been to the West Bank, let alone anywhere outside these territories. This begs the question: does the reconciliation agreement aim to unify two political factions or all segments of the Palestinian people? The push among civil society activists is of course the latter: to unite, in some meaningful way, all segments of the Palestinian people; and they will exert pressure on the government to do the same.

For some activists, such a process must begin with Gaza – at least, it certainly cannot begin without Gaza. As one told me, "Gaza will fight for Jerusalem, Ramallah will not." Gaza is the political heart and strategic core of Palestine and Palestinian nationalism, the centre of political resistance historically and currently. As such, Gaza represents a political challenge or threat that goes well beyond – and long precedes – Hamas. Israel well understood this, which is why Gaza was cut off from the West Bank and isolated. The fundamental problem confronting Palestinians is not Hamas or political Islam but a redrawing of the social contract, i.e. redefining the relationship between the state and its citizens wherever they reside, which is impossible without re-engaging Gaza. Ultimately, unity will not come from a Fatah–Hamas reconciliation alone but from a new societal programme, which some officials argue will begin with the dissolution of the PA.

Strategic shift: External

Another strategic shift is occurring in Palestine's external relations, in which US exceptionalism is no longer tolerable. In repeated conversations, the author was told some version of: "The US can no longer impose its terms on us." One striking illustration of Palestinian determination is seen in the following account by a key official involved in the UN initiative. Apparently there was enormous pressure on the Palestinian delegation on the eve of Abbas's appearance at the General Assembly to withdraw their bid for membership. This pressure, which was quite intense, came not only from the Americans and the Europeans but also from "all the Arab States". Refusal to give into the pressure was absolute. According to one official: "It felt like a fist fight, like a physical struggle. We were standing alone, really alone but we were determined to go ahead."

Another possible factor characterising the external strategic shift lies in an approach that appears to welcome a US role in some measure, but in a role that is defined in larger part by Palestinians and in which the US is no longer a strategic pillar. Prior to the UN, there was a battle between those Palestinians who wanted to pursue a legal and multilateral path (consolidate international recognition and become part of the international system) by first approaching the General Assembly, and those, including Abbas, who wanted to pursue a political and bilateral option by first approaching the Security Council. By going to the Security Council first, where the Palestinians knew they would encounter a US veto or certain defeat, Abbas was, arguably, keeping the bilateral (US–Palestinian) door, once wide open, slightly but not indefinitely open before it was closed. By November 2011 the Security Council was deadlocked with eight out of fifteen members approving Palestine's admission, which meant the US did not have to use its veto. Abbas indicated that he would return to the UNSC multiple times in his quest for full membership. There also have been reports that the PA has initiated a process that would upgrade Palestine's status via the General Assembly.

Whether this reflects a new commitment on the part of the leadership to a programme of nationalist reconstruction remains to be seen, but it does suggest an attempt to shift from the revolutionary legitimacy of the past to a new form of international legitimacy. This international legitimacy is characterised by another important strategic change: a shift by the Palestinian leadership away from American political elites, who are considered similarly obstructionist, to a more direct relationship with American civil society groups. According to a BBC poll, 45 percent of Americans support the Palestinian bid for UN membership, with 36 percent opposing. The same strategy will likely be used in Europe, where public opinion in three EU states was strongly supportive: France – 54 percent (20 percent opposed); Germany – 53 percent (28 percent opposed); and the UK – 53 percent (26 percent opposed).[50]

Is US Policy Becoming Less Relevant?
Another New Dynamic

According to Geoffrey Aronson of the Foundation for Middle East Peace in Washington, the almost two-year diplomatic effort on the part of the Obama administration "to build a solid foundation for final status negotiations by winning meaningful concessions from Israel on settlement expansion [had by December 2010] been declared a failure by the administration itself".[51] In December 2010 Hilary Clinton called for the resetting of US policy away from temporary reductions in settlement expansion toward final status issues despite Netanyahu's reluctance to engage in a process that addresses those issues.

Aronson further argues that the administration has been unwilling to confront Israel meaningfully on the issues of settlements, the ten-month settlement construction moratorium that ended in September 2010 notwithstanding. With the end of the moratorium, Israel began construction on 1,500 new settlement units in the West Bank, on both sides of the separation barrier.[52] Furthermore, Netanyahu's rejection of the US's "unprecedented package of incentives aimed at moving diplomacy beyond a short-lived settlement moratorium" effectively forced the US to declare an end to the settlement freeze initiative, which is no longer a "key weapon in the arsenal of American and international peacemakers".[53] On 7 December 2010 President Obama decided to abandon his policy, suspending American efforts to resume direct negotiations between Israel and the PA. The Palestinians remain opposed to restarting direct negotiations as long as Israel continues to build settlements and as long as the construction moratorium excludes East Jerusalem.

Clearly American power (and unilateralism) to shape regional events in its own interests is weakening, particularly with regard to preventing outcomes the US government does not want.[54] Furthermore, not only are the Palestinian and Arab peoples unwilling to succumb to US pressure as they once did but so are America's traditional (and highly reliable) European allies, as seen in the UN voting around Palestine's membership. Despite US objections, for example, the French voted in favour of Palestine's admission to UNESCO while the British abstained. Similarly, in the UNSC vote, only Germany voted "no" while the remaining European countries abstained.[55]

Some Reflections on the US Position

The paradigm for negotiations since 1967 has been land-for-peace, but what happens when there is no land? Because it is becoming less tenable for the US to explain the lack of political progress or credible alternatives to the status quo, the fiction of two states continues to be pursued; in order to pursue it, the US emphasises continued negotiations over real outcomes, which are, in effect, already predetermined – a Palestinian state that is weak and lacking real sovereignty.

A successful UN vote on Palestinian membership would isolate and humiliate the US, especially in a changing regional context where Arab peoples are fighting and dying daily for their freedom and liberty, further eroding America's public image if not its influence.[56] But there is another, less obvious but critically important dimension to the US position mentioned earlier, one that is characterised by anger over its diminishing control over the political process. In private meetings between US and Palestinian officials held in early 2011, the Palestinians expressed their desire to pursue a more autonomous policy, as seen in the UN initiative, and engage more directly with other players – be they regional, European or multilateral. They were met with considerable hostility from some American officials. Other colleagues in the PA described hostile, threatening phone calls from US officials.

Perhaps the US desires a peaceful settlement with security for Israel and a state for Palestinians, but US policymakers do not possess the will to do what is necessary to ensure that outcome, that is, challenge Israeli policies. There are many reasons for this, including the oft-cited influence of the Israel lobby, which treats Israel and its security as a domestic (and hence structural) issue. But as one American official confided: "This explanation, while real, is too simplistic and categorical. It's like pushing against an open door [which] is characterised by a predisposition toward Israel that derives from sympathy over the Holocaust, the rise of Arab terrorism, and the rise of anti-Muslim sentiment especially after 9/11."

A State Department official with fifteen years' experience of working on the Israeli–Palestinian issue provided the following assessment:

It should come as no surprise that key decision makers and Congress generally find Israeli arguments persuasive and can readily imagine that Israel is dealing with legitimate security concerns such as those they genuinely believe will arise from a unity agreement between Fatah and Hamas. Personal threats to Israel are seen as real and are felt. There is little acceptance that Israel is a large part of the problem and is the stronger party. Similarly, there is a belief that the West Bank territory that Israel wants to retain is not a big deal, poses no serious problem even if it degrades the territorial contiguity of a Palestinian state. The US does not fundamentally understand or care about the issues of injustice that form the Palestinian reality ... Like their Israeli counterparts, US policymakers fundamentally believe that the existence of the State of Israel is predicated on the denial of Palestinian nationhood. Palestinians are seen as intruders. Palestinians do not matter and have little to offer the US especially when viewed against our strong alliance with Israel economically, militarily, and politically. They are not respected and are considered weak and reactive, easily pushed around.

Despite official rhetoric, the Arab Spring is seen by many inside the administration as a threat to Israel. When Palestinians crossed the Syrian border into Israel, administration officials saw them as barbarians coming over the border. It apparently is a deeply held belief among US policymakers that the Arab people are not mature enough for democracy and there is a real fear that the Muslim Brotherhood will take over in different Arab countries. [Hence, for many inside the administration] Israel is right when they say there is no reliable partner to deal with.[57]

The question remains, of course, how will the US respond to the emerging sense of political empowerment in the Arab world including Palestine? Will it try to reduce the deepening gap between American policy as it has historically been defined and new Palestinian and Arab aspirations? Will the US be willing to work with those countries that support policies it does not, such as the Fatah–Hamas unity agreement?[58] And perhaps most importantly, will democracy in the Arab world be cast as adverse to American and Israeli interests?

A Changing Discourse in Israel: 1967 Borders and Social Protest – Emerging New Dynamics?

In calling for a return to 1967 borders, the Palestinian leadership is not without its supporters in Israel. It is also important to highlight the changing dialogue around 1967 borders within certain sectors of Israel itself, which opposes Netanyahu's position.[59] Strikingly, key figures in Israel's security establishment, including former chiefs of Israel's main security services – Mossad, Shin Bet and the Israel Defense Forces (IDF) – are calling for a two-state agreement with the PA based on 1967 borders and similar to the 2002 Arab League peace initiative, in addition to ending all calls for an attack against Iran. In fact, on 6 May 2011 Shaul Mofaz, a former IDF chief and ex-defence minister (and now Chairman of the Knesset's foreign affairs and defence committee) called for an immediate recognition by Israel of a Palestinian state, "followed by negotiations between the two states over borders, security arrangements and the like". He also stated that the unity pact between Fatah and Hamas was an "opportunity" for Israel, "predicting that if Israel seized the initiative now, it might well push Hamas into accepting Israel and swearing off terrorism".[60]

Furthermore, on 1 April 2011 the so-called Israel Peace Initiative, consisting of Israeli notables – former security officials, ex-diplomats, academics, artists, celebrities and business leaders (including Yitzchak Rabin's children, who are part of the Initiative's leadership) – signed a petition supporting a two-state solution based on the 1967 borders (with mutually agreed upon adjustments).[61] For years, talk of returning to the 1967 borders was unacceptable in the general discourse (except for the extreme Left) but it is increasingly becoming the norm in certain limited social and political sectors in Israel.

The summer of 2011 also saw massive protests in Israel around issues of social and economic justice parallel to those in America. Known as the J14 movement, this could be said to be Israel's "Arab Spring". The protestors have largely been silent on the connection between the social welfare crisis and the occupation, for supposedly strategic reasons.[62] Despite its importance as a potential social and political force, the question the J14 movement must ultimately ask is this: what does social justice mean within a state that oppresses and dispossesses another people under its control?

Are Egypt and Turkey Becoming More Relevant?

Writing in April 2011, an analyst in Gaza argued:

> The raising of the Palestinian flag in Tahrir Square in front of the Israeli embassy in Cairo was an important reason why the recent [March 2011] aggression on the Gaza Strip stopped after it became clear to the Israeli government that Egypt, its leadership and people, reject any Israeli aggression on Gaza. Also the role played by the Egyptian Foreign Ministry in curbing the attacks was very important as well as the decision made by the Arab League asking the UN Security Council for a no-fly zone over Gaza.[63]

He later wrote that during the March 2011 offensive on Gaza, Egypt sent a message to Tel Aviv through the EU, which stated the following: "Gaza is the backyard of Egyptian national security. Therefore we consider any attack on Gaza now as a direct threat to Egypt. ... War on Gaza is not allowed anymore."[64] Egyptian intervention also ended Israel's retaliatory attack against Gaza in August after eight Israelis were killed and another thirty wounded in an attack by militants in southern Israel.

The revolution in Egypt removed Hosni Mubarak and his regime as the bulwark of Israel's position in the region, releasing popular anger at Israel over its treatment of the Palestinian people, an issue that resonates deeply throughout the region. The attack on the Israeli embassy in Cairo in September 2011, which forced the Israeli ambassador and most of his staff to flee and which followed earlier protests and the burning of the Israeli flag in response to an attack in southern Israel where three Egyptian police officers were killed by Israel, was not something the Egyptian government wanted. According to the *New York Times*: "For Egypt's interim military rulers, allowing the invasion of a foreign embassy is an extraordinary breach of Egypt's international commitments that is raising security concerns at other embassies as well."[65] Yet despite the clear problems caused, the army refused to stop the attack because to do so would likely have been viewed as illegitimate by the Egyptian people. Unlike in the past, the Egyptian government and other Arab governments, including the PA in Gaza and Ramallah, must increasingly account for popular opinion in their quest for legitimacy while maintaining popular order and the rule of law.

After the embassy attack, however, the military government greatly increased its emergency powers, suppressing popular protest and further threatening personal freedoms. This in turn led to large-scale demonstrations against the government's growing authoritarianism and brutality, and the resignation of the Egyptian cabinet in November 2011. It is clear that the "Arab Spring" can take all kinds of directions and the times ahead, while dynamic, are uncertain.

The expulsion from Turkey of the Israeli ambassador in September 2011 and the deteriorating (military but not trade) relations with one of Israel's most important regional allies, something whose history predates the current situation, suggests further change *vis-à-vis* Israel and the Palestinians that remains hard to predict. Among other measures, Turkey has indicated that it will increase its naval presence in the eastern Mediterranean, which potentially could be a serious source of friction, given that gas fields have been found some sixty-eight nautical miles from the Gazan coast. In fact, Israel is in negotiation with British Petroleum for the exploration arrangements of this gas field. Under the pre-Hamas government, the Fatah authorities in Gaza reportedly ceded a large percentage of the yield to Israel.

In private talks with Palestinian officials, Turkey also has indicated its willingness to give Gaza direct access to its port in Izmir as part of its promise to engage more directly with Gaza's economy, while Cyprus has made a similar offer for use of its port in Limassol. Just before the UN meeting, Turkish Prime Minister Recep Tayyip Erdogan told Arab League Ministers that recognition of a Palestinian state was "not a choice but an obligation", thereby increasing pressure on the US and Israel.

Furthermore, as Turkey's old allies, Syria and Israel, fall into deeper isolation and US influence diminishes, Turkey is strengthening its alliance with Egypt, a new ally. Turkey's foreign minister, Ahmet Davutoglu, has indicated that Egypt will become the focus of Turkish efforts "as an older American-backed order, buttressed by Israel, Saudi Arabia and to a lesser extent, pre-revolutionary Egypt, begins to crumble".[66] Improved ties between Egypt and Turkey have already impacted on Hamas and

Palestinians generally – witness the Egyptian and Turkish roles in brokering the prisoner exchange between Israel and Hamas.

A Concluding Note

The political, economic and strategic implications for Palestine, Israel, the region and beyond, of the measures discussed remain to be seen. But they do point to two critically important facts: that the status quo ante is no longer possible, and change is inevitable if not irreversible; and that the resolution of the Israeli–Palestinian conflict must lie in the rule of law, which, the scholar Norman Finkelstein argues, is "the dominant language of our epoch",[67] an epoch now defined by an awakened and combustible Middle East.

FOUR

The Power of Narrative: Reimagining the Palestinian Struggle

Saree Makdisi

As it has done periodically over the years – in 1968, 1974, 1987, 1988 and 2001 – the Palestinian struggle is reinventing itself in 2012. It is slowly emerging from the carapace of an older self in a newly invigorated form: one more adapted, as though by a kind of evolutionary process of political selection, to the exigencies of the present. Viewed while still in the middle of this metamorphosis, the movement might seem – and indeed it is – split, especially between those Palestinians who cling to what is manifestly an outmoded form of political thought (one centred on the nation-state as Europeans defined it for their own purposes a couple of centuries ago), and those who are coming to embrace a new political logic, one in which identity is no longer seen as conferred by, or restricted to, the scale or apparatus of the nation-state; and hence one in which the traditional state form is no longer the ultimate objective of the Palestinian cause.

On the one hand, then, there are Palestinians who still believe in the idea of creating an independent Palestinian state alongside Israel, in deference to the logic that every people must have its own state. These include the cadres and leaders of all the major established political parties, from Fatah to Hamas. They cling to this logic even if there is no conceivable way in which such a state could fulfil the needs of all Palestinians. This is especially pressing given that the vast majority of Palestinians do not live in the territory deemed acceptable for such a state – some permutation of the territories Israeli occupied in 1967 – and could not be accommodated there even if a state was actually created in a viable form.

And on the other hand, there are increasing numbers of

Palestinians who are more interested in actually achieving their rights and in securing a just peace in the form of a one-state solution than they are in abstractly fulfilling the criteria for national independence as it was formulated by European writers (Theodor Herzl among them) in the eighteenth and nineteenth centuries.

Although the traditional language of Left and Right doesn't capture the nature of this split among Palestinians, it is worth noting that most of the advocates of a one-state solution are not affiliated with official parties, though they are increasingly clustered around the still-developing Boycott, Divestment and Sanctions (BDS) movement, itself inhabiting neither a hierarchical nor a formal party structure.

Indeed, on this point in particular, it might be worth borrowing from Edward Said's discussion of intellectual amateurism to describe the proponents of the one-state solution. For Said, amateurism is defined not by a lack of skill or capacity but, on the contrary, by a sense of intense care and commitment born out of freedom, in particular freedom of thought as generated by a relative degree of freedom from institutional-political entanglements. Whereas the professional-ised intellectual is all too willing to surrender insight and analysis in the service of institutional or career considerations, and hence adheres reflexively to certain approaches or lines of thought while refusing to contemplate others, the amateur is not so constrained: his or her approach is determined by care rather than career – and indeed, if need be, care at the expense of career. This necessarily opens up rather than closes down intellectual horizons, since lines of argument can be tried and contested on their merits rather than in terms of the good or harm they might do to one's standing within a party, institution or profession.

One last point by way of introduction: it is worth considering the extent to which those Palestinians who still cling to the two-state solution do so out of institutional or party affiliation rather than on the merits of the argument itself.

The Palestinian bid for statehood at the United Nations in the autumn of 2011 is perhaps the clearest recent example of the bid to sacrifice political principle in order to safeguard party affiliation and personal ambitions. In the wake of Mahmoud Abbas's UN General Assembly speech in September of that year, it was clear to many

Palestinians that the statehood bid was not really intended to address or secure the rights of all Palestinians, but rather to reassert the failing political fortunes of Mr Abbas himself, to tactically reframe rather than strategically transform the pointless negotiations game that he and his associates have been playing for two decades now. For their work, they saw the population of Jewish colonists triple while the Palestinians were more deeply immobilised and immiserated.

Moreover, the statehood gambit carries enormous political risks for the entire Palestinian people, into which Mr Abbas and his associates have entered without even consulting them. As many legal observers (including Guy Goodwin-Gill and more recently a team of Palestinian legal scholars whose declaration was published by the *Maan* News Service) have pointed out, there is a pointed danger that if the place of the PLO as the sole legitimate representative of the *entire* Palestinian people is taken at the UN by a putative Palestinian state representing only that minority of the Palestinian people who actually live in the Occupied Territories, the majority of Palestinians might find themselves excluded from the representation at the world body for which they struggled in the 1960s and 1970s.[1] There is also the attendant danger that if Palestinian rights are rewritten in the UN system on the basis of the much narrower set of claims concerning statehood in the territories occupied in 1967, the exercise of the right of return of the refugees and their descendants as well as the civil and political rights of the Palestinian citizens of Israel might be placed in jeopardy.

Mr Abbas and his associates have repeatedly shown themselves to be prepared to accept the sacrifice of the rights of the majority of Palestinians in return for being "given" a state in parts of the West Bank. If there were any lingering doubts around this question, surely they were put to rest by the Palestine Papers leaked to Al Jazeera and the *Guardian* earlier in 2011, which documented in minute and excruciating detail how far Abbas and the disgraced Saeb Erekat (who seems to have come back from the dead) were willing to go in pursuing their quest for an illusory statehood.[2] Not to mention that, even as Mr Abbas was presenting his stirring speech at the UN, his Israel-armed and American-trained security forces were busily cracking down on any sign of dissent in the towns and refugee camps of the West Bank (just as, it should be pointed out, Hamas forces were cracking down on any celebrations of the event in Gaza). "Security co-operation with the Palestinians is excellent at the moment and we do not want to jeopardise that," a senior Israeli military official told the British newspaper *The Independent*. This alone should remove any doubts about the extent to which the Palestine Authority (PA) has become what Israel always intended it to be: a full-blown collaborationist apparatus whose main function is to facilitate the ongoing occupation and colonisation of the West Bank.[3]

I raise all these by now familiar criticisms in order to make the point that Mr Abbas and his associates seem not to have noticed the resurgence of popular democratic activism in the intifadas sweeping across the Arab world from Maghreb to Mashreq. For all the claims to transparency and accountability and institutional development claimed by the PA, in actual fact it remains a profoundly undemocratic institution. Earlier suggestions of the PA's financial corruption have been replaced by the much more serious charge of its out-and-out collaboration with the Israeli occupation. The unelected leadership in Ramallah – which, having been swept from office in popular elections in 2006, was brought back to power almost literally on the turret of an Israeli tank – remains completely uninterested in any accounting for the scandal of the Palestine Papers or anything else for that matter. Mr Abbas and his associates have made zero effort to reach out and explain to their people their vision and strategy in any detail, much less to try to secure popular legitimacy for the high-stakes poker game they are playing at the UN, in which all Palestinians, and not simply an unrepresentative and unelected clique of middle-aged men, have a stake.

As they have done since entering into the disaster at Oslo in 1993, they keep only their own counsels, making no effort to engage the prominent and global body of Palestinian expertise in water rights, international law, negotiating strategy, refugee rights, demographics and so on. Above all, they still cling to the empty shell of precisely the same hopeless programme, the same meaningless jargon of "final status negotiations" and road maps and quartets, and the same failed two-state strategy, to which they have been committed for two decades with absolutely nothing to show for their effort. In the age of the Arab Spring, they look like left-behind and diminished versions of Ali Abdallah Saleh, Hosni Mubarak and Zein al Abidine Ben Ali.

The idea that the rights of some Palestinians can be addressed in a two-state solution that ignores or actually undermines the rights of the majority of Palestinians is doomed to failure. It should never have been embarked upon in the first place. The mere fact that the loudest champions of the creation of a Palestinian state in parts of the West Bank are Israelis, running the gamut from soft-core, liberal Zionists to seasoned and wily politicians like Ehud Olmert and Tzipi Livni, should be the clearest warning necessary that there is something profoundly flawed with this idea from a Palestinian perspective. "The Palestinian declaration of independence practically constitutes a victory for Israel's declaration of independence, and this is why Israelis must celebrate in the streets and be the first to recognise Palestinian independence, calling on the world to follow suit," wrote Sefi Rachlevsky in the Israeli paper *Yedioth Ahronoth*.[4] If Palestinians officially declare that all they seek is a state in the West Bank and nothing else, that relieves Israel of the challenge of democratic and equal rights for all citizens, including returned refugees.

Let us be absolutely clear about this. Palestinians living inside Israel today face a mounting set of legal, ideological, religious, political and material forms of repression unlike anything they have faced in the past, including the martial law under which they lived for their first two decades as putative citizens of the state. A new wave of explicitly racist laws targets them as a reviled non-Jewish minority, and strips them of their right to land, to family unification, to education, to housing, and even to historical memory (witness the recent law banning commemorations of the *Nakba* of 1948).

Nowhere is the repression of Israeli Palestinians more starkly evident than the Naqab desert, where Palestinian Bedouin have been subjected to a form of relentless victimisation that seems to recapitulate week after week and even day after day the experience of the *Nakba*, indeed, to remind us that the *Nakba* began but did not end in 1948. Every single structure in the Bedouin village of Araqib has been demolished by Israeli bulldozers not once or twice or three times but over twenty times in the last year alone.[5] More recently, the Israeli government prepared new plans to *transfer* 30,000 Palestinian Bedouin in the Naqab from their ancestral homes to new concentration points in order to safeguard the nakedly racist Zionist vision of a Negev free of Arabs.[6]

What would a Palestinian state in the West Bank do for the residents of Araqib and the other 1.5 million Palestinians inside Israel, other than condemn them all the more to their status as reviled and degraded non-Jews cluttering up the space of the Jewish state?

Meanwhile, the Palestinian refugees (the single largest component of the Palestinian people) continue to languish in the exile to which they have been condemned for over six decades; not only living in disgraceful circumstances in wretched refugee camps in Lebanon, Syria and Jordan but also ever more subject to the political violence sweeping through the Arab world. We are reminded of this by the total obliteration of the Nahr el Bared refugee camp in the north of Lebanon a couple of years ago, and the more recent bombardment to which Palestinian refugee camps in Syria have been subjected.

What would a state in the West Bank do for the residents of Sabra or Shatila or Nahr al Bared, other than confirm their condemnation to a fate of being left to their own devices as permanent human flotsam and jetsam, the detritus of a catastrophe whose making we are to believe can be taken off the table of history?

Here, we are clearly on the familiar terrain of the argument between the dwindling number of Palestinians still espousing a two-state solution and the increasing number advocating a one-state solution. My position on the debate is that the Palestinians are one people, who share one cause, and the only path to a just peace is one that addresses the rights of all Palestinians, not just the minority who have suffered under occupation since 1967.

It is true that the one-state solution, which I personally advocate, in which all Israelis and all Palestinians would live as equal citizens of a single democratic and secular state, is not the only way to address and guarantee the rights of all Palestinians. In principle, there could be a two-state solution that also guaranteed the right of return of the refugees, including the refugees of Gaza, to their homes inside what is today Israel, and the rights of present-day Palestinian citizens of Israel. But that is not the two-state solution that is now or has ever been under discussion, because the Israelis have made it abundantly clear that they will never accept a state in which Jews would be outnumbered by non-Jews.

Precisely on this point – about what the Israelis say they will or won't accept – it is necessary to mention realism, pragmatism and expectations, a set of terms that often comes up in the one-state / two-state debate. The worst habit of the advocates of a two-state solution is that they never stop congratulating themselves on how pragmatic and realistic they are, as opposed to those supposedly dreamy and unrealistic, if not downright romantic, one-staters (Mouin Rabbani recently indulged in this in a piece he wrote for the *London Review of Books*[7]). One reason they congratulate themselves is that they say a two-state solution is more realistic because the Israelis will never accept a one-state solution; therefore, they say, we must be pragmatic and accept this as fact. But the Israelis are no more willing to accept a two-state solution that recognises and embraces the Right of Return and the equal rights of present Palestinian citizens of Israel than they are willing to accept a one-state solution that treats all citizens as equals. What, then, is a partial two-state solution worth, if it leaves the majority of Palestinians high and dry?

Is it really "realistic" and "pragmatic" to expect Palestinians to determine their rights and articulate their aspirations on the basis of what Israelis deem to be acceptable? Is it really realistic to say that what the Palestinians can achieve depends on what the Israelis are willing to have addressed? I think not. Those who claim to be so realistic and pragmatic seem not to have even a passing familiarity with the documented empirical reality of historical experience, which teaches us over and again that no privileged group in the history of the world has ever voluntarily renounced its privileges: not King Charles I of England, who was executed by his people in 1649; not the British aristocracy in the nineteenth century, who faced a popular challenge to transform an aristocratic country into a representative democracy; not the slave-owning classes of the American south; not the white elites of the United States in the civil rights era of the 1960s; and not the white beneficiaries of Apartheid in South Africa in the 1970s and 1980s.

History – real, hard history – teaches us that privileged groups relinquish their privileges only when they have no other choice—and that, historically speaking, such abandonments of privilege have been brought about non-violently at least as often as they have been brought about through violence. If we want to be realistic and pragmatic, we have to begin by realising that the Israelis will never relinquish their privileges until they are *compelled* to do so, preferably by non-violent means. And it is at least as realistic to seek to compel them to accept the parameters of a single democratic state, a state that guarantees the rights of minorities, as it is to compel them to accept a cobbled together two-state solution that properly addresses Palestinian rights, which, by creating an "Israel" with a Jewish minority, one consequence of a complete return of refugees, would totally obviate the need to have two separate states to begin with.

So much for the realism of our expectations. A few more points are in order about the other claims to realism made by advocates of a partial two-state solution. Citing UN Resolutions 242 and 338, they continually repeat the claim that their vision is more realistic than the one-state vision because it has a basis in international law and in an international consensus. This again is facile: there is an equally strong basis in international law for the one-state solution, namely Resolution 194 and the wide range of international legal covenants prohibiting the forms of racial discrimination and Apartheid on which the very notion of an exclusively Jewish state – at least insofar as it is erected in land that has never been exclusively Jewish – depends for its existence. As for this international consensus about which we have heard so much, it would be folly for the advocates of Palestinian rights to forget that this so-called consensus was not something the family of nations agreed on and presented to the Palestinians. Palestinians maintained an earnest and dedicated struggle not to put but force it onto the world's agenda, in the 1960s, 1970s and 1980s.

Have people seriously forgotten the moment, a mere twenty years ago, when the very idea of a Palestinian state and even of a two-state solution seemed laughable? Do people think that a Palestinian state recognised, for all its flaws, by an overwhelming majority of the countries and populations of the world, was simply dropped out of the sky by a passing friendly alien spaceship? The very talk of a Palestinian state is something that the Palestinian people made happen, against the established global powers of the time, in the face of entrenched Israeli and American government positions and the indifference of Europe, through their sheer determination, sacrifice and force of will. The only thing stopping the Palestinians from demanding their full spectrum of rights today are the Palestinians themselves or, rather, the completely outmoded and worn-out leaderships in both Ramallah and Gaza, whose political projects have now, we can safely say, run their course.

Let me clarify what I am trying to say by going back to the standing ovation that Mr Abbas received at the United Nations. On that day, the representatives of the vast majority of the human race stood and celebrated for the people of Palestine and for the Palestinian cause in a way that is almost unimaginable for any other people or cause. And what do you call the ability, without any other inducement than an appeal to the imagination, to move hundreds and hundreds of millions of people around the entire world, who have over and over again, for six decades, steadfastly demonstrated their support and solidarity with the Palestinian people and their cause? What do you call that capacity, that potential?

In a word, you call it *power*.

My point here is really quite simple: the Palestinian people have far, far more power than they sometimes allow themselves to think or believe; certainly and demonstrably, far more power than Mr Abbas felt comfortable wielding at the UN.. However, the Palestinians' power does not function at the polite diplomatic negotiating table, or on the battlefield, where Palestinian fighters don't have a chance against a vastly better equipped enemy. Indeed, it is not merely useless, it is altogether a liability.

Switch the terrain, however, from the negotiating table and the battlefield to the realm of ideas, of ideals and of the imagination, and ask yourselves in all seriousness who has the upper hand there. Is it the Israelis, engaged in a hopeless defence of a brittle, racist, outmoded, ethno-religious colonial state project that is a fish out of water in the twenty-first century? Or is it the Palestinians, who have over and over again demonstrated their ability to reach and touch the hearts and minds of a global audience of hundreds of millions of people? From the first intifada of the 1980s to the current non-violent protests along the Apartheid Wall in the West Bank, a struggle that engages and activates a global imaginary realm from Hollywood films to the work of the London street artist Banksy, the Palestinians have repeatedly made clear that at the level of symbols and the imagination, the Israelis

– for all their vast and paid armies of hasbara agents, web crawlers, Wikipedia writers, Facebook propagandists, Tweeters, campus agitators and so on – can't even touch them.

It is not just pointless but altogether a doomed strategy for the Palestinians to try to achieve their rights in the domains and registers in which they hold no cards and in which the deck is in fact stacked against them, when they could be operating at the level of the symbolic and inspirational, where they completely outclass their opponents. Let me just add one or two further details before turning to my conclusion.

In shifting their struggle from the plane of state diplomacy to the plane of the symbolic and the imaginary, the Palestinians must make it absolutely clear, in the simplest, most straightforward and easily digestible form, what it is that they demand. Here, the one-state solution is far, far more readily transmissible and understandable than any other formulation of what a just and lasting peace would look like. In capsule form, it simply and neatly outlines and expresses a vision of rights – rights for all Palestinians: those inside Israel, those in exile, and those under occupation; while also embracing and encompassing the rights of Jewish Israelis – that is not only unimpeachable but also irrepressible, irresistible.

Don't just take my word for it. Here is former Prime Minister Olmert, speaking in November 2003, and explaining the then unfolding Ariel Sharon scenario:

> There is no doubt in my mind that very soon the government of Israel is going to have to address the demographic issue with the utmost seriousness and resolve. This issue above all others will dictate the solution that we must adopt ... We don't have unlimited time. More and more Palestinians are uninterested in a negotiated, two-state solution, because they want to change the essence of the conflict from an Algerian paradigm [of armed resistance to occupation] to a South African one. From a struggle against "occupation," in their parlance, to a struggle for one-man-one-vote. That is, of course, a much cleaner struggle, a much more popular struggle – and ultimately a much more powerful one.[8]

This is an argument that Olmert went on to reiterate in 2006 and again in 2007.

So what are the Palestinians waiting for? Why should they continue to play along in the self-mutilating role assigned to them by an Israeli narrative of domination, when they are in a position to throw that narrative into total disarray, especially when all they have to do in order to do so is to claim rights that *even their enemy acknowledges* it would be impossible to go on denying them forever?

One last point. When I speak of the Palestinian struggle embarking in this new direction, I am speaking not about a future condition but a present one. The regular non-violent protests including Israeli and international participation along the Wall in the West Bank; the global campaign for BDS (boycotts, divestments and sanctions), modelled on the campaign that was successful in ending Apartheid in South Africa; new movements such as Gaza Youth Break Out; and a new generation of Palestinian activists, fluent and comfortable speaking in English to a global audience to an extent that their parents never were, and savvy in new media and social media such as Facebook and Twitter, in the realm of music (hip hop bands like Dam), and cinema (think of the historic accomplishment of Hani Abu Asad winning the Golden Globe for *Paradise Now*): all these groups are already leading the way in charting the future of the Palestinian struggle, taking it to the terrain of language, symbols and the imagination where Palestinians are a force to be reckoned with.

FIVE

Protest and Privilege

Joseph Dana

As the funeral procession of Mustafa Tamimi weaved through the narrow streets of Ramallah in late December 2011, the emotional pain of the angry group was barely concealable. Tamimi, a twenty-eight-year-old Palestinian resident of the West Bank village of Nabi Saleh, had been shot and killed by an Israeli tear gas canister during an unarmed demonstration against the Israeli occupation just days earlier. His village, just west of Ramallah and directly adjacent to one of the oldest Israeli settlements in the West Bank, Halamish, has become the current symbol of the nascent unarmed resistance movement.

Among the faces present at the Ramallah funeral were a handful of Israeli peace activists from Tel Aviv. An unusual sight in the de facto West Bank capital, these activists carried themselves with a sense of belonging and familiarity. This belonging has been hard won, as for the past ten years Israeli activists have played a crucial albeit small role in the development of the unarmed resistance movement. Their participation has not sufficiently changed the power dynamics between the Israeli army and occupied Palestinians, however.

Despite its small size, the joint-struggle protest movement presents one of many current challenges to the Zionist narrative coming from inside Israeli society. The act of breaking down the carefully guarded physical and psychological barriers between Israelis and Palestinians through Palestinian-led protest is the central challenge to one of Zionism's most carefully guarded principles: separation. Radical Jewish settlers in the West Bank, who attack Israeli military positions and soldiers before demolitions of outposts, present another challenge to the overarching Zionist national ethos in Israel – but from the other end of the political spectrum. Both movements are 'anti-State' and necessarily anti-Zionist in practice, with various degrees of extremity.

These challenges to the liberal Zionist dogma of present-day Israel cannot compare in size to recent protest movements, which challenged the policies of the state but not its ideology. The Israeli tent protesters – who burst onto the scene in the middle of 2011 demanding social justice and lower rent – present the most concrete affirmation of Zionism in the past twenty years. Willingly dismissing the occupation as a "political" issue in mainstream media outlets, the majority of the tent protesters attempted to focus on the social justice rights of Israelis outside the paradigm of the Israeli–Palestinian conflict. Missing in the sea of placards which filled the streets of major Israeli cities during the protests was any mention of an end to the occupation. The result was a confirmation of the carefully created "separation principle" that has typified Zionist thinking and practice since its inception.

While separation permeates the Israeli psyche, the situation on the ground reflects a level of Israeli control over the area between the Jordan River and the Mediterranean Sea the like of which has not been seen in the past sixty years of conflict. Currently, Israel is the sole sovereign force over the entire area. A system of unequal citizenship prevails in Israel, while Palestinians in the West Bank and Gaza are governed directly or indirectly by a military occupier. Actual separation, in fact, exists in the minds of Israelis.

There has always existed a small but vocal portion of Israeli society which has voiced opposition to the state's policies regarding Palestinians. Since the beginning of construction on Israel's controversial West Bank separation barrier at the height of the second intifada in 2003, a small group of Israeli activists have taken their protest actions against Israeli occupation to a dangerous and intimate level. Standing in front of armed soldiers or earth-shattering bulldozers, these activists have adopted an unarmed resistance model which highlights solidarity with occupied Palestinians through direct action. The costs have been high, for both Palestinians and members of the activist groups. Yet after ten years of struggle, the Israeli side of the movement is listless and directionless.

It was small pockets of Palestinians who initiated actions aimed at reformulating the nature of their confrontation with Israel in terms of rights as opposed to security. The demonstrations were understood as a strategic move, which would highlight the desperate nature of Israeli control in the occupied West Bank in a spirit similar to that of the first Palestinian intifada. Of course, the human and emotional costs of the second intifada were becoming increasingly evident to West Bank Palestinian leaders. While reserving the right to armed resistance, Palestinian civil society leaders in small villages directly affected by the creation of the separation barrier appealed to their people to adopt unarmed resistance.

"We felt as though we had no other choice," Ayed Morrar, a veteran leader from the village of Budrus, said. "We wanted to change the way that Palestinians approached the conflict and unarmed protests were the way to do this. The Israeli activists only came later but I am happy that they came."

At the start of the joint protests, many Palestinian communities had not seen extended, large-scale unarmed demonstrations against the occupation since the first intifada, which ended in the early 1990s. The second intifada began in October 2000 with unarmed protests at Israeli checkpoints, but after dozens of Palestinians were killed by massive Israeli firepower – according to Israeli army estimates over one million bullets were fired by Israeli forces in the first month of the second intifada alone – it gradually took the form of an armed struggle carried out by small cells of militants and aimed at Israeli soldiers, settlers and civilians. Israel eventually crushed the uprising by using all its military power, and the violence left thousands of casualties in both societies. This deepened hostility between Israelis and Palestinians and handed the once strong Israeli Left a near-fatal blow in its pursuit of the Oslo peace process.

The key turning point in the joint struggle occurred when protests erupted in 2003 in Budrus, a small village west of Ramallah and close to the 1967 Green Line. The proposed route of the separation barrier in Budrus would have resulted in the loss of nearly forty acres of the village's farmland, which are crucial to its survival. As Israeli bulldozers started destroying the ancient olive trees, Budrus residents held a series of nonviolent demonstrations, drawing on a long Palestinian tradition of civil disobedience and popular protest. This led to the formation of a committee of village leaders, who decided to invite Israelis as well as international activists to participate. From 2003 to

2005, dozens of Israelis and internationals joined the demonstrations in Budrus and surrounding villages. Despite a fierce response by the Israeli army, including the use of live ammunition, nightly raids on the village and curfews, the protests grew stronger. Eventually, – after the Israeli high court ruled that its route was illegal, the Israeli military decided to request a different route for the separation barrier – one that would not annex any of Budrus's farmland. The joint popular struggle had its first victory.

Founded in a haphazard way in 2003, the Israeli group Anarchists Against the Wall (AATW) has consistently been at the forefront of the joint struggle over the past ten years. AATW was formed as the first parts of the separation barrier were being built, at the height of the second intifada when violence and tensions were high. The activists were repeatedly arrested and injured. It also took time for them to gain the trust of Palestinians. "Some worried, and for a good reason, that we were Shin Bet [Israel's internal security agency]," recalls Jonathan Pollak, who was one of the first activists to take part in the demonstrations and is now the media coordinator for the Popular Struggle Coordination Committee, a Palestinian umbrella organisation of local committees. "I remember one demo in which I was taken aside and searched by the *shabab* young [Palestinian men]. With time, when they saw us standing shoulder to shoulder with them, and especially when they saw how the Israeli army treated us, more trust was gained."

Israeli protesters have been injured and arrested, and a few have been sentenced to short jail terms. Lately, some have been summoned by Israeli internal security services to receive warning lectures. Yet there is no way to compare this to the far harsher treatment routinely meted out to Palestinians. The anarchists often refer to their privileged status, which seems to increase their urge to act.

Israelis activists usually meet in the heart of Tel Aviv on Friday mornings – demonstrations almost always take place on Friday afternoons – and pile into private cars on their way to the villages. In the early days of the struggle, the Israeli military would set up a network of checkpoints forcing the activists to use back roads, some of which are in a state of ill repair. These days, the journey is open and activists arrive in villages like Nabi Saleh within forty-five minutes of leaving

Tel Aviv. A march towards the Wall or contested area of the village, as in the case of Nabi Saleh, is followed by heavy-handed Israeli army crowd control measures including the firing of rubber bullets and tear gas.

"By an Israeli activist, I mean that I am rooted in my place as an Israeli," twenty-three-year-old Matan Cohen noted in a hip coffee shop in Jaffa. "I understand that this means that I have a certain responsibility in the situation. I can't shy away from the power dynamics which exist between us but at least I am trying to work through them." Cohen is a prominent Israeli activist who has most recently been involved in international boycott campaigns of Israel. Early in the work of the AATW, he lost his eye after being hit directly with a rubber bullet fired by an Israeli border police officer.

At the core of the power dynamics of which Cohen speaks is the dominant ideology in Israeli society, Zionism. For the majority of activists in AATW, Zionism is not an issue they devote any time to. Action occupies their minds. According to Mairav Zonszein, a journalist and translator living in Tel Aviv and a member of the joint struggle group Ta'ayush, Zionism is not a topic spoken about often among activists – but Jewish identity is. "Sometimes debates have arisen [about Zionism] among Ta'ayush activists, but usually when the day in the West Bank is over and we are already on the way back to the comfort of our daily lives or talking over a beer. But they are not necessarily debates about Zionism so much as about Jewish identity on a whole."

Ta'ayush works mostly in the south West Bank, in the arid desert surrounding the holy city of Hebron. Its actions don't draw as much violence as those of the Anarchists Against the Wall. Violence does not originate from activists, who maintain a strict adherence to non-violent resistance. Rather, the violence often comes from hard Israeli army crowd control measures, which are more often apparent in AATW protests than those of Ta'ayush. This stems from the fact that AATW often works with Palestinians who throw stones, which provides the army with a pretext for using measures like tear gas and live bullets. Ta'ayush, by contrast, does not associate with any Palestinians who throw stones.

"In Israel, Zionism is not treated the same as it is outside – there aren't necessarily discussions about the merits of the concept since we are Israeli citizens and choose to deal with the very real detrimental actions [which] take place all the time," Zonszein continues. "Assuming there is a lack of debate about Zionism, I think it is mostly due to the fact that actions speak louder than words. The moment someone decides to engage in direct actions and joint struggle in the West Bank, he has already made a significant statement about his ideology and positioning *vis-à-vis* this country."

After the success in Budrus, dozens of Palestinians and a few Israelis began weekly marches toward the Separation Wall in Ni'lin. Weekly protests also currently take place in Nabi Saleh, al Mas'ara, Beit Ummar, Hebron, Iraq Burin, various villages in the South Hebron Hills and in Walaje, just south of the Jerusalem municipal border. Walaja is about to be completely surrounded by the Wall, leaving only a narrow gate in what will become an open-air prison for its two thousand residents. Dozens of Israelis and Palestinians have been arrested while attempting to disrupt the Wall's construction there. The deteriorating ability to protest and the narrowing space for political activism against the Israeli occupation, Pollak says, have coincided with a growing space for racism and nationalism.

Over the course of current Israeli Prime Minister Benjamin Netanyahu's term, Israeli society has moved firmly to the right in both ideology and political aspirations. The Israeli parliament has successfully passed legislation which effectively curtails legitimate political speech against the occupation or Israel's policies towards Palestinians. Most notable among the current batch of anti-democratic laws is the anti-Boycott law, which criminalises Israeli support of non-violent boycott initiatives against settlements in the occupied West Bank and/or economic boycotts of the state. This corrosive legislation, coupled with rising attacks on mosques, Palestinian institutions and property, has created a dangerous climate of racism and nationalism on the ground.

Palestinians still debate the usefulness of cooperating with Israelis – some claim that even if the Israelis mean well, working with them ultimately legitimises Israel. Recently, Palestinian activists both in Palestine and abroad, have renewed attention to so-called normalisation projects. According to the activists, these projects often provide a skewed picture of the relationship between Israelis and Palestinians. The argument is that normalisation programmes in the form of conferences on co-existence as well as youth groups like Seeds of Peace ignore the asymmetric nature of the conflict, in which one side is under occupation and the other is the occupier.

But this debate does not spill over into the villages where joint protests take place; the spirit of cooperation is evident. It is even common to see Palestinians hiding Israeli activists from soldiers in their houses during demonstrations. The reason for this partnership is simple in the eyes of Dianne Alzeer, a Palestinian activist from Ramallah. "The Israelis come in solidarity with our cause. They understand our struggle and do not try to dictate its terms."

Unlike traditional Israeli peace rallies, the West Bank demonstrations are led by Palestinians. The Jewish participants arrive at the invitation of local Palestinian committees, and they must accept the political and tactical choices of the local leadership. Although there is coordination, it is the Palestinians who decide on the course of action and the level of confrontation with the army. The Israelis see themselves as guests.

"The joint struggle opens up a way for us to be supportive of the Palestinians without silencing them and appropriating their suffering," says Ayala Shani, a long-time activist who regularly attends protests. "It means that Palestinians are leading their own struggle for freedom, and Israelis have the opportunity to stand with them in solidarity."

Under Israeli military law, Palestinians are not allowed to protest the occupation without special permits, which are almost never requested – partly as a matter of principle, but also because they are almost never given. The unarmed demonstrations are usually met with heavy-handed measures, including tear gas, rubber-coated bullets and even live ammunition. Since 2005 twenty-one Palestinians have been killed in these demonstrations, including ten children under the age of eighteen, with thousands injured. Many international activists have been injured, including American Tristan Anderson, who was left paralysed after being hit in the head by an Israeli tear gas canister shot at close range. Israelis and international activists have been injured too, but so far no Israeli Jews have been killed. The Israeli protesters claim that their presence restrains the army and helps draw media attention. Many Palestinians agree, and over the years they have come to see the Israeli activists as partners.

"The participation of Israelis in demonstrations, unfortunately, does make a difference," says Pollak. "It makes a difference because of the racist nature of our situation. Open-fire regulations, for instance, are a lot more stringent, officially, when Israelis are present. It is, however, important to remember that we are not much more than a side-note in the movement, and that it is the Palestinians who are at its centre. People are often fascinated by the fact that a handful of Israelis cross the lines this way. But currently this is what we really are, a handful, and the real question, in my opinion, is, how come only so few do so? The sad answer is that most Israelis simply don't care; to most Israelis, Palestinians simply don't really exist."

While the ability of Palestinians and Israelis to come together in unarmed protest against Israeli occupation is clear, genuine projects of co-existence have been few and far between. "I think that the difference between our actions and the current ones is that one of these kids will end up getting killed," noted Akiva Orr, one of the founders of the Matzpen political movement, which promoted Arab–Jewish partnership through a socialist platform in the early 1960s. "The boldness of their actions is a response to the facts on the ground but they lack the necessary work in building co-existence projects. They really don't spend time with each other outside of the protests."

Orr's observation may be only partially correct. The joint struggle is changing life in the village of Nabi Saleh. According to Ben Ronen, a veteran Israeli activist who currently works in the law firm of a prominent Israeli lawyer who regularly represents Palestinians from the unarmed struggle, Israelis and Palestinians are building a common life in Nabi Saleh. "I never really spent time in other villages the way that I do in Nabi Saleh," Ronen noted in a café near his home in Jaffa. "Something about the warmth of the people or the nature of the struggle, I just feel at home there. I spend more time in Nabi Saleh now than I do in Tel Aviv."

Ronen, like Matan Cohen, has been seriously injured in West Bank demonstrations. During the summer of 2011 he was hit at close range by a high-velocity tear gas canister, which resulted in a double fracture in this hand. The case is currently under review in the Israeli courts, due to clear video footage of the incident captured on cameras provided by B'tselem, the Israeli centre for human rights in the Occupied Territories.

Palestinians remain at the forefront of changes taking place in the joint struggle. Recently, more and more Palestinians have joined social networking platforms like Twitter and Facebook as a way of spreading their stories from the ground. "We understand the need to challenge the Israeli narrative of peace and security with one about rights," Dianne Alzeer noted in a conversation in Ramallah. She, like other activists, has developed a large following on Twitter with constant updates from demonstrations.

Despite the interest and enthusiasm around the joint struggle, many Palestinians are becoming more interested in reforming Palestinian politics as a way of challenging the occupation. "The Palestinian Authority no longer represents our interests," said Fadi Quran, a youth leader in Ramallah. "The joint struggle is an important component of our struggle just like BDS [Boycott, Divestment and Sanction] advocacy is but it is just one part of a bigger strategy. People understand that we have to get rid of the current leadership in the West Bank if our struggle is going to grow."

Since its inception, the joint struggle in the West Bank has been on the periphery of the Israeli–Palestinian conflict. When it began, the second intifada demanded the mainstream attention of foreign eyes, due to the horrible cycle of violence which engulfed the region. As the second intifada cooled, the joint protests have garnered more attention from international journalists dying to grab a story infused with some form of violence – which western audiences are accustomed to seeing on the ground. Currently, the protests continue but they are not well supported, either by Fatah – the governing party of the Palestinian Authority – or the mainstream Israeli Left. In recent months, Hamas members have mentioned public support for the protests but have not put any action behind their words.

While support in terms of numbers is currently lacking for the joint struggle protests in the West Bank, many Palestinians agree that the next outbreak of violence will be an unarmed one. The general sentiment in Ramallah as well as Nablus is that a version of the first

intifada – the intifada of stones, not suicide bombs – will return to
the Israeli–Palestinian conflict in the next five years. If this is indeed
what is to be expected in years to come, joint-struggle villages like
Nabi Saleh will be natural sources of motivation and inspiration for a
wider West Bank rebellion.

The internationalization of the unarmed Palestinian struggle also
has a serious impact on the joint struggle movement. The success of
the global Boycott, Divestment and Sanction (BDS) movement has
certainly encouraged it, on the grounds that unarmed and non-violent resistance to the occupation works. Founded in 2005, the BDS
movement has quickly inflicted significant damage on Israel through
boycotts of Israeli products, academic institutions and artists which
meet specific criteria of complicity in Israel's occupation.

The Gaza aid flotilla movement is another component of the internationalisation of the Palestinian unarmed struggle. Despite visible
incompetence in planning, activists from all corners of the globe have
been able to highlight Israel's strict control over Gaza through the
simple and non-violent act of sailing to the besieged Strip.

The goal of all of these actions, from the joint struggle in Nabi
Saleh to BDS events in London, seeks to highlight Israel's bellicose
strategy towards the Palestinians and the unequal nature of the conflict between the two sides. From the point of view of activists and
even some mainstream politicians in Israel and Palestine, meaningful
change is increasingly likely to be achieved only with external pressure
and not internally.

The Tent Protest

In the dead heat of a humid Tel Aviv summer, a small group of young
urban professionals set up a cluster of tents in the heart of the city's
most expensive street. Mere metres away from the Habima Hebrew
National Theatre, attractive young Israelis demanded better allocation of economic resources, lower rents and social justice for the
citizens of Israel. Within weeks, their movement had stolen the heart
and imagination of Israeli society. What began as a small tent protest
mushroomed into a tent city, with half-a-million-strong protests on

the streets of major cities in Israel against the economic direction of the country and under the banner of social justice.

Initially, the radical leftists which compose the ranks of the Anarchists Against the Wall approached the tent protesters with caution. For sure, many lived in Tel Aviv, paid high rent and understood the effect of poor Israeli economic policies on the country. But the issue of the occupation remained a difficult hurdle to overcome. Despite the loud proclamations of many in the streets that the "Israeli spring" had arrived, the social justice movement was reticent about issues concerning Palestinians, both inside and outside of the West Bank as well as Gaza. Quickly, the occupation was labelled a "political issue", one which had no place in the debate concerning the social justice rights of Israelis.

Why was it so easy for the tent protesters to dismiss the occupation? The answer to this question can quickly be found in Israeli societal patterns of the last ten years. Since the outbreak of violence of the second intifada, Israeli society has successfully distanced itself from its Palestinian counterpart. From 1967 until the mid-1990s, Palestinians would often work in Israeli cities, while borders between the two places were relatively open and porous. This openness engendered a certain familiarity among the two peoples. Indeed, many Palestinian men over the age of thirty-five speak Hebrew with a level of fluency, and many older Israelis have a more developed understanding of Arabic.

The second intifada ended this relationship and the next generation of Israelis – those demanding social justices in Tel Aviv – has no understanding of Palestinians outside of its military service. Of course, Palestinians still must deal with the Israeli army on a regular basis and thus do not have the luxury of separation which Israelis enjoy.

Interestingly, as the tent protest movement gained steam in Israel, there was no noticeable increase in the numbers of participants in the joint demonstrations in the West Bank. However, there was an increase in the number of Israeli settlers in locations like the settlement of Ariel, home to the only settler university in the West Bank, who demanded their "social justice" and held protests in loose connection with the main tent protests in Tel Aviv and Jerusalem.

For many in Israel, the tent protests signalled the possibility of a resurgence of the Israeli Left which routinely occupied Rabin Square in the 1990s in support of a two-state solution with Palestinians. In recent years, the mere mention of the Israeli Left will generate laughter in many Tel Aviv bars. "In fact, the Israeli Left never recovered from Rabin's assassination," says former Knesset Speaker Avraham Burg. "Later, Ehud Barak came and presented his personal failure in Camp David [in 2000] as the failure of the entire way. When the head of the peace camp declared that there was no partner on the other side, it opened the door for unilateralism." Burg, the son of one of Israel's legendary religious leaders, was a prominent voice in the Israeli Left during the 1980s and '90s, a member of Peace Now and one of the leaders of the Labour Party. Since his retirement from the Knesset in 2003, his criticism of liberal Zionism and its exclusively Jewish nature has deepened. Recently, he called for Israeli Jews to explore alternative historical narratives and political models.

"There was something unilateral in Zionism from the start, but it became the only way after Camp David," says Burg. "We built the fence unilaterally, and we left Gaza unilaterally. Barak brought us back to the days of Golda Meir, who denied there is such a thing as a Palestinian people." At the same time, the closures on the West Bank – introduced by Israel in the early 1990s and vastly tightened with the second intifada and construction of the Separation Wall a decade later – ended the daily direct contact, much of it commercial, that was common between Israeli and Palestinian civilians. Today, most Israelis do not travel to the West Bank, except as part of their military service or on settler-only bypass roads, while a new generation of Palestinians knows Israelis only as soldiers in uniform or as settlers.

The physical separation barrier is only one aspect of the distance between Israeli and Palestinian society; others include legislation outlawing public commemoration of the *Nakba* – the Palestinian marking of the creation of the state in 1948 – and proposed measures to remove Arabic as an official language and other attacks on Palestinian citizens of Israel that are currently gaining steam in Israel's parliament.

The separation principle described in this piece, which has guided Zionist thinking since its inception, was clearly demonstrated in the tent protest movement. Israelis, desperate for a sense of normalcy, demanded to participate in the wave of global upheaval connected with falling markets and emerging democracies, simply refusing to allow pesky issues like the Palestinians get in their way. Indeed, Israelis, fed up with the economic situation in Tel Aviv, demanded to change the game unilaterally, with no discussion of the occupation or the deep-seated separation principle which has taken over Israeli society. The simple fact apparently lost on many Israelis is that Israeli and Palestinian society is more connected now than at any other time. Israelis have been able to maintain their society and its willing ignorance of the situation in the West Bank only through collective cognitive dissonance. This explains the bitter reaction of many tent protesters when presented with the paradox of demanding social justice without discussion of the occupation. It also explains the generally negative sentiment towards the joint struggle, as well as the low numbers of Israelis who join the protests.

What is unavoidably clear from the protest climate in Israel/ Palestine is that pockets of civil society are taking political matters into their own hands. Whether it is the failed peace process or the economic disintegration of Israel, civil society has time and again proven itself capable and willing to engage in non-violent demonstrations. However, the tent protests confirm that at the core of the conflict remains the Zionist dilemma, or the ability or need of the Jewish population of Israel to adhere to an exclusivist national ideology which, by definition, places Palestinians on the outside.

Given the incredible power Israel holds over the peace process, the ability of Israeli civil society to sow change on the ground is a thorny issue. It requires a genuine challenge to the overarching discourse which predicates withdrawal from the territories on the whims of Israeli comfort levels. With Israeli social justice movements controlling undue attention in the international media cycle, the question of joint Palestinian–Israeli social movements, which directly confront Israel's hold on the West Bank, is now more important than ever. The joint struggle demonstrates that some in Israel are ready to live in a bi-national state, while the tent protests confirm that this state is still a distant aspiration.

If we are to believe the majority of Palestinians, who predict that the conflict is headed for another West Bank rebellion of stones and mass rallies, the likelihood of increasing numbers of Israelis joining the joint struggle is low. The number of Israelis who join these movements, like those which joined Matzpen in the 1960s and 1970s, is simply too small to argue that there is a serious movement inside of Israeli society which is ready – or able – to challenge the occupation. The dismissal of the occupation by the tent protesters is yet more confirmation that Israeli society is unable at the present moment to change its policies regarding the Palestinians.

In the current climate of immediate and intimate communication as well as Middle Eastern revolution, the fact that Israelis are uninterested in changing the situation on the ground might not matter. The international community is increasingly aware of the separate and unequal situation in the West Bank. While observers might not understand what it feels like to stand in line at the Qalandia checkpoint separating Jerusalem and Ramallah, they are aware that something is wrong in Israel/Palestine. The success of the BDS movement coupled with hysterical Israeli reactions to non-violent actions like the flotilla confirms that the trend of Israeli isolation will continue. In this climate, the presence of Israelis in the joint struggle can serve in a similar way to the presence of white leftists in the anti-Apartheid movement. They can reaffirm the fact that the Palestinians are fighting against the occupation structure which deprives them of their rights, and not against Israelis or Jews, in the very same way that the African National Congress was fighting the Apartheid structure and not the white population.

SIX

Beyond Regional Peace to Global Reality

Jeff Halper

The Israeli Committee Against House Demolitions (ICAHD), the organisation I co-founded and have headed since 1997, is a non-violent, direct-action, peace and human rights group dedicated to ending the Israeli Occupation and establishing a just peace between Israel and the Palestinians, in whatever form that might take. The focus of our work, and the vehicle through which we expose and resist Israel's policies and the workings of the Occupation, is Israel's policy of demolishing Palestinian houses – about twenty six thousand in the Occupied Territories since 1967. Since the root of the conflict lies in 1948 and not in the occupation of 1967 ICAHD resists the demolition of homes of Israeli citizens, Palestinian and Bedouin, as well.

The ICAHD Model of Strategic Activism

From the outset, ICAHD has considered itself a political actor rather than merely a protest group. Believing that as a civil society organisation we can indeed insert ourselves into the political process, we have developed strategies of parlaying our actions "on the ground", particularly those having to do with house demolitions, into effective advocacy. To avoid diverting our attention from the political task before us, every action, programme or campaign in which we engage must address the question: *Is it contributing to an end of the Occupation?* If not, if it is merely an act of documentation or protest or humanitarian aid, then it is not at the centre of our work. This is at the heart of what we call "strategic activism".

ICAHD's approach to peace-making, developed over the past decade and a half, reflects my own anthropological background.

Indeed, without anthropology I do not believe my work would have been nearly as effective. Whether in establishing rapport with Palestinians and creating trust that bridges the chasm between our situations, in "reading the lay of the land" and in arriving at a grounded analysis, or in the ability to effectively present the situation, my anthropological tools have been indispensable. The basic question that anthropology posits – what in the hell is going on here? ("the hell" part being the critical element) – leads one to the essential causes of the conflict.

The ICAHD approach can be broken into five parts:

(1) A Rights-Based Yet Political Approach to Peace-Making. A discourse based on human rights avoids the necessity of "taking sides", since they are universal in nature. By invoking universal rights, we pursue a win-win approach, one that is much more useful for reaching a just resolution of the conflict than those based on win-lose, us-them framings. Focusing on human rights and humanitarian issues without addressing the political causes of conflicts can, however, be ineffectual and even perpetuate conflict – focusing on "food insecurity" in Gaza, for example, cannot ignore its source: the Israeli blockade. ICAHD is *both* a political and a human rights organisation.

(2) Being There/Resistance. "Being there" means resistance to occupation in real time, that is, when events are happening. ICAHD's main form of resistance is our active opposition to Israel's policy of demolishing Palestinian homes. ICAHD activists physically stand in front of bulldozers sent by the Israeli authorities to demolish homes. Over the past decade and a half we have also rebuilt 185 demolished Palestinian homes, some having been demolished two, three or four times. We do so as *political acts of resistance*, not humanitarian gestures. Volunteers – Israeli and international – join with local Palestinian families and communities to rebuild the homes. "Being there" is a crucial element in any attempt on the part of an Israeli organisation to work with Palestinians across the divide of power and oppression.

(3) From Activism to Grounded Analysis. Activism, as an integral component of "being there", is a necessary but nevertheless limited element of grassroots peace-making. Since ICAHD aspires to influence policy rather than merely protest, we parlay our experiences "on the ground" into analysis, literally *grounded* analysis, that makes the connection between specific policies and actions and the bigger political picture. Why, we ask, is Israel demolishing homes, and in particular this family's home? What political intentions lie behind that act and policy? What are its implications for future peace? How, for example, does the demolition policy fit into Israel's larger Matrix of Control over the Occupied Territories, and in what ways do these "facts on the ground" determine (and limit) the possibilities of a just and workable political solution? Both the questions themselves and the answers arise from the ground up.

(4) "Reframing." The success of the Israeli government in promoting a framing of the conflict based solely on security constitutes a major obstacle to any attempt to get across a message of just peace and an analysis of what it would mean. The Israeli framing is compelling, simple and brief. It consists of one sentence: Israel is a small Western democracy besieged by Muslim/Arab terrorism. Period. The sentence contains every self-explanatory and emotional buzzword necessary, and pointedly leaves out one: occupation (which Israel officially denies exists). The framing places Israel squarely on the side of the West ("us") in the clash of civilisations, while casting it as an innocent victim, an image which intentionally exploits historic Jewish suffering (although Zionism had originally tried to counter that stereotype).

Rather than attempting to argue each part of the Israeli framing – indeed, such loaded terms as "terrorism" or the underlying contention that the Arabs are Israel's interminable and irrational enemies make constructive dialogue impossible – we believe that only an alternative framing based on human rights can address the underlying causes of the conflict while offering a way out, one based on the reality of two peoples living in Israel/Palestine, each possessing rights of self-determination. True to ICAHD's principle that it is the Palestinians' prerogative to specify what solution to the conflict is acceptable to them, the reframing can be applied to any number of arrangements, from a two-state solution through a bi-national or democratic state and on to a regional confederation. Our only caveat is that any solution be inclusive of all the people residing in Israel/Palestine.

ICAHD's reframing rejects the fundamental premise of Israel's security paradigm: that Muslims and Arabs as a whole, and Palestinians in particular, are its enemies. Insisting that the conflict be conceived as a political one, that must therefore have a solution, it rejects attempts to mystify it through claims that Jews and Arabs have been enemies "from time immemorial" or, indeed, that the conflict has anything to do with some "clash of civilisations". It also rejects the notion that terrorism lies at the root of the conflict. While we condemn any attack on civilians, we recognise that such violence is a symptom of intolerable oppression that will end only when the peoples' underlying claims and grievances are resolved.

The contrast between the two framings, which comprises ICAHD's main strategy of advocacy, may be presented as follows:

The Israeli Security Framing	ICAHD's Rights-Based Framing
The Land of Israel belongs exclusively to the Jewish people; there is no other people that has legitimate rights or claims.	Two peoples reside in Israel/ Palestine and each has rights of self-determination.
Israel's policies are based on concerns for security.	Israel pursues a proactive policy of expansion into the Occupied Territories based on settlement and control.
The Arabs don't want peace; the Palestinians are our enemies.	The Palestinians recognize Israeli sovereignty over 78 percent of the country; the Arab world has offered Israel regional integration.

There is no occupation; the problem is Arab terrorism. Since Israel is the victim fighting for its existence, it is exempt from accountability for its actions.	The problem is Israel's occupation; Palestinian violence is a symptom of oppression. In human rights language, all attacks on civilians are prohibited, whether from non-state or state actors.
Any solution must leave Israel in control of the entire country.	Israel is a major regional superpower that must be held accountable for its actions.
Israel needs a Palestinian state, but only one that is truncated, non-viable and semi-sovereign.	A Palestinian state has to be viable and truly sovereign, not merely a Bantustan.
The conflict is a win-lose proposition: either we "win" or "they" do.	Only a solution based on human rights and international law ensures a win-win solution.
The answer to anti-Semitism is a militarily strong Israel aligned with the United States.	Anti-Semitism is a form of racism; only respect for human rights will effectively address anti-Semitism and Israel's security concerns. Problem is Arab terrorism.

(5) Strategic Advocacy seeks ways in which a critical peace perspective can influence policy and prod unwilling or reluctant governments to do the right thing. Realising that activism must be translated into a strategy of change, it mixes resistance on the ground with an array of other tactics. Reframing and the production of informational materials are integrated with the Boycott, Divestment and Sanctions (BDS) movement and other campaigns. ICAHD staff conduct speaking tours throughout the world in order to reach broad audiences and to mobilise our civil society partners: churches, trade

unions, university circles, political and human rights organisations, professional associations (such as Architects for a Just Peace) and critical Jewish organisations. We also engage with decision-makers – government officials, members of parliaments and UN officials, staffs of embassies and consulates present in Israel/Palestine and political delegations visiting the country – and opinion-makers such as journalists, intellectuals, film-makers and public figures.

An Approach to Peace in Israel/Palestine: Seven Key Elements

As an Israeli peace and human rights organisation belonging to what we call the "critical Left", we have worked for many years with like-minded Palestinian counterparts, many of whom are members of the Palestinian NGO Network (PNGO), the roof organisation of 132 progressive Palestinian organisations. In 2000 PNGO issued a Civil Society Call that conditioned an end to the conflict upon Israel meeting "its obligation to recognise the Palestinian people's inalienable right to self-determination" and complying with "the precepts of international law by:

1. Ending its occupation and colonisation of all Arab lands and dismantling the Wall;

2. Recognising the fundamental rights of the Arab-Palestinian citizens of Israel to full equality; and

3. Respecting, protecting and promoting the rights of Palestinian refugees to return to their homes and properties as stipulated in UN resolution 194."

Since no end-game has been agreed upon and accepted by all our Palestinian partners, PNGO's *approach* to a just resolution of the conflict is useful. While it could accommodate a wide range of solutions from two-state to one-state to regional confederation, it sets out basic parameters and red lines according to which any particular solution can be evaluated. ICAHD does not advocate a particular solution, since we believe that is the Palestinians' prerogative. We do, however, advance an *approach* to peace that complements, if fleshed out, the PNGO conditions. (I have also suggested a solution that goes beyond the one-state/two-state framework, which I offer below, since thinking "out of the box" is essential to eventually formulating a just and lasting peace, even if it does not constitute an end-game to advocate for at this stage.)

The ICAHD approach rests on seven key elements. In our view, any solution that embodies *all* of them can resolve the conflict, while solutions skipping even one cannot work, no matter how compelling they may seem on paper. They are as follows:

1. A just peace must be inclusive. Two peoples reside in Israel/Palestine. That reality must be accepted and built into the resolution of the conflict. Only then can the unavoidable process of reconciliation and historic accounting be undertaken.

2. National expression must be provided for both Palestinians and Israelis. These two peoples are not merely ethnic groups in a larger national society, or merely a collection of individual voters, but national entities in themselves. This constitutes the strongest argument for a two-state solution, though Israel has likely eliminated that option, but it also argues for a bi-national state, which Israel refuses even to consider. Nevertheless, this is the reality and must be incorporated into any workable solution.

3. Economic viability. This principle, enshrined in the Road Map, would, if implemented, foreclose an Apartheid "solution".

4. Conformity to human rights, international law and UN resolutions. Any process based on the two sides negotiating over specific issues (settlements, borders, water, refugees, Jerusalem, sovereignty, etc.) will fail if it is not based on these three foundations. Only they can create parity between the sides. The Oslo process failed primarily because it was based only on power, and if power alone determines the outcome, then Israel wins.

5. The refugee issue must be addressed squarely. It is negotiable, but it requires two pre-conditions: acceptance of the refugees' right to return, so that it is not merely a "goodwill" or "humanitarian" gesture on the part of Israel; and acknowledgement by Israel of its responsibility for driving out half the Palestinian people in 1947–8 as well as for the expulsions of 1967. It is Israel's steadfast refusal to accept the refugees' rights and to make that symbolic yet crucial acknowledgement of responsibility that makes the resolution of this fundamental issue impossible.

6. A just peace must address the security concerns of all in the region. Israeli Prime Minister Benjamin Netanyahu wants to begin the negotiations by addressing Israel's security concerns before the issues of occupation and Palestinian sovereignty. This will not work because no party's security can be guaranteed before a political settlement; indeed, the very point of a political settlement is to resolve the conflict and thereby bring security to all parties. Security is a critical issue, but it must be applied to all parties (the Palestinians, after all, have had many more civilian casualties and have suffered more from house demolitions and other threats to their security than have the Israelis). It must be embedded, however, in an overall solution.

7. A just peace must be regional in scope. Israel/Palestine is too small a unit to cram all the elements of peace into. Refugees, water, security, economic development, environmental sustainability – all these are regional issues that can only be addressed by a process that includes, at a minimum, Egypt, Jordan, Syria and Lebanon. Such a broadening of the peace process may wait on meaningful movement between Israelis and Palestinians, but it is part and parcel of the overall equation.

Adopting these elements in a comprehensive approach to peace gives us a powerful filter through which to evaluate the course of negotiations or any future peace process. If we cannot be present in the negotiations, we can ensure that the process actually produces a just peace.

Thinking Out of the Box: A Regional Economic Confederation

Just as the essential elements of a just peace can be formulated in the absence of an agreed-upon solution, so too can the outlines of a workable outcome. Variations of two solutions are usually raised: the two-state or the one-state. The first has already disappeared; the second contains serious pitfalls. Yet another "solution", that of warehousing, is in fact being implemented: because of its horrendous implications, this cannot even be given the status of a legitimate option. Let's review them briefly before we move on to consider what, in my humble opinion, is the only truly sustainable solution: a regional economic confederation, even though it has hardly been explored.

- The traditional two-state solution, in which a Palestinian state emerges within the entirety of the Occupied Territories (with minor adjustments), has been the preferred solution of the international community since 1967. It has been pursued by the Palestinian Authority since 1988 at least, and has long been promoted by the Zionist Left and liberal communities in Israel and the Diaspora. Given Israel's massive "facts on the ground", coupled with American recognition of its major settlement blocs, I contend that the two-state solution has been eliminated by Israel itself. In fact, I suggest we should stop talking about the two-state solution altogether, since it only obfuscates an already complex discussion.

- An "Israel Plus – Palestine Minus" two-state solution, pursued by both Labour and Likud governments and now advocated by the US as well, constitutes nothing less than Apartheid. Needless to say, it is totally unacceptable to the Palestinians. This "solution" envisions a semi-sovereign, semi-viable Palestinian state arising in the nooks and crannies among Israel's major settlement blocs, a territory truncated into at least four cantons (without Jerusalem) and comprising only 15 percent of historic Palestine. Whatever illusions Israeli leaders had that military defeat, pacification, impoverishment, transfer, political isolation and an "Iron Wall" of settlements and barriers would coax a compliant post-Arafat leadership to agree to a Bantustan were dashed in September 2011 when Abbas approached the UN to request the recognition of Palestine within the 1967 borders.

- A single democratic state seems on the surface the most natural and just alternative to the two-state solution. "One person, one vote", just as in post-Apartheid South Africa. Certainly the one-state solution represents the ultimate vision of the vast majority of Palestinians (and the ultimate nightmare of Israeli Jews). It is a compelling solution since it envisions a unitary Palestine – or the Greater Land of Israel, since Israel itself sees the entire country as one entity and has de facto rendered it such through its settlement enterprise. This is precisely the problem in imposing a unitary democratic state on a bi-national entity: to whom does the state "belong", especially in the absence of a cross-cutting civil identity? Still, by transforming their struggle for national liberation into one for civil rights, akin to that of South Africa, the Palestinians could put Israel in a very difficult situation. "Israel has eliminated the two-state solution," they could say convincingly, "now give us the vote." It is hard to see on what basis such a struggle could be opposed, especially by Diaspora Jews – for whom civil rights are a religion – or by the American or European governments who are busy pushing "democracy" on everyone. Yet by the same token, it is hard to see them, not to mention the Israeli Jewish public, accepting the transformation of Israel from a "Jewish" state into a democratic one (with a Palestinian majority moreover).

- Of the various one-state solutions, a single bi-national state makes the most sense, in my view, because the socio-political reality in Israel/Palestine is a bi-national one: both Palestinian Arabs and Israeli Jews constitute national entities that cannot be reduced to a mere collection of individual voters. The difficulty here, beyond the fact that bi-national states do not work very well and tend to be highly conflictual, is that the Israeli and Palestinian populations are so intertwined within such a small country. Without fairly discrete areas in which each national group is concentrated, it is difficult to see how a bi-national state would actually function.

- Another one-state model is, of course, Algeria: once liberation takes place the colonial population simply leaves and the indigenous retake their country. This was the PLO's position before it adopted the two-state solution in 1988 and it remains that of Hamas. Interestingly, just as Zionism is increasing being characterised as a European settler colonial movement by the Palestinian Left and the Jewish national narrative is being entirely dismissed, many of our Palestinian partners are moving, albeit not in so many words, towards the Algerian model.

- Warehousing. Israel knows that neither the Palestinians nor the international community will accept Apartheid. So it has moved beyond occupation, which is defined as a temporary military situation, and past Apartheid as well, to warehousing, the permanent if de facto imprisonment of the Palestinian people in tiny, disconnected and impoverished enclaves. Since any of the other options are unacceptable – including the Israel Plus – Palestine Minus two-state solution or even Apartheid; both of which, for the Israeli Right, give away too much of the Land of Israel – warehousing has simply becomes a method of avoiding any negotiations that would require Israel to make meaningful concessions, while giving it time to create irreversible facts on the ground.

Working Around the Occupation:
A Two-Stage Approach to a Middle East
Economic Confederation

Given the fatal flaws in each of the six solutions reviewed above, only one other option remains that seems capable of incorporating the essential elements of peace I outlined earlier: a regional economic confederation. A "Two-State Plus" solution, this approach envisions a two-stage process in which self-determination is disconnected from economic viability. Less elegant than the others, more complex, more difficult to present in a soundbite, it is also far more workable. Like the European Union – or even a looser confederation, as in the early days of the European Economic Community – it preserves a balance between national sovereignty and the freedom to live anywhere within the region. Rather than eliminating the occupation, it neutralises it by compensating the Palestinians' readiness to compromise on territory with the economic, social and geographic depth afforded by a regional confederation. Not only is a confederational approach just and sustainable, it offers a win-win solution as well.

In contrast to the two-state solution, which is limited in scope, technical in conception and unable to address many of the underlying issues of the conflict, the "two-stage" approach emphasises processes – of peace-making, trust-building, economic development, the establishment of strong civil societies and reconciliation leading to a genuine resolution of the conflict – while taking into account the national identities and needs of all the peoples in the region. Its outlines are straightforward and transparent.

Stage 1: A Palestinian State Alongside Israel

Recognising that Palestinian demands for self-determination represent a fundamental element of the conflict, the first stage of the confederational approach provides for the establishment of a Palestinian state. This meets the Palestinians' requirements for national sovereignty, political identity and membership in the international community. Statehood, however, does not address the crucial issue of viability. If it were only a state the Palestinians needed, they could have one tomorrow – the Bantustan offered by Netanyahu and former Israeli Prime Minister Ehud Barak. But being locked into a non-viable prison-state cannot possibly address the needs of their people, now or in the future.

The "two-stage" approach offers a way out of this trap, even if the Israeli presence is reduced but not significantly eliminated. The Palestinians might be induced to accept a semi-viable state on something less than the entire Occupied Territories (with or without some territorial swaps) *on condition* that the international community guarantees the emergence of a regional economic confederation within a reasonable period of time (five to ten years). So while the first stage, the establishment of a Palestinian state on most of the Occupied

Territories (including borders with Jordan, Syria and Egypt) addresses the issue of self-determination, the second stage, a regional confederation, would address that of viability. It would give the Palestinians a regional "depth" in which to meet their long-term social and economic needs.

Stage 2: A Regional Confederation

Following upon the emergence of a Palestinian state, the international community would broker a regional confederation among Israel, Palestine, Jordan, Syria and Lebanon, thus recreating the historic economic and geographical unit of that part of the world. Over time, Egypt and other countries of the region might enter into the confederation as well.

The key element of this approach is the ability of all members of the confederation to live and work anywhere within the confederation's boundaries. This breaks the Palestinians out of their prison. Rather than burdening the small emergent state with economic responsibilities it cannot possibly fulfil, the confederational approach extends that burden across the entire region. It also addresses the core of the refugee issue, which is individual choice.

Palestinians residing within the confederation would have the choice of becoming citizens of the Palestinian state, retaining citizenship in their current countries of residence or leaving the region entirely for a new life abroad. They could choose to return home to what is today Israel, but they would do so as Palestinian citizens or citizens of another member state. Israel would be under no obligation to grant them citizenship, just as Israelis living in Palestine (former "settlers" who choose to remain in the now-integrated Ma'aleh Adumim or Hebron, for example) would retain Israeli citizenship. This addresses Israeli concerns about the integrity of their state, although the internal struggle for an Israel of all its citizens would continue. As in Europe, the Middle East Economic Confederation would have a regional layer that would guarantee the economic and legal rights of all citizens of the region regardless of where they lived – together with the task of restoring land to its Palestinian owners or negotiating compensation.

In such a confederation, even a major influx of Palestinian refugees into Israel would pose no problem. It is not the presence of the refugees themselves that is threatening to Israel. After all, 300,000 foreign workers reside in Israel today. The threat to Israeli sovereignty comes from the possibility of refugees claiming Israeli citizenship. By disconnecting the Right of Return from citizenship, the refugees would realise their political identity through citizenship in a Palestinian state while posing no challenge to Israeli sovereignty, thus enjoying substantive individual justice by living in any part of Israel/Palestine or the wider region they choose. And since a confederational solution does not require the dismantlement of settlements – although they will be integrated and issues of Israel's confiscation of Palestinian lands would have to be resolved – it is not dependent upon "ending the occupation", which is the main obstacle to the two-state solution. It will simply neutralise it, rendering all the walls, checkpoints, by-pass roads and segregated cities irrelevant.

The two-stage solution will encounter opposition. Israel, perceiving itself as a kind of Singapore, has no desire to integrate into the Middle East region, relinquish its control over the entire country or accommodate Palestinian refugees. But it does offer the Israeli people – willing, unlike the government, to truly disengage from the occupation – a way out of an untenable situation. The autocratic regimes of the region might resist such a project out of fear of the democratisation it would entail, but the advantages of an end to the conflict in the region are obvious and clearly promote the visions of the "Arab Spring". International pressures and economic inducements, combined with a strong civil society initiative, could persuade the region's countries to participate.

And for the Palestinians there are only advantages. The two-stage approach offers them much more than the two-state solution, and is far more achievable than a single state since it builds upon the concept of discrete nation-states already accepted by the international community.

Although such a confederation sounds like a pipe dream in the present context of intense conflict, the infrastructure is in place. Peace treaties already exist (though limited to inter-government relations) among Israel, Egypt and Jordan, not to mention the formal and semi-formal ties with most of the states in the Middle East, North Africa and the Muslim world. The Arab Peace Initiative extends that base even further. Europe, with its experience of the past half century and its close (colonial) ties to the countries of the region, could mentor the process over a ten-year or so period. The United States, which has demonstrated its inability to broker a just peace, would simply be bypassed, as is already beginning to happen. (As I write this, the EU has announced it will initiate programmes to help Palestinians stay and develop the West Bank "as if Israel is not present".) In general, we need to develop a "working around America" strategy.

Where Are We Headed?

As I write this piece in early 2012, we find ourselves at an extremely fluid political moment in the history of Israel/Palestine. The occupation continues to expand and be fortified daily; in the past few months the Israeli government has announced the construction of more than five thousand housing units in East Jerusalem and other parts of the West Bank. While it seems clear that the negotiations of the past twenty years have reached their end and that the international community (the US and parts of Europe excepted) has acknowledged the need to recognise a Palestinian state within the 1967 borders, it seems equally clear that the two-state solution has disappeared under the weight of Israel's irreversible "facts on the ground". Talk of the resignation or collapse of the Palestinian Authority is rife, despite PA attempts to reconcile with Hamas and hold elections. Besides acting as Israel's policeman, the PA only perpetuates the occupation by keeping the illusion of negotiations and an ever-renewing "political process" alive. Were it to leave the scene, the occupation would be thrown back squarely into Israel's lap where it belongs, thereby creating an unsustainable situation that would likely force the international community, including the BRICS states and Third World countries sympathetic to the Palestinian cause, to intervene. "After Zionism" may be more than the title of a book: the whiff is in the air.

The international community has been mobilised. My impression from travels throughout the world is that the Palestinian issue has reached the proportions of the anti-Apartheid struggle in South Africa. It is one of the two or three leading international issues. Even governments, including many in Europe, are moving in the direction of Palestinian self-determination, while the US finds itself increasingly isolated.

What is lacking at the moment is Palestinian agency, particularly from our partners on the Left. The Palestinian "street", from resistance to Zionist settlement more than a century ago through several intifadas (the first being the Great Revolt of 1936–9) and on to constant daily struggle against occupation, has provided an important form of agency of active resistance. But the masses cannot articulate a plan for resolving their suffering; that is up to the political leadership and, pushing it, civil society movements and organisations. Non-Palestinian civic players, numerous, articulate and active though they may be, can neither represent the Palestinians nor take an independent leadership role. It is the Palestinians themselves who must provide the leadership and direction. The events leading up to the PLO/PA's approach to the UN in September 2011 highlight this strategic shortcoming.

During the months before the decision of the Palestinian Authority to ask for UN recognition of a Palestinian state, we of the Israeli peace camp and other international actors received mixed messages from our Palestinian partners. Most Palestinians in the Occupied Territories and Israel simply sat out the initiative. Some of our partner organisations characterised it as a "non-event" and a "farce" (an evaluation I strongly disagree with), expressing various levels of opposition. Respecting our partners' views, we at ICAHD announced that we were also "sitting it out", although we also expressed our pain at having to do so, since we see ourselves as political players and do not believe in sitting out political events or processes.

An incipient campaign for new universal elections for a genuinely representative PLO is currently under way and is certainly in order. The PLO, after all, currently represents the *only* Palestinian political agent that can bring about a just peace. But political events do not wait upon such matters. The September UN initiative backed us, willingly or not, into a potentially historic moment, but one which leaves the issue of agency open. Who, exactly, is to achieve Palestinian rights? If the PA under the leadership of President Mahmoud Abbas does not have the authority to pursue an end to the conflict, and a reconstituted PLO pressing an agreed-upon solution is still in the indeterminate future, from whom are we to take our marching orders?

This is the moment when we, the non-Palestinians, desperately need the guidance and leadership of Palestinian civil society. The struggle – and it certainly is a struggle – to re-establish representative Palestinian institutions is crucial, but it is internal to the Palestinian community. In the meantime the train of history moves on with or without us. It is a shame that the fierce debate over Palestinian agency erupted only now, a few weeks before the UN vote, and not a year ago, when it might have been resolved. Not from today was it evident that the PA is not on our side. But paralysing activists on the cusp of a major political moment is not acceptable.

A parallel and urgent agenda thus arises. Palestinian civil society, or at least the organisations of the Left with whom we work most closely, must begin to offer us, if not an end-game (one democratic state, one bi-national state, two states, a regional confederation – whatever), then at least a political programme. The popular committees and other activists may play a key role in keeping the struggle alive and focused, and BDS may provide a powerful vehicle for mobilising people abroad, but even together they do not constitute a political strategy capable of delivering liberation. If not a programme or a particular solution, at least we non-Palestinians deserve a *vision* of where our partners are headed. A far-reaching and urgent discussion of our post-September political programme is desperately needed.

The Issue of Inclusivity

Part of the uncertainty of post-September has to do with "inclusion", an extremely sensitive issue to which I alluded earlier. Over all the years of joint struggle, the assumption of the Israeli peace camp was that any solution must be inclusive of all the peoples living in the country, as citizens if not as national groups. The example of post-Apartheid South Africa was often invoked. Yet over the past few years, as the occupation grew stronger and the prospect of a two-state solution receded, a subtle, unspoken shift began to take place among our Palestinian partners, especially those on the Left. A process of withdrawal from joint actions with Israeli groups started to manifest itself, usually under the rubric of anti-"normalisation". This was true in regard to ICAHD and other Left Israeli groups, even those (such as ICAHD) that were explicitly post- or even anti-Zionist, and despite the fact that we conformed to the principles of the Civil Society Call.

As the Palestinian Left moved towards a one-state solution, an anti-colonial discourse began gaining ground. Zionism and any form of a Jewish national narrative were categorically rejected, as was the notion that Israeli Jews would form part of a bi-national entity. Whether or not Israeli Jews would even have a place in the future Palestine (/Israel) has so far been left unsaid, but one can discern movement from an inclusive South African model to an exclusive Algerian one.

For the record, I do not consider Zionism a colonial movement. It did contain a fatal element of exclusivity, to be sure, deriving both from the Bible and from the nineteenth-century tribal nationalism of Central and Eastern Europe, where most Jews lived. It therefore became colonial as soon as it sought to deny the national rights and very existence of a Palestinian people, embarking on a campaign of displacement that continues to this day. But the initial impulse of Zionism was genuine: the notion of returning to one's ancient home-land and reviving a national culture that could not be sustained in the Diaspora. As an anthropologist, I understand that the Zionist narrative was constructed and "invented"; but in that, Zionism was no different from any other national movement, including the Palestinians'. Self-determination means just that.

I would argue that "after Zionism" means to *de-colonise* Zionism. Whether it should have come into existence or not, an Israeli-Jewish national entity exists and we must work towards integrating it into a bi-national reality that reflects a genuine Israel/Palestine, existing within a multi-national, multi-religious Middle East. Regardless of whether Palestinians ever accept Zionism as a legitimate national movement (and there is no reason why they should, given the crimes committed over the past century), I must insist on inclusiveness as a fundamental principle of a just and lasting peace – conditional on the de-colonisation of Zionism and the transformation of Israel into a broader, inclusive political entity, be it a bi-national state or a regional confederation.

Global Palestine

The political implications of the Israeli–Palestinian conflict extend far beyond any particular geography. In many ways, the Israeli–Palestinian relationship represents in microcosm the global relationship between the western "core" countries that dominate the world system and the vast majority of humanity doomed to exist on its "peripheries"; suppliers of raw materials and cheap labour, warehoused and subject to military attack whenever they attempt to resist. The Occupied Territories have never constituted a significant military threat to Israel, and "security" plays no genuine role in Israel's insistence on retaining control over it. Instead, it has become a laboratory for the testing of weapons and tactics of "counterinsurgency", one which has propelled Israel to the top ranks of military exporters (Israel ties with France as the world's third largest seller of arms); and this does not include its homeland security industry, which has eclipsed its military sales.

To be sure, Israel specialises in weapons and components of weapons systems used in conventional warfare: electronics, optronics and electro-optics; avionics; precision-guided weapons; unmanned aerial vehicles and other forms of robotics; tanks, armoured vehicles and modular armour; small arms; accessories and equipment for soldiers; and future warfare weaponry such as cyberwarfare (already used on Iran) and the integrated technologies of GNR (genetics, nanotechnology and robotics).

Much of this technology, however, has arisen from or been adapted to what is known in military parlance as "warfare amongst the people". It is this reality of having millions of trapped people, upon whom it can experiment with virtually any weapon – including new-generation cluster bombs, flechettes and anti-personnel devices, white phosphorous and tungsten-based DIME explosives, all of which are prohibited by international law for use in densely populated areas like Gaza – that gives Israel the edge in the tremendously profitable, yet tremendously competitive, arms and security industries.

Israel is the world's leader in the use of surveillance and killer drones (UAVs or unmanned aerial vehicles), which are appearing so prominently in Afghanistan but are also being adopted by increasingly militarised police forces. It is exporting its matrix of control to places like Iraq, where house demolitions is a common practice of counter-insurgency; or Brazil, where Israeli tactics and weapons (such as drones) are being used to "pacify" the favelas in anticipation of the World Cup in 2014 and the Olympics in 2016; or to western nations, who increasingly use Israeli biometrics in their airports and police forces.

Activists on the Palestinian issue have long proclaimed: "We are all Palestinians!" By this, we mean that we stand in solidarity with the Palestinian people. Increasingly, however, as Israel's occupation becomes globalised, the people of the earth – favela dwellers, Occupy Wall Street protesters, those that resist the exploitation of their labour and resources, women and child workers in the global factory, victims of remote-controlled drone strikes by missiles fired from Las Vegas – are literally becoming Palestinians. Don't think what happened to the people of Gaza remains with them alone. Whether through armies, security agencies or your local police, the road from Gaza leads directly to your door.

Without deflecting attention from the actual conflict "on the ground" in Palestine and the struggle for Palestinian rights, a lot is riding on the just resolution of the Israel/Palestine conflict: the prospect of regional and world peace, to be sure, but beyond that the possibility of replacing the militarism and exploitation on which the world system is presently based with a more human reality of human rights, inclusiveness, economic justice and peace. Writ large, from the micro of Palestinian and Israelis to the macro of global society, "After Zionism" holds out a vision of where we all should be headed.

SEVEN

The Future of Palestine:
Righteous Jews vs. the New Afrikaners[1]

John J. Mearsheimer

One of the most important issues in world politics today is the future of Palestine. By that I mean the future of the land between the Jordan River and the Mediterranean Sea, or what was long ago called Mandatory Palestine. That ground is now broken into two parts: Israel proper, or what is sometime called "Green Line" Israel; and the Occupied Territories, which include the West Bank and Gaza. In essence, the future of Palestine revolves around the relationship that develops between Israel and the Occupied Territories.

We are not just talking about the fate of those lands, of course; we are also dealing with the future of the peoples who live there, who include the Jews and the Palestinians who are Israeli citizens, as well as those Palestinians who live in the Occupied Territories.

My story is straightforward. Contrary to the wishes of the Obama administration and most Americans – and this includes many American Jews – Israel is not going to allow the Palestinians to have a real state of their own in Gaza and the West Bank. Regrettably, the two-state solution is now no more than fantasy. Instead, those territories will be formally incorporated into a Greater Israel, which will be a full-blown Apartheid state bearing a marked resemblance to white-ruled South Africa. Yet a Jewish Apartheid state is not politically viable over the long term. In the end, it will become a democratic bi-national state, whose politics will be dominated by its Palestinian citizens. In other words, it will cease being a Jewish state, and this will mean the end of the Zionist dream.

Potential Ways to Configure Palestine

Given present circumstances, there are four possible futures for Palestine. The outcome that gets the most attention these days is the two-state solution, which was described in broad outline by President Bill Clinton in late December 2000 and would involve the creation of a Palestinian state operating side by side with Israel. For this to be viable, Palestine would need to control 95 percent or more of the West Bank and all of Gaza, with East Jerusalem as its capital. There would also have to be territorial swaps to compensate the Palestinians for any small pieces of the West Bank that Israel was allowed to keep in the final agreement. The Clinton Parameters envisioned certain restrictions on the new state's military capabilities, but it would control the water beneath it, the air space above it, and its own borders – to include the Jordan River Valley. Finally, the Palestinians and Israelis would have to use clever language to deal both with Palestinian claims to "Right of Return" and with Israeli culpability for the hundreds of thousands of Palestinians who were expelled from their homes in 1948. A small number of those refugees and their descendants might be allowed to return to their homes inside Israel for symbolic purposes, but the overwhelming majority would live in either the new Palestinian state or another country.

There are three possible alternatives to a two-state solution, all of which involve creating a Greater Israel – an Israel that officially includes the West Bank and Gaza. In the first scenario, Greater Israel would become a democratic bi-national state in which Palestinians and Jews enjoy equal political rights. This solution has been suggested by a handful of Jews and a growing number of Palestinians. However, it would mean abandoning the original Zionist vision of a Jewish state, since the Palestinians would eventually outnumber the Jews in Greater Israel.

Second, Israel could expel most of the Palestinians from Greater Israel, thereby preserving its Jewish character through an overt act of ethnic cleansing. This is what happened in 1948 when the Zionists drove roughly 700,000 Palestinians out of the territory that became the new state of Israel, and then prevented them from returning to their homes. Following the Six Day War in 1967 Israel expelled

between 100,000 and 260,000 Palestinians from the newly conquered West Bank and drove 80,000 Syrians from the Golan Heights.
This time, however, the scale of the expulsion would have to be even
greater: there are now about 5.6 million Palestinians living between
the Jordan River and the Mediterranean Sea.

The final alternative to a two-state solution is some form of
Apartheid, whereby Israel would increase its control over the
Occupied Territories whilst allowing the Palestinians to exercise
limited autonomy in a set of disconnected and economically crippled
enclaves.

The two-state solution is the best of these alternative futures. By
no means an ideal solution, it is nonetheless by far the best outcome
for the Israelis and the Palestinians, as well as the United States. That
is why the Clinton, Bush and Obama administrations have all been
deeply committed to it. Nevertheless, the Palestinians are not going
to get their own state any time soon. They will instead end up living in
an Apartheid state dominated by Israeli Jews.

Israel and the Two-State Solution

The main reason that a two-state solution is no longer a serious option
is that most Israelis are unwilling to make the sacrifices that would be
necessary to create a viable Palestinian state. There is little reason to
expect them to have an epiphany on this issue. To begin with, there are
now around 500,000 settlers in the Occupied Territories, who have
brought with them a huge infrastructure of connecting and bypass
roads, not to mention settlements. Much of that infrastructure and
large numbers of those settlers would have to be removed to create a
Palestinian state – and the settlers would fiercely resist any attempt to
roll back the settlement enterprise.

A March 2010 poll conducted by the Truman Institute at Hebrew
University found that 21 percent of settlers believe that "if the government decides on a comprehensive evacuation of settlements", Israelis
should "resist it by all means". Presumably this would include the use
of arms. In addition, the pollsters found that 54 percent of settlers do
not recognise the government's "authority to decide to evacuate or

not evacuate settlements"; even if there was a referendum sanctioning a withdrawal, 36 percent of settlers said they would not accept it.

Those settlers, however, have no need to worry about the present government trying to remove them. Prime Minister Netanyahu is committed to expanding the settlements in East Jerusalem and indeed throughout the West Bank. Of course, he and virtually everyone in his cabinet are opposed to giving the Palestinians a viable state of their own.

One might argue that there are prominent Israelis like former Foreign Minister Tzipi Livni and former Prime Minister Ehud Olmert who openly disagree with Netanyahu and advocate a two-state solution. While this is true, it is by no means clear that either of them would be willing or able to make the concessions necessary to create a legitimate Palestinian state. Olmert certainly did not do so when he was prime minister, although he was serious about negotiating with the Palestinians in pursuit of a two-state solution.

Even if some Israeli leader was seriously committed to creating a Palestinian state in the Occupied Territories, it is unlikely that he or she could garner enough public support to make a deal work. Over the past decade the political centre of gravity in Israel has shifted sharply to the Right, and there is no sizeable pro-peace political party or movement that they could turn to for help. Perhaps the best single indicator of how far to the Right Israel has moved in recent years is the shocking fact that Avigdor Lieberman is employed as its foreign minister. Even Martin Peretz of the *New Republic*, who is well known for his unyielding support for Israel, describes Lieberman as "a neo-fascist" and equates him with the late Austrian fascist Jorg Haider. There are other individuals in Netanyahu's cabinet who share many of Lieberman's views about the Israeli–Palestinian conflict; they just happen to be less outspoken than the foreign minister.

Even if someone like Livni or Olmert were able to cobble together a coalition of interest groups and political parties that favoured a genuine two-state solution, they would still face fierce resistance from the sizeable forces that stand behind Netanyahu and his allies today. It is even possible, which is not to say likely, that Israel would be engulfed by civil war if some future leader made a serious attempt to give the Palestinians a real state of their own. An individual with the stature of David Ben Gurion or Ariel Sharon – or even Yitzhak Rabin – might be able to stand up to those naysayers and push forward a two-state solution, but there is nobody with that kind of standing in Israeli politics today.

In addition to these practical political obstacles to creating a Palestinian state, there is an important psychological barrier. From the start, Zionism envisioned an Israeli state that controlled all of Mandatory Palestine. There was no place for a Palestinian state in the original Zionist vision of Israel. Even Yitzhak Rabin, who was determined to make the Oslo peace process work, never spoke about creating a Palestinian state. He was merely interested in granting the Palestinians some form of limited autonomy, what he called "an entity which is less than a state". Furthermore, he insisted that Israel should maintain control over the Jordan River Valley and that a united Jerusalem should be the capital of Israel. Also remember that in the spring of 1998 when Hillary Clinton was First Lady, she was sharply criticised for saying that: "It would be in the long-term interests of peace in the Middle East for there to be a state of Palestine, a functioning modern state on the same footing as other states."

It was not until after Ehud Barak became prime minister in 1999 that Israeli leaders began to speak openly about the possibility of a Palestinian state. Still, not all of them thought it was a good idea and hardly any of them were enthusiastic about it. Even Barak, who flirted seriously with the idea of creating a Palestinian state at Camp David in July 2000, initially opposed the Oslo Accords. Indeed, he has been willing to serve as Netanyahu's defence minister for the past three years, knowing full well that the prime minister and his allies are opposed to creating an independent Palestine. All of this is to say that the core beliefs of Zionism are deeply hostile to the notion of a Palestinian state, and this mindset makes it difficult for many Israelis to embrace the two-state solution.

In short, it is difficult to imagine any Israeli government having the political will, much less the ability, to dismantle a substantial portion of its vast settlement enterprise and create a Palestinian state in virtually all of the Occupied Territories, including East Jerusalem.

President Obama and Israel

Many advocates of a two-state solution recognise this problem, but think that there is a way to solve it: the Obama administration needs to come up with a clever strategy for putting pressure on Israel to allow the Palestinians to have their own state. Once the right strategy is found, it should be a relatively easy task to move Israel in the right direction. After all, the United States is the most powerful country in the world and it should have great leverage over Israel because it gives the Jewish state so much diplomatic and material support.

But this is not going to happen, because no American president can put meaningful pressure on Israel to force it to change its policies toward the Palestinians. The main reason is the Israel lobby, a remarkably powerful interest group that has a profound influence on US Middle East policy. Harvard law professor Alan Dershowitz, a staunch supporter of Israel, was spot on when he said: "My generation of Jews ... became part of what is perhaps the most effective lobbying and fund-raising effort in the history of democracy." That lobby, of course, makes it impossible for any president to play hardball with Israel, especially on the issue of settlements.

Let's look at the historical record. Every American president since 1967 has opposed settlement building in the Occupied Territories. Yet no president has been able to put serious pressure on Israel to stop building settlements, much less dismantle them. Perhaps the best evidence of America's impotence is what happened in the 1990s during the Oslo peace process. Between 1993 and 2000, Israel confiscated 40,000 acres of Palestinian land, built 250 miles of connector and bypass roads, doubled the number of settlers, and established thirty new settlements. President Clinton did hardly anything to halt this expansion. Instead, the United States continued to give Israel billions of dollars in foreign aid each year and to protect it at every turn on the diplomatic front.

It is tempting to think that Obama is different from his predecessors, but there is hardly any evidence to support that belief and much to contradict it. Consider that during the 2008 presidential campaign, Obama responded to charges that he was "soft" on Israel by pandering to the lobby and repeatedly praising America's special relationship with Israel. In the month before he took office in January 2009 he was silent during the Gaza massacre – at a time when Israel was being criticised around the world for its brutal assault on that densely populated enclave.

Since taking office, President Obama has clashed with Prime Minister Netanyahu four times: in each case Obama backed down and Netanyahu won the fight. Shortly after the administration came to power, the president and his principal foreign policy advisors began demanding that Israel stop all settlement building in the Occupied Territories, to include East Jerusalem, so that serious peace negotiations with the Palestinians could begin. After calling for "two states for two peoples" in his Cairo speech in June 2009, President Obama declared: "it is time for these settlements to stop." Secretary of State Hillary Clinton had made the same point one month earlier when she said: "We want to see a stop to settlement construction, additions, natural growth – any kind of settlement activity. That is what the president has called for." George Mitchell, the president's special envoy for the Middle East, conveyed this straightforward message to Prime Minister Netanyahu and his advisors on numerous occasions.

In response, Netanyahu made it clear that Israel intended to continue building settlements and that he and almost everyone in his government opposed a two-state solution. He made but a single reference to "two states" in his own speech at Bar Ilan University in June 2009, and the conditions he attached to it made it clear that he was talking about giving the Palestinians a handful of disconnected Apartheid-style Bantustans, not a fully sovereign state.

Naturally, Netanyahu won this fight. Not only did the Israeli prime minister refuse to stop building the 2,500 housing units that were under construction in the West Bank; just to make it clear to Obama who was boss, in late June 2009 he authorised the building of 300 new homes in the West Bank. Netanyahu refused even to countenance setting any limits on settlement building in East Jerusalem, which is supposed to be the capital of a Palestinian state. By the end of September 2009 Obama conceded publicly that Netanyahu had beaten him in their fight over the settlements. The president falsely denied that freezing settlement construction had ever been a precondition for resuming the peace process, and instead meekly asked Israel to please exercise restraint while it continued colonising the West Bank. Fully aware of his triumph, Netanyahu said on 23 September: "I am pleased that President Obama has accepted my approach that there should be no preconditions."

Indeed, his victory was so complete that the Israeli media was full of stories describing how their prime minister had bested Obama and greatly improved his shaky political position at home. As Gideon Samet wrote in *Ma'ariv*: "In the past weeks, it has become clear with what ease an Israeli prime minister can succeed in thwarting an American initiative."

Perhaps the best American response to Netanyahu's victory came from the widely read author and blogger, Andrew Sullivan, who wrote that this sad episode should: "remind Obama of a cardinal rule of American politics: no pressure on Israel ever. Just keep giving them money and they will give the US the finger in return. The only permitted position is to say you oppose settlements in the West Bank, while doing everything you can to keep them growing and advancing."

The Obama administration was engaged in a second round of fighting over settlements in March 2010, when the Netanyahu government embarrassed Vice President Biden during his visit to Israel by announcing plans to build 1,600 new housing units in East Jerusalem. While that crisis clearly revealed that Israel's brutal policies toward the Palestinians are seriously damaging US interests in the Middle East, Netanyahu rejected President Obama's request to stop building settlements in East Jerusalem. "As far as we are concerned," he said on 21 March, "building in Jerusalem is like building in Tel Aviv. Our policy on Jerusalem is like the policy in the past forty-two years." One day later at the annual AIPAC Conference he said: "The Jewish people were building Jerusalem three thousand years ago, and the Jewish people are building Jerusalem today. Jerusalem is not a settlement; it's our capital." Meanwhile, back in the United States, AIPAC got 333 congressmen and 76 senators to sign letters to Secretary of State Clinton reaffirming their unyielding support for Israel and urging the administration to keep future disagreements behind closed doors. By early July, the crisis was over. Obama had lost again.

The third fight came soon thereafter in September 2010. Ten months earlier, the Israelis had agreed to a partial building freeze in the

West Bank, although not in Jerusalem. That gesture had been enough to convince the Palestinians to resume negotiations that September with the Israelis over the future of the Occupied Territories. Talks began in early September. However, there was a major problem: the partial building freeze was due to expire in late September. Obama went to great lengths to convince Netanyahu to extend the freeze so that the talks could continue. Netanyahu refused and the negotiations collapsed just as they were getting started.

The fourth round of fighting took place in May 2011 when President Obama gave a major speech calling for the establishment of a Palestinian state based on the 1967 borders. The Netanyahu government, however, had made it clear beforehand that talking specifically about the 1967 borders was unacceptable, even though everyone has long understood that any meaningful agreement would have to be based on those borders with minor adjustments where necessary. Netanyahu and his American supporters responded by lambasting the president; this included a televised meeting where the Israeli prime minister lectured the president about the flaws in his thinking about the peace process. Subsequently, Netanyahu went to Capitol Hill, where he was treated like a conquering hero. Obama, facing a tough election in 2012 and deeply fearful of losing support in the American Jewish community, quickly backed off from pressuring Israel and instead decided to offer unconditional support.

The president's toadying quickly became apparent in the summer of 2011 when it became clear that Palestinian President Mahmoud Abbas intended to approach the United Nations in September to ask for formal recognition of a Palestinian state based on the 1967 borders. This move was consistent with Obama's goal of achieving a two-state solution. But the Netanyahu government, which has no interest in seeing the Palestinians get a viable state of their own, was adamantly opposed to the plan, and put enormous pressure on the Obama administration to thwart the Palestinians. Not surprisingly, the United States went to great lengths to discourage Abbas from going to the United Nations; when that failed, Obama vowed to veto the application in the Security Council.

It is manifestly clear that President Obama is no match for the lobby. The best he can hope for is to re-start the so-called peace process, but most people understand that these negotiations are a charade. The two sides engage in endless talks while Israel continues to colonise Palestinian lands. Henry Siegman got it right when he called these fruitless talks "The Greater Middle East Peace Process Scam". And whether Obama is re-elected or a Republican moves into the White House, this situation is not going to change after the 2012 presidential election.

There are two other reasons that there will not be a two-state solution. Deeply divided among themselves, the Palestinians are not in a good position to make a deal with Israel and then stick to it. That problem is fixable with time and help from Israel and the United States. But time has run out and neither Tel Aviv nor Washington is likely to provide a helping hand. Then there are the Christian Zionists, a powerful political force in the United States, especially on Capitol Hill. They are adamantly opposed to a two-state solution because they want Israel to control every square millimetre of Palestine, a situation they believe heralds the "Second Coming" of Christ.

Israel's Future

The inevitable conclusion all of this will be the formation of a Greater Israel between the Jordan River and the Mediterranean Sea. In fact, I would argue that de facto it already exists, as Israel effectively controls the Occupied Territories and rules over the Palestinians who live there. The West Bank and Gaza have not yet been incorporated de jure into Israel proper, but that will eventually happen – certainly in the case of the West Bank. When it does, that will complete the transformation of Green Line Israel into Greater Israel.

But who will live there and what kind of political system will it have? It is not going to be a democratic bi-national state, at least in the near future. An overwhelming majority of Israel's Jews have no interest in living in a state that would be dominated by the Palestinians. And that includes young Israeli Jews, many of whom hold clearly bigoted views toward the Palestinians in their midst. Furthermore, few of Israel's supporters in the United States are interested in this outcome at this point in time. Most Palestinians would, of course, accept a democratic bi-national state without hesitation if it could be achieved quickly. But that is not going to happen, although, as I will argue shortly, it is likely to come to pass down the road.

Then there is the possibility of ethnic cleansing, which would certainly mean that Greater Israel would have a Jewish majority. But that murderous strategy seems unlikely, because it would do enormous damage to Israel's moral fabric, its relationship with Jews in the Diaspora, and to its international standing. Israel and its supporters would be treated harshly by history, and it would poison relations with Israel's neighbours for years to come. No genuine friend of Israel could support this policy, which would clearly be a crime against humanity. It also seems unlikely because most of the 5.6 million Palestinians living between the Jordan River and the Mediterranean Sea would put up fierce resistance if Israel tried to expel them from their homes.

Nevertheless, there is reason to worry that Israelis might adopt this solution as the demographic balance shifts against them and they start to fear for the survival of the Jewish state. Given the right circumstances – say a war involving Israel that is accompanied by serious Palestinian unrest – Israeli leaders might conclude that they can expel massive numbers of Palestinians from Greater Israel and depend on the lobby to protect them from international criticism and especially from sanctions.

We should not underestimate Israel's willingness to employ such a horrific strategy if the opportunity presented itself. It is apparent from public opinion surveys and everyday discourse that many Israelis hold racist views of Palestinians, and the Gaza massacre in the winter of 2008–9 makes clear that they have few qualms about killing Palestinian civilians. It is difficult to disagree with Jimmy Carter's comment in June 2009 that "the citizens of Palestine are treated more like animals than like human beings." A century of conflict and more than four decades of occupation will do that to a people. And, of course, the Israelis engaged in a massive cleansing of the Palestinians in 1948 and again in 1967. Still, I do not believe Israel will resort to this horrible course of action.

The most likely outcome in the absence of a two-state solution is that Greater Israel will become a fully fledged Apartheid state. As anyone who has spent time in the West Bank knows, Israel essentially has an Apartheid system up and running there, with separate laws, separate roads, and separate housing for Israelis and Palestinians. The latter are essentially confined to impoverished enclaves that they can leave and enter only with great difficulty. However, because the Occupied Territories have not been fully integrated into Israel, one can plausibly argue that the Tel Aviv has not yet gone all the way down the Apartheid road.

Israelis and their American supporters invariably bristle at the comparison to white rule in South Africa, but that is their future if they create a Greater Israel while denying full political rights to an Arab population that will soon outnumber the Jewish population in the entirety of the land. Indeed, two former Israeli prime ministers have made this very point. Ehud Olmert, who was Netanyahu's predecessor, said in late November 2007 that if "the two-state solution collapses," Israel will "face a South African-style struggle." He went so far as to argue that, "as soon as that happens, the state of Israel is finished." Former Prime Minister Ehud Barak said in February 2010: "As long as in this territory west of the Jordan River there is only one political entity called Israel it is going to be either non-Jewish, or non-democratic. If this bloc of millions of Palestinians cannot vote, that will be an Apartheid state."

Other Israelis, as well as Jimmy Carter and Archbishop Desmond Tutu, have warned that if Israel does not pull out of the Occupied Territories it will become an Apartheid state like white-ruled South Africa. But if I am right, the occupation is not going to end and there will not be a two-state solution. That means Israel will complete its transformation into a full-blown Apartheid state over the next decade. In the long run, however, Israel will not be able to maintain itself as such. Like racist South Africa, it will eventually evolve into a democratic bi-national state whose politics will be dominated by the more numerous Palestinians. Of course, this means that Israel faces a bleak future as a Jewish state.

Selling Apartheid in the West

One problem that Israel will face is that the discrimination and repression that are the essence of Apartheid will be increasingly visible to people all around the world. Israel and its supporters have been able to do a good job of keeping the mainstream media in the United States from telling the truth about what Israel is doing to the Palestinians in the Occupied Territories. But the Internet is a game changer. Not only does it make it easy for the opponents of Apartheid to get the real story out to the world; it also allows Americans to learn the story that the *New York Times* and the *Washington Post* have been hiding from them. Over time, this situation may even force these two media institutions to cover the story more accurately themselves.

The growing visibility of this issue is not just a function of the Internet. It is also due to the fact that the plight of the Palestinians matters greatly to people all across the Arab and Islamic world, and they constantly raise the issue with westerners. The Arab Spring is likely to intensify this support for the Palestinians, because future Middle East leaders will be fearful of alienating their publics if they do not back the Palestinian cause to the hilt. It also matters very much to the influential human rights community, which is naturally going to be critical of Israel's harsh treatment of the Palestinians. It is not surprising that hard-line Israelis and their American supporters are now waging a vicious smear campaign against those human rights organisations that criticise Israel.

The main problem that Israel's defenders face, however, is that it is impossible to defend Apartheid, because it is antithetical to core western values. How does one make a moral case for Apartheid, particularly in the United States, where democracy is venerated and segregation and racism are routinely condemned? It is hard to imagine the United States having a special relationship with an Apartheid state. Indeed, it is hard to imagine the United States having much sympathy for one. It is much easier to imagine the United States strongly opposing that racist state's political system and working hard to change it. Of course, many other countries around the globe will reach the same conclusion, probably before the United States, because of the power of the lobby in Washington. This is surely why former Prime Minister Olmert said that going down the Apartheid road would be suicidal for Israel.

Apartheid is not only morally reprehensible, it also guarantees that Israel will remain a strategic liability for the United States. Numerous American leaders, including President Obama, Vice President Biden and CIA director David Petraeus, have emphasised that Israel's colonisation of the Occupied Territories is doing serious damage to American interests in the Middle East. As Biden told Prime Minister Benjamin Netanyahu in March 2010 during the vice president's controversy-filled visit to Israel: "This is starting to get dangerous for us. What you're doing here undermines the security of our troops who are fighting in Iraq, Afghanistan and Pakistan. That endangers us, and it endangers regional peace." This situation will only get worse as Israel becomes a fully fledged Apartheid state. And as that becomes clear to more and more Americans, there is likely to be a serious erosion of support for the Jewish state on strategic grounds alone.

Hard-line Israelis and their American supporters are aware of these problems, but they are betting that the lobby will defend Israel no matter what, and that its support will be sufficient to allow Apartheid Israel to survive. It might seem like a safe bet, since the lobby has played a key role in shielding Israel from American pressure up to now. In fact, one could argue that Israel could not have got so far down the Apartheid road without the help of organisations like AIPAC and the Anti-Defamation League. But that strategy is not likely to work over the long run.

The problem with depending on the lobby for protection is that most American Jews will not back Israel if it becomes a fully fledged Apartheid state. Indeed, many of them are likely to criticise Israel and support calls for making Greater Israel a legitimate democracy. That is obviously not the case now, but there are good reasons to think that a marked shift in the American Jewish community's thinking about Israel is in the offing. This is not to deny that there will be some diehards who defend Apartheid Israel; but their ranks will be thin and it will be widely apparent that they are out of step with core American values.

American Jews and Greater Israel

American Jews who care deeply about Israel can be divided into three broad categories. The first two are what I call "righteous Jews" and the "new Afrikaners", clearly definable groups that think about Israel and where it is headed in fundamentally different ways. The third and largest group is comprised of those Jews who care about Israel, but do not have clear-cut views on how to think about Greater Israel and Apartheid. Let us call this group the "great ambivalent middle".

Righteous Jews have a powerful attachment to core liberal values. They believe that individual rights matter greatly and that they are universal, which means that they apply equally to Jews and Palestinians. They could never support an Apartheid Israel. They understand that the Palestinians paid an enormous price to make it possible to create Israel in 1948. Moreover, they recognise the pain and suffering that Israel has inflicted on the Palestinians in the Occupied Territories since 1967. Finally, most righteous Jews believe that the Palestinians deserve a viable state of their own, just as the Jews deserve their own state. In essence, they believe that self-determination applies to Palestinians as well as Jews, and that the two-state solution is the best way to achieve that end. Some righteous Jews, however, favour a democratic bi-national state over the two-state solution.

On the other side, we have the new Afrikaners, who will support Israel even if it is an Apartheid state. These are individuals who will back Israel no matter what it does, because they have blind loyalty to the Jewish state. This is not to say that the new Afrikaners think that Apartheid is an attractive or desirable political system, because I am sure that many of them do not. Surely some of them favour a two-state solution and some of them probably have a serious commitment to liberal values. The key point, however, is that they have an even deeper commitment to supporting Israel unreservedly. The new Afrikaners will of course try to come up with clever arguments to convince themselves and others that Israel is really not an Apartheid state, and that those who say it is are anti-Semites. We are all familiar with this strategy.

The key to determining whether the lobby can protect Apartheid Israel over the long run is whether the great ambivalent middle sides with the new Afrikaners or the righteous Jews. The new Afrikaners have to win that fight decisively for Greater Israel to survive as a racist state.

There is no question that the present balance of power favours the new Afrikaners. When push comes to shove on issues relating to Israel, the hardliners invariably get most of those American Jews who are concerned about Israel to side with them. The righteous Jews, on the other hand, hold considerably less sway with the great ambivalent middle, at least at this point in time. This situation is due in good part to the fact that most American Jews – especially the elders in the community – have little understanding of how far down the Apartheid road Israel has travelled and where it is ultimately headed. They think that the two-state solution is still a viable option and that Israel remains committed to allowing the Palestinians to have their own state. These false beliefs allow them to act as if there is little danger of Israel becoming South Africa, which makes it easy for them to side with the new Afrikaners.

This situation, however, is unsustainable over time. Once it is widely recognised that the two-state solution is dead and Greater Israel has become a reality, the righteous Jews will have two choices: support Apartheid or work to help create a democratic bi-national state. I believe that almost all of them will opt for the latter option, in large part because of their deep-seated commitment to liberal values, which renders any Apartheid state abhorrent to them. Of course, the new Afrikaners will fiercely defend Apartheid Israel, because their commitment to Israel is unconditional, so it overrides any commitment they might have to liberal values.

The critical question, however, is this: what will happen to those Jews who comprise the great ambivalent middle once it is clear that Israel is a fully fledged Apartheid state and that facts on the ground have made a two-state solution impossible? Will they side with the new Afrikaners and defend Apartheid Israel, or will they ally with the righteous Jews and call for making Greater Israel a true democracy? Or will they sit silently on the sidelines?

I believe that most of the Jews in the great ambivalent middle will not defend Apartheid Israel but will either keep quiet or side with the righteous Jews against the new Afrikaners, who will become increasingly marginalised over time. Once that happens, the lobby will be unable to provide cover for Israel's racist policies toward the Palestinians in the way it has done in the past.

There are a number of reasons why there is not likely to be much support for Israel inside the American Jewish community as that country looks increasingly like white-ruled South Africa. A despicable political system, Apartheid is fundamentally at odds with basic American values as well as core Jewish values. This is why the new Afrikaners will claim that security concerns explain Israeli discrimination against and oppression of the Palestinians. But as we have seen, we are rapidly reaching the point where it will be hard to miss the fact that Israel is becoming a fully fledged Apartheid state and that those who claim otherwise are either delusional or disingenuous. Simply put, not many American Jews are likely to be fooled by the new Afrikaners' arguments.

Furthermore, survey data shows that younger American Jews feel less attachment to Israel than their elders. This is due in part to the fact that the younger generations were born after the Holocaust and after anti-Semitism had largely been eliminated from American life. Also, Jews have been seamlessly integrated into the American mainstream, to the point where many community leaders worry that rampant inter-marriage will lead to the disappearance of American Jewry over time. Not surprisingly, younger Jews are less disposed to see Israel as a safe haven should the goyim go on an anti-Semitic rampage, because they recognise this is not going to happen in the United States. That perspective makes them less inclined than their elders to defend Israel no matter what it does.

There is another reason that American Jews are likely to feel less connected to Israel in the years ahead. Important changes are taking place in the demographic make-up of Israel that will make it more difficult for many of them to identify closely with the Jewish state. When Israel was created in 1948, few ultra-orthodox Jews lived there. In fact, ultra-orthodox Jews were deeply hostile to Zionism, which they viewed as an affront to Judaism. Secular Jews dominated Israeli life at its founding and they still do, but their influence has been waning and is likely to decline much more in the decades ahead. The main reason is that the ultra-orthodox are a rapidly growing percentage of the population, due to their stunningly high birthrates. It is estimated that the average ultra-orthodox woman has 7.8 babies. In fact, in the 2008 mayoral election in Jerusalem, an ultra-orthodox candidate boasted: "In another fifteen years there will not be a secular mayor in any city in Israel." Of course, he was exaggerating, but his boast is indicative of the growing power of the ultra-orthodox in Israel.

An additional dynamic is changing the make-up of Israeli society. Large numbers of Israelis have left the country to live abroad and the majority are not expected to return home. Several recent estimates suggest that between 750,000 and one million Israelis reside in other countries, most of them secular. On top of that, public opinion surveys indicate that many Israelis would like to move to another country. This situation is likely to get worse over time, because many secular Jews will not want to live in an Apartheid state whose politics and daily life are increasingly shaped by the ultra-orthodox.

All of this is to say that Israel's secular Jewish identity – which has been so powerful from the start – is slowly eroding and promises to continue eroding over time as the ultra-orthodox grow in number and influence. That important development will make it more difficult in the years ahead for secular American Jews – who make up the bulk of the Jewish community in the United States – to identify closely with Israel and be willing to defend it when it becomes a full-blown Apartheid state. Of course, that reluctance to back Israel will be reinforced by the fact that American Jews are among the staunchest defenders of traditional liberal values.

The Bottom Line

It seems clear that Israel will not be able to maintain itself as an Apartheid state over the long term, because it will not be able to depend on the American Jewish community to defend its loathsome policies toward the Palestinians. Without that protection, Israel is doomed, because public opinion in the West will turn decisively against it. Thus, I believe that Greater Israel will eventually become a democratic bi-national state, and the Palestinians will dominate its politics, because they will outnumber the Jews in the land between the Jordan River and the Mediterranean Sea.

What is truly remarkable about this situation is that the Israel lobby is effectively helping Israel to commit national suicide. What makes this situation even more astonishing is that there is an alternative outcome which would be relatively easy to achieve and is clearly in Israel's best interests: the two-state solution. It is hard to understand why Israel and its American supporters are not working overtime to create a viable Palestinian state in the Occupied Territories and why instead they are moving full-speed ahead to build Greater Israel. It makes no sense from either a moral or a strategic perspective. Indeed, it is an exceptionally foolish policy.

There are obviously great dangers ahead for the Palestinians, who will continue to suffer terribly at the hands of the Israelis for years to come. But it does look as though the Palestinians will eventually get their own state, mainly because Israel seems bent on self-destruction.

EIGHT

Israel's Liberal Myths

Jonathan Cook

In the Israeli newspaper photograph, Ahmed and Fatina Zbeidat could be mistaken for models recruited to a government promotional campaign. Young, slim and attractive, they clutch their beaming toddler daughter between them. They are in celebratory mood on a patch of rough ground, their joyous smiles suggesting that they may have just won the national lottery.

However, the image obscures more than it reveals. It cannot show that the Zbeidats are as clever as they are photogenic: both are architects who graduated with distinction from one of Israel's leading arts colleges, Jerusalem's Bezalel Academy of Arts and Design. It cannot explain the real reason for their smiles; they have just been awarded the piece of land on which they are standing, in the rural community of Rakefet in northern Israel, as the place to build their home. It does not hint at the relief masked by the smiles; they have fought for six years to be allowed access to the land. Or the humiliation they have endured to reach this point; their neighbours in Rakefet have repeatedly refused them a home in the community, judging them to be "social misfits".[1]

Rakefet's admissions committee, asked to define more precisely what its assessment meant, claimed Fatina was "too individualistic" and that Ahmed "lacked interpersonal sophistication and has difficulty integrating naturally into society". Those judgments surprised friends, family and work colleagues. Ultimately, Israel's leading judges were unpersuaded too, ruling in September 2011 that the couple be allowed a home in Rakefet.[2] To everyone involved in the case, it was always clear – even if it was never admitted by Israeli officials – that Ahmed and Fatina's "social failings" were code for the fact that they are not Jews.[3]

The Zbeidats are Israeli citizens but they also belong to the country's large Palestinian minority. They are descendants of some of the
150,000 Palestinians who were not expelled or forced to flee during
the 1948 war that established a Jewish state on most of historic
Palestine. Today, Palestinian citizens number about 1.5 million, nearly
a fifth of Israel's total population. The Jewish majority usually refers to
them dismissively as "Israeli Arabs".

Since Israel's creation more than six decades ago, members of the
Palestinian minority have been forced to live in a self-declared Jewish
state that systematically discriminates against them – a fact that even
Israeli leaders are increasingly prepared to concede, though they have
failed to take any meaningful action to correct such injustice.[4] Poverty
among the Palestinian minority exists at a rate four times higher than
among Jewish citizens, propped up by a system of segregation in
education, in many areas of the economy and in housing and land
allocation. Contrary to the view of Rakefet's admissions committee,
the Zbeidats and Palestinian families like them are inspiring examples
of talent and determination triumphing within a system designed to
marginalise them.

It was built into the very DNA of Rakefet that Arabs should be
excluded from its leafy streets. It is one of seven hundred villages –
known formally as "community associations" – that were founded
according to a Zionist vision that desired the permanent dispossession of the Palestinian population in their native homeland. Today,
most of the habitable land in Israel is controlled by these small communities whose admissions committees are designed to weed out
"undesirables": chiefly the country's Palestinian citizens, but also Jews
who are seen as "weak" from a Zionist perspective, such as Middle
Eastern Jews, single mothers, gays and the disabled.

Rakefet is a modern, middle-class community of eight hundred
residents whose spacious, mostly characterless, suburban homes sit
on the lower slopes of the rocky hills of the central Galilee. Its name,
"cyclamen", is for the clusters of pretty flowers that adorn these
hills in winter. The air is clean, the views magnificent, especially for
the young professionals and middle-managers who have chosen to
move north to escape the stress and high prices of Tel Aviv and its
environs.

If the Zbeidats could speak freely, Rakefet is probably not exactly the stuff of their dreams, at least not quite in the manner it is for many of their new Jewish neighbours. In an early interview with the *Washington Post*, in a rare instance of the foreign media taking an interest in the couple's plight, Fatina explained: "If they won't develop our villages, then we will choose where we want to live. The problem lies not with us, but with Jewish society that does not accept the other."[5] Meanwhile in 2011, as the Supreme Court ruled in their favour, the pair diplomatically told the Israeli media: "Every move is difficult but we have no problem living in a Jewish community. We will be able to handle life in Rakefet. We wanted to live in a quiet, developed place."[6]

The couple's first test after the ruling may have come sooner than they expected: in April 2012, before they had even begun building their home, members of Rakefet placed an Israeli flag – with the symbol of the Star of David at its centre – on their land. The Zbeidats carefully folded up the flag and returned it to Rakefet's officials, who quickly denounced them for an "unacceptable act" and demonstrating "a moral and ethical lapse".

Given the Zionist, exclusivist ethos of the community, it is possible to conjecture that the couple might have preferred to live in a welcoming modern Palestinian community, sharing in its vibrant Arab culture. But such a possibility is denied them. Despite the Palestinian population growing more than eight-fold since the state's establishment, Israel has not allocated land to build a single new Arab town or village in that time (though it has belatedly recognised a handful of Bedouin communities it criminalised soon after Israel's establishment).

Nor is it a big move for the Zbeidats. It is less than two miles from the home they rented for many years close to Ahmed's family in Sakhnin, an Arab town of some twenty seven thousand inhabitants. The Zbeidats may be successful and aspiring but Sakhnin was never going to be a place where they could hope to escape the overcrowding and squalor that is an integral part of life for a Palestinian citizen. Most of the Palestinian minority are crowded into some 120 legal communities across Israel, and a few dozen more villages the state has refused to recognise.[7]

It is not surprising that the options available to the Zbeidats are limited. Through the use of complex legal tools, Israel has effectively penned its Palestinian minority into ghettos. First, it nationalised most of the territory in the years following 1948. Palestinian citizens, who lived under martial law for the first two decades of Israel's existence, could do little to prevent the state confiscating their outlying lands on a variety of flimsy legal pretexts.[8] Today 93 percent of Israel is owned by the state or an international Zionist organisation, the Jewish National Fund (JNF), and held in trust for the Jewish people worldwide rather than the country's citizens (which would include people like the Zbeidats). Strict territorial segregation ensures that only Jews have access to what are termed "national lands".[9] The minority, meanwhile, is restricted to the 2.5 percent of Israel's territory it owns – chiefly the land on which its communities sit.[10]

Second, Israel adopted the Planning and Building Law in 1965, which tightly delimited the expansion of Arab towns and villages. A thick blue line was marked on official maps around the communities' built-up areas, making expansion for most of them all but impossible over the past four decades. Planning committees are staffed by Jewish officials whose Zionist mission has turned the process of house-building by Palestinian citizens into a Kafkaesque nightmare.[11] The result has been tens of thousands of their homes declared illegal, with their owners subject to heavy annual fines to ward off demolition.[12]

The same planning committees, meanwhile, have ensured the rapid approval and expansion of small, land-hungry Jewish settlements across Israel. According to Adalah, the Legal Centre for Arab Minority Rights, 5 percent of Israel's population – the Jewish inhabitants of the hundreds of community associations – control 81 percent of the territory, acting as a bulwark against Palestinian citizens gaining access to "national lands".[13]

The significance of this form of discrimination has been explained by Mordechai Kremnitzer, a law professor at Hebrew University in Jerusalem: "The issue in question is not just the liberty of a resident to choose his neighbours. It is also the way the state allocates its economic assets. In such allocations, the state has no right to discriminate on a national-ethnic basis." Kremnitzer was also dismissive of claims often made by Israeli Jews that segregation is justified as a means to preserve Jewish identity: "This difference between majority and minority justifies settlements for Arabs or vegans alone, but not for Jews only. Since Jews are the majority, there is no concern about the preservation of their group identity, [whereas] the Arabs are a minority, and their collective identity is threatened."[14]

Despite its outward pretensions of respectability, Rakefet is one small link in the Zionist continuum of aggressive Jewish settlement in heavily Palestinian-populated areas that came to be officially termed "Judaisation".[15] Rakefet's origins can be traced to pioneer Zionist communities founded in the 1920s and 1930s, such as one thirty miles to the south called Tel Amal, close to the town of Beit Shean. Tel Amal was a wooden "tower-and-stockade", now accurately reconstructed in its original location close to the Nir David kibbutz. It is often visited by Israeli schoolchildren who ascend the high watch-tower to scan the horizon, mimicking their armed ancestors whose job was to terrify away the Bedouins who farmed the land until Tel Amal's construction. Such tower-and-stockades marched across Palestine in the pre-state years, dispossessing the native population. Moshe Sharrett, who later became one of Israel's first prime ministers, described the aim of the tower-and-stockades as: "to change the map of Eretz Israel ... to make it as difficult as possible to solve the problems of this land by means of division or cantonisation."[16]

But Rakefet, established in the early 1980s, can also trace its lineage to the more recent phenomenon of the West Bank settlements. The same blueprint has been adopted for the settlements and for Rakefet, with the same goal in mind. Their true purpose is hinted at by the fact that both types of settlement, in Israel and the West Bank, are perched on hilltops in heavily Palestinian-populated areas.

In the West Bank, the 120 settlements and their offspring – more than one hundred tiny unauthorised outposts, established over the past fifteen years – make headlines for their terror tactics against Palestinians. In particular, the outposts' occupants, mainly young Jewish religious fanatics calling themselves the "hilltop youth", regularly descend into the West Bank's valleys to burn Palestinian crops, attack village residents and torch their mosques. But the settlements' more mundane tasks are to break up Palestinian territorial contiguity, thereby foiling the chance of statehood and undermining the Palestinians' ability to organise and resist their dispossession.

A clue to Rakefet's true purpose is to be found in the name of its style of community association: the *mitzpim* (lookouts).[17] They were the brainchild of Ariel Sharon, an infamous army general who was appointed agriculture minister when the Right-wing Likud Party came to power for the first time in the late 1970s. Sharon understood that the traditional model of Judaisation of the Galilee – the cooperative agricultural communities such as the *kibbutzim* and *moshavim* – was dying. Few middle-class Israeli Jews of European origin – the Ashkenazim often referred to by officials as a "strong Zionist population" – were still prepared to labour in the fields or wanted to adopt a communitarian model of self-sacrifice and material privations.

Equally, Sharon saw a threat in the new-found assertiveness of the Galilee's Palestinian population, who dominated the northern region. Likud had formed a government in the wake of the Land Day strike of 30 March 1976, the first general strike in the Palestinian minority's history, called to protest against a wave of confiscations by the state of their farming lands. The focus of the one-day protest was Sakhnin and neighbouring Arab towns in the central Galilee. The Labour government of Yitzhak Rabin responded by declaring a curfew and sending in the army, backed by tanks. In what amounted to a military operation against Israel's own citizens, six unarmed protesters were shot dead and dozens more injured.[18]

As he took office, angered by the effrontery of Land Day, which had served only to heighten long-standing Zionist fears that the Galilee's Palestinian population might try to secede or make alliances with Lebanon or Syria, Sharon explained the need to recruit a new generation of Jews to the Judaisation programme. "The region is again the Galilee of the gentiles [non-Jews]," he said. "I've begun intensive activity ... to prevent control of state lands by foreigners [the country's Palestinian citizens]."[19]

The *mitzpim* offered the Ashkenazi middle classes a fast track to a rural life-style, with the state heavily subsidising their privileges in a Faustian pact that required in return – implicitly, at least – that they serve as spies on their Palestinian neighbours. The aim of Rakefet's teachers and bankers is little different from that of the hilltop youth: to help intimidate and contain their Arab neighbours, excluding them from the vast majority of land which Israel wants reserved solely for Jews.[20] Only the methods differ. Rakefet's residents don't pick up flaming torches or rocks when Palestinians upset them; they pick up the phone and call a relevant official to warn him or her that a resident of nearby Sakhnin is trying to build outside the developed area or is failing to tend an olive grove (under the Fallow Lands Law, uncultivated land can be expropriated by the state).[21]

Fatina and Ahmed Zbeidat, like the other inhabitants of Sakhnin, are the victims of some twenty-nine *mitzpim* – collectively known as the Misgav Regional Council – that surround and watch over the valley in which the town is located. Not only have these *mitzpim* been built on lands that once belonged to Arab communities like Sakhnin, but the state has even awarded to Misgav council municipal jurisdiction over much of what remains of Sakhnin's surrounding agricultural land.

Contained on all sides, young couples like the Zbeidats are unable to find new land on which to build. If they manage to rent or buy a home inside Sakhnin, it will invariably be in an overcrowded neighbourhood with unplanned and potholed roads, deprived of pavement, street lighting and public parks. However beautiful their home, it will still be within a local authority whose budgetary resources and allocations from the central government in Jerusalem are a fraction of those of Misgav's.[22]

But while the Zbeidats appear to have been successful in their struggle to live in Rakefet, it would be foolhardy to declare a victory for equality and justice for Palestinians in Israel, even on the limited issue of land. This is still just a tiny crack in the monolithic facade of Zionism that confronts the Palestinian minority. The six-year battle by the Zbeidats followed a lengthier and even more acrimonious struggle to exclude another Palestinian family, Adel and Iman Kaadan and their four daughters. The Kaadans had tried to buy a plot of land in the community association of Katzir, another front in Sharon's renewed Judaisation programme.

Katzir was established in Israel's Wadi Ara, a heavily Palestinian-populated region which hugs the north-western corner of the West Bank, and is located between two large Arab towns in Israel, Umm al-Fahm and Baqa al-Gharbiyya. It is one of more than a dozen so-called "star points", small communities built along the Green Line that formally separates Israel from the West Bank. Sharon hoped that the "star points" would erode the Green Line's significance, blurring for Jewish citizens the distinction between Israeli communities and the settlements, and ultimately act as a magnet drawing Israeli Jews deeper into the West Bank.

The Kaadans seemingly made legal history in 2000 when the Supreme Court ruled tentatively in their favour against Katzir, whose admissions committee had excluded them five years earlier based on their ethnicity. In demanding only that the committee "reconsider" its decision, Aharon Barak, president of the Supreme Court, described his ruling as "one of the most difficult of my life".[23] With a heavy heart, he suggested that the principle of equality should be considered as important as the Zionist goal of Judaisation. Some observers declared it the court's first "post-Zionist" decision.

In fact, the case dragged on for many more years as Katzir continued to reject the Kaadans, this time creating a new criterion of "social suitability" – later to be adopted by Rakefet when dealing with the Zbeidats. The court held back from imposing a judgment, though it expressed increasing frustration with Katzir. The Kaadans finally started work on their home in Katzir in 2007 – after twelve years of legal struggle – though not directly because of a court ruling. Instead, in 2006, a day before an important hearing on the case, government officials agreed they would give the family a plot of land in Katzir, apparently as a way to avoid a court decision that might create a legal precedent and open the floodgates to other Palestinian applicants.[24] After a series of delays, the Kaadans finally moved in to their home in 2011.

Ever since the Kaadan case, the state and the hundreds of community associations have been seeking ways to justify keeping out other Palestinian citizens like the Zbeidats. Leading the way has been the Jewish National Fund (JNF), a Zionist organisation that was awarded quasi-governmental powers following the establishment of Israel. The JNF owns 13 percent of Israeli territory, much of it refugee property bought by the Fund from the state for a relative pittance in the 1950s. The advantage to the Israeli state in transferring the refugees' lands to the JNF was that the Fund was not even formally obligated by the commitments towards equality made – although rarely honoured

– by Israel. The JNF's charter requires instead that it serve only the interests of worldwide Jewry, not Israel's citizens.[25]

The JNF had long been in a position to effectively dictate land policy in Israel, ensuring that most of the country was reserved for Jewish settlement only. It owned much of the rural land on which the community associations were built, and where it did not it still maintained control through its heavy representation on the admissions committees and the government's land management body, the Israel Lands Authority (ILA).

The JNF had good reason to be concerned by the Katzir case. The Supreme Court sided with the Kaadans chiefly because the discriminatory policy barring the family from Katzir was being enforced, as it was in other community associations, in the name of the state through the ILA. The JNF had accepted that all its lands would be managed by the ILA under an agreement reached in 1962. Until the Katzir case, the deal had suited both sides: the ILA got to manage all the territory in Israel, while the JNF was largely able to direct the ILA's policy through its dominance of the Authority's board of directors. The Katzir case made that convenient alliance look like a liability: the ILA might be forced under pressure from the courts to end the exclusion policies it enforced against Palestinian citizens on behalf of the JNF.

The legality of the relationship looked certain to be tested again as new cases emerged in the wake of the Kaadan ruling. In early 2005 the attorney general, Menachem Mazuz, declared that the JNF's prejudicial policies violated Israel's anti-discrimination laws: "The ILA is obligated to market JNF land to Arabs, too."[26] His change of position was apparently driven by the fear that a court ruling in favour of a Palestinian family might set a legal precedent against discrimination in land allocation. In response, the JNF threatened to withdraw from its arrangement with the ILA.

As panic mounted, Yehiel Leket, head of the JNF, declared: "We are still fighting for our future existence as a Jewish state. In order to strengthen the Jewish state it's justified to have a Jewish organisation strengthening our presence here."[27] Israeli legislators agreed: in 2007, they passed by an overwhelming majority the first reading of a bill to ensure that all JNF lands be allocated to Jews only,[28] though the bill was later dropped. At around the same time a poll revealed that 81 percent of Israeli Jews wanted JNF land to be reserved for Jews.[29]

In the meantime, the government found a less flagrantly racist solution to the problem than the 2007 JNF Lands Bill. It signed a deal with the JNF in 2009 to ensure that none of the Fund's lands would be turned over to non-Jews. The agreement meant that if a Palestinian citizen won an ILA-run tender for a plot of land at a JNF-owned site, the state would compensate the JNF with a new piece of land. As Adalah pointed out, such an exchange, while potentially ending some of the discrimination in principle, would actually increase it in practice. Not only would the JNF continue to own 13 percent of land in Israel, from which it excluded all Palestinian citizens, but it would also gradually own more land in the peripheral regions where most Palestinian citizens live.[30]

While the agreement averted any danger of JNF lands being "lost" to non-Jewish control, the struggle to exclude Palestinian citizens from state lands simply shifted to new battlegrounds. The sense of urgency to find water-tight grounds for such exclusion intensified as the Adalah Legal Center for the Arab Minority in Israel, which represented the Zbeidats, pressed during that period for a hearing of the family's still-unresolved case before the Supreme Court. Adalah wanted the Court to end its dithering and rule on the legality of the admissions committees.

In early 2009 several communities in Misgav, close to Rakefet, made a hasty counter-move, announcing that they were planning to change their bylaws to include a loyalty oath for new families hoping to move in. Manof's changes were typical: the village's new bylaws required applicants to share "the values of the Zionist movement, Jewish heritage, settlement of the Land of Israel ... and observance of Jewish holidays". They also demanded that the community's children be encouraged to join the Zionist youth movement and the Israeli army.[31] One of the few residents who opposed the change, Arik Kirschenbaum, told the liberal *Haaretz* newspaper: "It suddenly seems as if we adopted bylaws from the settlements."[32]

The oath was a thinly veiled attempt to replicate a scheme proposed by the far-Right party of Avigdor Lieberman, the foreign minister, to require a pledge of loyalty to Israel as a Jewish state from all non-Jews applying to become Israeli citizens. Ron Shani, elected

Misgav's mayor in 2008, had made opposition to the Zbeidats' bid
to live in Rakefet a major platform in his campaign. He defended the
bylaw change to the Israeli media. "The [regional] council's position
is that it is appropriate to strengthen the character of the community
– a community in which Zionist values and Jewish heritage stand at
the heart of its way of life. We don't see this as racism in any way."[33]
"Character" and "Zionist values" were transparently being used as
code for "Jewishness".

The loyalty measure, however much it revealed about the Zionist
attitudes that still prevailed among Israel's Jewish middle classes, was
a mere skirmish before the real battle. That was to be conducted elsewhere, chiefly in legislative moves by the government and private
Knesset members to privatise parts of Israel's state lands and to protect
the future role of the admissions committees.

In 2009 Benjamin Netanyahu, Israel's prime minister and an arch-
neoliberal, turned his privatising zeal to Israel's "national lands", one
area of life that was still very much a relic of the country's original
Zionist ethos of statist control on behalf of worldwide Jewry. During
the 1980s, as the Right held the reins of power, Netanyahu and his colleagues prised control of large parts of the Israeli economy from the
grasp of the Histadrut, a Labour party-affiliated trade union federation that for many years was also a series of monopolistic companies
in charge of the banking sector, the media, construction, agriculture
and much else.

The Right's remedy for Israel's Soviet-style, centrally commanded
economy was to break up the Histadrut's monopolies and replace
them with a series of cartels overseen by Jewish private business interests, both Israeli and foreign. The privatisation programme, as conceived by Likud party apparatchiks like Netanyahu, was not about
opening up Israel's economy to global market forces but shifting power
and capital away from the Labour party and toward a newly emerging
elite of business families in Israel that, it was correctly assumed, would
work to keep Likud in power (the increasing power of the cartels led
to large cost-of-living rises that fuelled an unprecedented wave of protests demanding social justice in summer 2011).

But Israel's "national lands" were a far more contentious choice
for privatisation than the economy, especially among traditional

Labour Zionist groups. With a strong Right-wing majority government behind him, Netanyahu finally took on the issue at the end of the 2000s. He announced a programme of what was termed "land reform" to allow Israeli Jews, almost all of whom were living in homes and on land on the basis of a long-term lease from the ILA, to buy their properties outright. The sell-off was expected to appeal most strongly to middle-class Jews living in the hundreds of rural community associations. One of the Right's motives in pushing the measure through was to win over to the Likud party Israeli home-owners in these rural communities who had traditionally identified with Labour Zionism.[34]

The area of land in question was not especially large: some 800,000 hectares, or about 4 percent of Israel's territory. But it had dramatic ramifications, as well as potential obstacles, related to the native Palestinian population. The first was that Israel's ownership of the much of this land was of dubious standing, at least according to international law. Many of these exclusivist Jewish communities, especially the *kibbutzim* and *moshavim* (collective communities founded originally on agriculture), had been built on "destroyed villages", the lands and homes of more than five hundred Palestinian communities emptied during the 1948 war. Most of the original inhabitants had been forced out of the new state of Israel and they and their descendants – numbering more than four million today – had been living ever since in exile, often in refugee camps in neighbouring Arab states. Yet more of the refugees were Palestinians internally displaced by the 1948 war as well as their descendants, estimated to number about 350,000 today. Despite having Israeli citizenship, these refugees, like those in exile, had always been refused the right to return to their lands.

In accordance with international law, the refugees' property was held in trust by an Israeli official known as the Custodian of Absentee Property. Netanyahu's plan was to revoke unilaterally the rights of the refugees and sell off their lands to private Israelis in a move designed to pre-empt a final peace agreement. One internal refugee from the destroyed village of Saffuriya, now a *moshav* called Tzipori, described the move as: "like a thief who wants to hide his loot. Instead of putting the stolen goods in one box, he moves it to seven hundred different boxes so it cannot be found."[35]

Despite the transparent violation of international law, little could be done to stop the sell-off. But there was a problem. What would prevent wealthy Arabs from abroad, including refugees, or Israel's own Palestinian citizens from outbidding Israeli Jews to buy the land? Would this not risk a reversal of Zionism's success in Judaising the land, as many Israeli Jewish groups feared?[36]

The first part of the problem was easily solved. Suhad Bishara, a lawyer with Adalah, explained of the land reform: "Only Israeli citizens and anyone who can come to Israel under the Law of Return – that is, any Jew – can buy the lands on offer, so no 'foreigner' will be eligible."[37] There was also a safeguard ensuring that Palestinian citizens continued to be barred from these rural communities: the admissions committees. These committees, which had been used to block the Zbeidats from Rakefet, would continue to oversee property transactions. Just as the Likud's privatisation of the economy had simply moved control from one group of Israeli Jews to another, Netanyahu's land reform would simply refashion the exclusion and discrimination imposed on Palestinian citizens.

The role of the admissions committees as a way to prevent the Palestinian minority from encroaching on "national lands" was already under threat from isolated cases such as the Zbeidats and the Kaadans. But the land privatisation made it even more apparent to Israel's leaders that the committees' role must be safeguarded at all costs. Suhad Bishara of Adalah clarified what was at stake: "There is nothing unique or special about the way of life in these communities [like Rakefet] to justify this kind of restriction on admission. Rather, the purpose of the selection system is to make sure 80 percent of the territory inside Israel is not accessible to Arabs, that the control of public resources stays exclusively in Jewish hands."[38]

In 2010 two separate initiatives were introduced in the Knesset to set in law the continuing viability of the admissions committees and pre-empt any decision against them by the Supreme Court. By late that year the two initiatives had been merged, and they attracted wide support in the Knesset. The bill – known formally as "Amendment to the Community Associations Law", and popularly as the Admissions Committee Law – gave small communities of up to four hundred families in the Galilee and Negev the right to reject new applicants if they were considered "unsuitable" or failed to "match the social-cultural fabric" of the community.[39] It also determined the composition of the admissions committees, specifying that they must include two representatives from the community; a member of the Zionist movement to which the community belongs; a representative from one of two Zionist agencies, the Jewish Agency or the World Zionist Organization; and a representative of the local Jewish regional council.[40] Israel Hasson, an MK with the centrist Kadima party who was among those who drafted the bill, said it "reflects the state's commitment to the achievement of the Zionist vision in the Land of Israel".[41]

The bill was passed at a late-night session in March 2011.[42] The Palestinian–Israeli MKs in the chamber were outraged. One, Taleb a-Sana, commented: "Imagine if Britain or France had made a law preventing Jews from living in certain communities." Another, Ahmed Tibi, provoked near-riots among his Jewish colleagues when he compared the law both to South African Apartheid and to Nazi laws against Jews: "You must read Jewish history well and learn which laws you suffered from."[43]

The Arab MKs were not alone in making such comparisons. Leading jurist Mordechai Kremnitzer argued that the law gave off the "foul odour of racism".[44] Zvi Barel, a columnist with the *Haaretz* newspaper, believed the new legislation was Israel's equivalent of the Group Areas Act, one of South Africa's Apartheid laws that determined "group regions" where each racial group could live.[45]

Similarly, Amnon Be'eri Sulitzeanu, of the Abraham Fund Initiatives, a coexistence group, pointed out that the new law would further contribute to the hardening of segregationist attitudes in most areas of Israeli life: "Visitors from abroad cannot believe their eyes: segregated education, segregated businesses, separate entertainment venues, different languages, separate political parties ... and of course, segregated housing."[46]

The law, both its supporters and opponents agreed, was a rearguard action to prevent the possibility that other Palestinian citizens might be inspired to follow the Kaadans' and Zbeidats' example. But neither side looked ready to let the matter rest. Human rights groups quickly submitted two separate petitions to the Supreme Court to void the legislation. In June 2011 the Court demanded that the state prepare an explanation as to why the law should not be disqualified for violating the principles of Israel's Basic Laws.[47] The case had yet to be decided at the time of writing.

But the admissions committees' supporters, which included most of the Israeli public and the Knesset members, were far from repentant. The Right-wing *Jerusalem Post* newspaper believed the law justifiably ensured that Israeli Jews had "the right to live in a community where they are not threatened by intermarriage or by becoming a cultural or religious minority".[48] In the same spirit, a group of Knesset members, including Avi Dichter, the former head of Israel's domestic intelligence agency, the Shin Bet, advanced a bill in late 2011 to strengthen the Jewish character of the state. Included in its provisions was a section formally sanctioning communal separation based on religious or national characteristics.

Contemplating the Admissions Committee Law, columnist Zvi Barel offered a vision of where Israel was heading:

> The remainder of communities [not covered by the new law], and especially the large cities, will have to continue, for the mean time, to make do with voluntary Apartheid. But the days will also come, as they did in South Africa, when an appropriate solution was found for its cities. It will be possible, for example, to grant homeowners' committees the authority to determine who can buy or rent an apartment in a building.[49]

It may not be surprising that the Supreme Court had a heavy heart as it ruled in favour of the Kaadans and the Zbeidats. The dispossession of Palestinians, and the subsequent exclusion from most state land of the few Palestinians who remained, lie at the heart of the Zionist project. The court rulings laid bare – in a manner that made Israeli Jews of the Left and Right equally uncomfortable – the logic of segregation that underpinned Israel's birth in 1948. For the first time, Zionism's core problem was forced out of the shadows: how could the circle of the Zionist mission to create a Jewish fortress be squared with the acceptance and integration of a large Palestinian minority?

The Supreme Court justices offered no solutions. All their

judgments served to do was set in motion a rearguard action – what, for most Israeli Jews, amounted to a clarification of what their Jewish state was all about. That process of clarification, as Barel suggests, is likely to deepen as the Jewish majority further entrenches and formalises the principle of segregation through additional and more blatantly racist legislation. The Admissions Committees Law is just one of several recent laws and legislative proposals being used to "strengthen" a Jewish Zionist identity against the non-Jewish "other". That is certain to be a painful process for the Palestinian minority, but it may also prove a revelatory one for those observers who still cling to the idea of Israel as a Jewish and democratic state.

The plight of the Zbeidats offers a clarifying insight into the contradictions inherent in a Zionist state; contradictions whose consequences Israel's Palestinian community have had to endure alone for decades. The international community has not only shown little interest in the situation of the Palestinian minority, it has also demonstrated a more troubling failure to understand that a Jewish state is incapable of offering a just or moral solution to the problem posed by families like the Zbeidats. Reforms, whether of the kind explicitly proposed by Netanyahu or alluded to by the Supreme Court, cannot mend the essential flaws in a state designed to provide privileges to some citizens based on their ethnicity or religious beliefs. Only a much more substantial and drastic reform – ending Israel's Jewish character – can hope to provide Palestinian citizens with the equality they demand.

NINE

The Contract

Phil Weiss

Al Walaje is a Palestinian village south of Jerusalem that Israeli settlers are slowly devouring. Bulldozers are moving across farmers' land
uprooting olive trees. Israeli soldiers stand by to make sure no one
stops them. Two years ago, I was at a demonstration on that sun-
baked hillside when I got into an argument about Zionism with an
older American Jewish woman with a steel cane. She came over to
hear what I was talking about with two high school students from my
hometown, Baltimore. So there were actually four Jews: me, her and
the two young men.

The settlement was illegal, she said, but that was not a reflection
on the Jewish state. There was no reason that it could not continue
to be a Jewish state, right over there, on the next hill. Many states in
the world discriminate on the basis of ethnicity, she said. Look at
Germany, Japan and Saudi Arabia. Yugoslavia had shattered into a
half-dozen ethnic pieces. Well, Israel and Palestine were no different.
Israel for the Jews, Palestine for the Palestinians. That is why it was so
urgent that the occupation be ended.

It was odd to hear that argument coming from a Left-wing American.
But she was older. She had surely seen Israel's creation as a necessary,
noble thing. And yet she was arguing for an ethnic state. She is hardly
alone, of course. The great bulk of America's Jewish community believes
that support for an ethnic state in Israel is a good thing – and only what
we deserve. Why shouldn't such a state have a right to exist? The system
of governance the world has arrived at in the twenty-first century is
an aggregation of countries, many of which reflect an ethnic desire to
form a community. The word nation has the word birth at its root – it
carries a sense of blood relation. France for the French, Germany for
the Germans. Slovakia for the Slovaks and Kazakhstan for the Kazakhs.

Why should Jews abandon this arrangement, and call for a multi-ethnic democracy where the United Nations said there should be a Jewish state? Why should we give up ours when so many other peoples – the Muslims of Pakistan and Hindus of India, for instance—have already shown that they are of no mind to forgive their neighbours their ethnicity? Those peoples want their majorities protected by the preservation of a solid social structure, a sovereign state. A flag, an army, a sense of cohesion.

I come to this conversation as an American Jew. American first, but Jewish, very Jewish: I grew up in an ethnically cohesive community with not a whole lot of mingling with the Christian world till I got to high school. And I think that American Jewish identity is a key to working the Israel/Palestine problem out.

In Gaza in 2009, I shared my struggle involving Jewish identity with my Arab-American roommate in our hotel room. It was six months after the Gaza onslaught, and we were together on a Left-wing delegation to the war-torn strip. Gaza was overwhelming – the rubble of the official buildings, the billboards with the many portraits of murdered policemen, the crippling injuries to people you saw on the street, the still-smoking white phosphorus. Often, the Jews on the trip would talk about their Jewish values. My roommate listened respectfully but he said that these matters were a "sideshow" to the main issue, American support for the brutality we saw at every hand.

And in light of the evidence of war crimes, it seemed to me he was right. So when our group came back and gave reports on the trip, I parked my Jewishness in the back lot. And still the question came up wherever we went. There were always agonised Jews in the crowd. The slaughter of Gaza – nearly four hundred children killed in a brutally efficient twenty-two days – had wakened American Jews. There was my new friend, Code Pink's Medea Benjamin, who had worked all her life on global political issues, but who grew up in a Zionist family and had long been held by that allegiance to say as little as possible about Israel. Horrified by Gaza, she had now thrown herself into the question and was doing more than anyone else to help the Gazans, defying the Israeli siege. Naomi Klein, the bestselling author, was also galvanised by Gaza. In an appearance on the West Bank after the onslaught, she had apologised to Palestinians for her "cowardice" in not being more forthright before.

These women were pioneers, but the entire community was in tumult over the question of Zionism. Even liberal Zionists were disturbed by what they saw. And it was foolish to deny that Jews were important in American society; we made up a significant portion of the liberal establishment, from newspaper columnists to university presidents to the hedge fund managers and real estate magnates who paid for all the non-profits. If you could get the Jews, you could get America. Or at least persuade the Democratic Party to alter its hard-line positions.

Grassroots organisers like to say that you must go to a community's self-interest, and I have come to understand that my chief concern about the Israel/Palestine issue is selfish: it goes to what Israel has required of the United States and the American Jewish community. In a word, it has required our blind support. Hannah Arendt saw all this sixty years ago, in the days when Israel was being formed by warfare. Right-wing Zionism was building a Sparta, she said, a warrior society that would be entirely dependent on the "protecting wings" of a great power. And because of this requirement, Israel would depend upon court Jews, well-placed supplicants to American power – the Israel lobby.

Sadly, American Jews had accepted this role, even to the point of standing up for Apartheid. We are the wealthiest and most-highly educated group in American society. We can brag of an unrivalled tradition of learning and achievement and political liberalism. Yet we have held the bag for Israeli crimes, forever. How did that happen?

I have never been a Zionist, but I realise that I was part of the problem. Left-wing Jews and hawkish Jews had reached a contract that was steeped in guilt and passivity on the Left-wing side. I'd made this contract myself; I'd kept my mouth shut about whatever they were up to in the Middle East.

The hawks were a distinct minority inside the Jewish community, the neoconservatives. They were always primarily concerned with the safety of Israel, and they became Right-wing militants during the 1970s in the wake of the two Israeli wars and the Vietnam War, because they feared that dovish Jews were fostering policies that would not serve

Israel in the crunch. The two founding fathers of neoconservatism left the Democratic Party over this very question. Irving Kristol wrote in 1973 that doves would "drive a knife into the heart of Israel":

> Senator McGovern is very sincere when he says that he will try to cut the military budget by 30 percent. And this is to drive a knife in the heart of Israel ... Jews don't like big military budgets. But it is now an interest of the Jews to have a large and powerful military establishment in the United States ... American Jews who care about the survival of the state of Israel have to say, no, we don't want to cut the military budget, it is important to keep that military budget big, so that we can defend Israel.

Kristol was writing just after Nixon had saved Israel with an emergency delivery of arms during the October war. A few years later Norman Podhoretz echoed Kristol:

> There was, to be sure, one thing that many of even the most passionately committed American Zionists were reluctant to do, and that was to face up to the fact that continued American support for Israel depended upon continued American involvement in international affairs – from which it followed that an American withdrawal into the kind of isolationist mood that prevailed most recently between the two world wars, and that now looked as though it might soon prevail again, represented a direct threat to the security of Israel.

This concern for American power deployed on behalf of Israel was one basis of the neoconservative movement. There is a direct line between these statements and the 2002 statement from a group put together by Irving Kristol's son William urging George W. Bush to invade Iraq and defeat Saddam:

> No one should doubt that the United States and Israel share a common enemy. We are both targets of what you have correctly called an 'Axis of Evil.' Israel is targeted in part because it is our friend, and in part because it is an island of liberal, democratic

principles – American principles – in a sea of tyranny, intoler-
ance, and hatred ... Israel's fight against terrorism is our fight ... For
reasons both moral and strategic, we need to stand with Israel in its
fight against terrorism.

It was a time when many Americans felt themselves to be in the
same boat as Israel. The trauma of 9/11 echoed the Israeli trauma
of the second intifada. Many American Jews were shocked by the
uprising, when Palestinian suicide bombers had blown themselves
up in Jerusalem and Tel Aviv. And of course, the tactic was deeply
unnerving to Israeli society. Spouses kissed goodbye to one another
in the morning with the sense that they might not see one another
ever again, and Israel responded with overwhelming military force,
sending its army into the West Bank in an effort to crush the resistance. And here was William Kristol and friends offering that militant
occupation as the model for America's dealings with Saddam Hussein.

Most liberal Jews had not supported the Iraq war, though the
liberal Democrats who represented them did – people like Chuck
Schumer, Dianne Feinstein and Hillary Clinton. And this brings me
back to the contract that we reached with neoconservatives. They
were family, and for the sake of Jewish unity it was important to go
along with their plans, or at least not speak out against them as they
related to Israel. I made just such a contract with a neoconservative
in college: Eric Breindel, a child of Holocaust survivors, who later
befriended Menachem Begin, served as a foreign policy advisor to
Daniel Patrick Moynihan and became editorial page editor of the
New York Post. One day I had the temerity to venture to Eric that
Israel had an "expansionist" policy of colonising occupied territory
in Gaza and the West Bank. Eric shook his head dismissively. He
said that to reach such a conclusion I would have to know about the
history of the Balfour Declaration and the formation of TransJordan
under the League of Nations mandate of 1922.

It was 1976, and we were standing in the newsroom of the Harvard
Crimson, not far from a poster of Chairman Mao. Eric's words were
so much gobbledygook, but I reflected that I had never encoun-
tered such a literacy test on any other issue. Were the question about
Vietnam or South Africa or El Salvador, I would not have had to

know the ins-and-outs of ancient treaties. But Eric imposed his literacy test, and the pity is that I withdrew, I deferred to Eric's expertise. For thirty years I never went to Israel because I knew I would disapprove of it, but I kept my disapproval to myself. I thought, "They know more about this issue than I do – who am I to speak out?" So I worked for Marty Peretz's New Republic, a feverishly Zionist publication, and never questioned that policy in the least. Again, I emphasise, this liberal deference was widely shared. Indeed, Michael Kinsley, the former editor of the New Republic, has written that he printed many articles supporting Israel that he questioned in his mind even as he edited them.

Why did Mike Kinsley, who never hesitated to offer his own thoughts on difficult matters, defer in this case? Well, his boss was a raving Zionist. And not just his boss. Many members of our community were ravers, and still there was a Jewish commandment of unity that we obeyed. We have got so far in history as a transnational minority facing persecution only by maintaining a strong sense of community when facing the outside world, the untrustworthy goyim. Now was not the time to break openly inside the family over Israel policy. Jewish lives were at stake.

And the hawks know more about this. They've been there. They are taking care of things.

Religious guilt played its part. Israel had become the way for Jews to be Jewish. Most American Jews were falling away from religious practice. Politically conservative Jews tended to be more observant and more concerned with community survival. Bill Kristol, Elliott Abrams and Jeffrey Goldberg, for instance, are all observant Jews, and all supported the Iraq war. Elliott Abrams wrote that liberal Jews had replaced the religious covenant between God and Abraham – and its 613 laws of conduct from eating kosher to marrying a Jew – with a sense of Jewish culture that we called Jewishness. Judaism would last, he said, but Jewishness would merely fade away with intermarriage and Americanisation. So I was betraying the Jewish people.

I didn't have much respect for Abrams, but I felt guilty about my lapses. I was married to a non-Jew. I wasn't supposed to do that. Oh but I met her at a Jewish friend's book party on the Upper West Side. We fell in love – how could I help myself? I would have married a

Jewish girl if the right one had only come along.

I am saying that a whole complex of attitudes about one's community came to bear when a Left-wing Jew even thought of criticising Israel. The guilt was deeply entwined with issues of survival. The neo-conservatives said they were doing what was good for the Jews. And maybe if there had been more militants in the Warsaw ghetto there would be twice the number of Jews today as there are. So the neocons were our id. And just as America's id prevailed in the presidential election that pitted George Bush against John Kerry in 2004 – that sense that at least Bush was doing something to protect us and we didn't know how Kerry would do at the job – there was a primordial feeling inside the Jewish community that the Israelis were doing what needed to be done in such a dangerous environment, and American liberals ought to put their liberalism aside in such circumstances. My mother, for instance, did so when she said, echoing Right-wingers, that Muslims taught their children to blow themselves up and our children would never do such a thing. There was no other area of political life where she parroted Right-wingers. But these were Jews. They were family.

This family contract ended for me during the 2003 Iraq war. I was sitting with my older brother in his living room in the run-up to the war when he said: "How do you feel about this war? I demonstrated against the Vietnam War, but my Jewish newspaper says this war could be good for Israel."

My liberal brother had never been to Israel, and I was shocked. I was demonstrating against the war plans, and the revelation that somehow this war had a footing in my Jewishness and might compel Jewish support was too much for me to handle. I might be the most guilty, intermarried, non-Hebrew reading, pork-eating, Sabbath-defiling Jew in the United States. Still I was a Jew, and I was proud of that, and I cared enough about my community to commence a battle for its soul. I didn't want Jewishness to go the way of militarism. And inevitably this battle for Jewishness led me to Israel, and then to Palestine, to the occupation. I went to Al Walaje and saw the conditions that we had imposed on the Palestinians, and was horrified by them.

I've stayed in touch with the two young Jews I met on the hillside in Al Walaje that day. They were working in a refugee camp and were as critical of the occupation as I am. Today there is growing panic within American Zionist ranks over the defection of young Jews like them, who are increasingly alienated from Israel. All the efforts to pack them off on free indoctrination trips to Israel with lots of other Jews may have slowed the tide but it hasn't reversed it. Many young Jews have come back to the U.S. talking about a society that is unrecognisable to them as liberal Americans. And many of them, like me, see no need for a Jewish national refuge. Anti-Semitism may surge again, but we see universal acceptance of human rights as our strongest protection. And so we want to build societies that respect human rights.

The split in the community that I have sought since 2003, when our community leadership did nothing to impede the rush to a disastrous war because it might be good for Israel, is finally happening. And the 2012 election campaign saw the beginnings of the politicisation of the Israel issue, something that the Israel lobby has worked to avoid at all costs. Mainstream political journalists are starting to address the role of Right-wing Jewish financial contributions on American policy. There is a prayer in the US that the American people will at last get to discuss this issue openly, and learn about Palestinian conditions, and end the "special relationship" between the superpower and the regional hegemony that has helped to cause so much unrest in the region.

This process will unfold too late for the two-state solution. Israel as a Jewish state is likely a casualty of this late awakening. For me this is no tragedy. I have never regarded anti-Semitism as an important condition of my experience in the West, and never seen the need for a place to run to – let alone a place on someone else's land. But it will be a tragedy to a great number of American Jews. Had they truly reckoned with the effect of the never-ending occupation on Palestinian aspirations, or reckoned with the unique opportunity of the Arab Peace Initiative of 2002, they would have pressed their favourite country to make concessions ten years ago so as to solidify the long-shaky partition of the land by establishing genuine borders. But they didn't. The contract held. They were obedient to a leadership that described the Palestinian desire for self-determination as a form of anti-Semitism. They listened to people like Alan Dershowitz, who described the former 1967 border as the "Auschwitz border". The colonisation process continued apace. The fervent colonisers became a crucial part of the Israeli government and of the Israel lobby organisations in the US. And the country is today unable to save itself. Even moderates warn of "national suicide".

Some day, an accounting will take place of American Jewish leadership and it will be understood that it required a breach of community loyalty to criticise the occupation. Sara Roy, the Harvard scholar who bore witness to the brutality of the occupation, had to stop speaking to family members in Israel once she did so. Henry Siegman, the former head of the World Jewish Congress who exposed the sham peace process, also says that he stopped speaking to members of his own family. Neither of these thinkers were opposed to the existence of a Jewish state. But their community did not want to hear from them. When it is asked "Who lost Israel?" I'd answer, liberal American Jews. We stood by.

In June 2009 I sat in the audience at Cairo University as Barack Obama told "the Arab world", as the media put it then, that the settlements must end and that the occupation is humiliating to Palestinians. In the years since, American Jewish organisations set out to undermine his push for a two-state solution, and they succeeded. Today the settlements continue at a brisk pace and Obama has stopped talking about the occupation. As one policy expert has said to me, the two-state solution is about as likely as my jumping off the ground and flying to the moon. Yet it remains an article of faith in Washington among people who do not seem to care that Palestinians have no rights.

The woman with the metal cane in Al Walaje is deeply disturbed by the possibility that the Jewish state will be lost. She wants to save it now. And I understand the power of her feelings. Especially when her case is framed against the great bloodletting of World War II and the Holocaust, when half of European Jewry was exterminated. Jews have a special reason to want a homeland, a place to go. Why must we give it up?

Or look around at Israel's Arab neighbours. None of them is doing a very good job of protecting the rights of all their citizens. The Arab Spring is transforming political culture, but this is a slow process.

When I was in Egypt in 2011 I attended Christian funerals where Copts pressed against me saying they were persecuted and asked what it would take to get America's attention. Shias and Sunnis have been killing one another in Iraq and Syria. Kurds have felt unsafe in several countries. Under these circumstances, who has the right to be utopian and prescriptive to Israel – or to deny the desirability of partition?

As Ali Abunimah has said to me, none of us is capable of dictating a solution here. His comment echoes a statement Theodor Herzl often made in his diaries: "Nothing happens as one fears, nor as one hopes." What you or I say will mean very little against the rough flow of history.

Still, these are questions that keep me up at night, and they deserve thoughtful answers. I'm an anti-Zionist. I don't believe in the need for a Jewish state. I know that this one exists and it isn't going anywhere any time soon. If I had my druthers, I'd wave a wand and there would be a federation in Israel and Palestine, a bi-national state. This stance flies in the face not only of reality but of most members of my own religious community. How will I persuade fellow Jews of the error of their ways?

Yes, I am singling Israel out for a special role to play. But Israel has long singled itself out. The creation of Israel was the great exception to the flow of bodies across the world after World War II, the period at the end of empire when colonialist structures were taken down and former colonials began migrating to the West. A largely immigrant western group was granted rights by the world in a place inhabited mostly by indigenous brown-skinned people, the Palestinians.

That exceptional land grant reflected an exceptional historical case. The Holocaust is a sacred chapter of Jewish history, and all American schoolchildren must study it. I remember when that history was being claimed, in the 1960s and 1970s, with books and movies and capital letters, The Holocaust. Before then, in my house, it was The Six Million (a number my mother wanted to answer, with six children).

But that recovery obligates us to recover the Palestinian story that followed closely on the Holocaust. Israel's creation involved actions that today are understood to be war crimes and crimes against humanity. These crimes reside in people's actual and historic memories, as the *Nakba*, or expulsion of hundreds of thousands of Palestinians from historic Palestine to create a Jewish majority. More than five hundred Palestinian villages were erased from the map. You can read many of their names at college campuses on Nakba Day, when this historical crime is remembered – in ceremonies that Israel supporters say represent a "delegitimisation" of Israel.

So my community and country have denied these crimes for generations. And still the injustice won't disappear, and the refugee problem won't go away. We must come to terms with the *Nakba*, and the only way is to offer the descendants of those who were cleansed a place in the future of that society.

Israelis like to point out that Americans did the same thing, two and three hundred years ago, to get a European majority in the settled portions of the United States. But today the extermination and transfer of Native Americans are recognised as a crime, the US has struggled to come to terms with those actions, and that awareness cannot justify doing such a thing again in the Middle East. There are now too many cameras and international laws to push ethnic cleansing under the rug.

Of course, the biggest way that Israel has singled itself out is its insistence that it is the only democracy in the Middle East. But what are the consequences of that brag? Jews like to argue that Israeli Palestinians have it better than their counterparts in the Arab world. But if that is the political value, why not uphold it all the way? Why not truly be a democracy that protects the rights and freedoms of all its citizens, and cause them to want to defend the place? Palestinians don't serve in the Israeli army. How many Americans know that Palestinian Israelis have not even got to the point that blacks in the US reached in 1948 with the integration of the armed forces. They are not required to serve, and almost none of them do, because Israel is afraid they will not be loyal. Oh my: what kind of democracy is it that fears that 20 percent of its population won't be loyal?

Well, because they're Arabs, and Israel is surrounded by Arab countries. The Arab world has so often been hostile to Israel. There has been one war after another. Yes, but what if Israel could truly become a democracy for all its citizens? Do you think that any Arab country would want to invade it? I don't.

So, again: be the thing you say you value. If you are going to be the only democracy in the Middle East, then be it in earnest. Show the people of the region and the world what democracy means. And I issue that challenge to American Jews too. We must be forward-thinking, endorse the idea of multi-ethnic democracy and guide Israelis toward the radical concept of equal rights.

In the United States we fought like the dickens to make democratic promises real. Jews were granted religious freedom by the founding fathers and though we faced social and political discrimination for more than a hundred years of eastern European emigrations, the last sixty years have seen an incredible success story. The Gentleman's Agreement (barring Jews from privileged jobs and neighbourhoods) has fallen to the wayside. Religion was the most important factor in New York law firms' hiring decisions, Alan Dershowitz has said. Not any more.

This is the path of history. So it is not really the case that the Jews of Israel would be giving up what no other people are giving up. All around us, we see western societies struggling with a definition of justice that grants equal rights to those whom the country's forebears would never have seen as the rightful inheritors of wealth and freedom and order. In the United States we have seen minorities attain the highest positions – including, notably, Jews, three of them on the Supreme Court right now. In Europe we see Muslim minorities fighting for the right to participate and for religious pluralism. And while there has been great push-back against that pluralism, especially since 9/11, democracies are headed toward greater tolerance. With the end of discrimination, rigid religious traditions begin to fall. Consider Dershowitz. He was Kosher once, he isn't any longer. The less objection that anyone voiced to a Jew covering his head, the fewer Jews chose to cover them.

The Arab world is setting out on the same path. Democracy is the actual living ideal of social organisation in Egypt, Tunisia and Libya. Who are Jews to forswear it? The only way forward is for Israel to begin to honour Palestinian human rights. It does not matter how many sovereign entities emerge in historical Palestine, what matters is that Israelis learn to treat non-Jews as equals.

Zionists say that to restore the rights of the Palestinians to their property would dismantle the Jewish state. This has yet to be seen.

How many refugees would even want to return? But this is policy-making by fear. And in the meantime Zionism and the "law of return" for Jews anywhere in the world has created a festering wound – of ethnocracy and ethnic cleansing and occupation. These abuses are known all over the Middle East and now the world, which is why the Israeli brand is spiralling. The status quo is unsustainable – even Hillary Clinton and Joe Biden say as much all the time. They know that Palestinians are oppressed. Who in their right mind would want to sustain these conditions? Well – the American Jewish leadership.

My focus has always been on my community because I believe American Jews hold the key. But to move them requires great lever-age. Changes in American political conditions will only come from the grass roots, from activists and social media, from Americans shut out by the Israel lobby and young Jews who are sick of being indoctri-nated to bless oppression.

All of us know that there are terrible risks in what lies ahead. We only need to look at South Africa or Zimbabwe or Egypt or Russia to understand that social transformations are extremely difficult. But some orders demand transformation. And not all revolutions are bloody. The more of my Jewish American community I can convince of the inevitability of democratic change and the horror of present conditions the more peaceful the transition will be. I urge my broth-ers and sisters to end the contract and take the risk.

TEN

Zionist Media Myths Unveiling

Antony Loewenstein

There are 101 different types of permits that govern the movement of Palestinians. Israel's Civil Administration, according to a document published in December 2011 by Israeli newspaper *Haaretz*, finds countless ways to restrict access for Palestinians, both in Israel proper and in the Occupied Palestinian Territories.[1] There is a permit for travelling to a wedding in the West Bank, a different permit for escorting a patient in an ambulance and another again for simply accompanying a patient.

Such restrictions may seem mundane to an outsider, yet more numbers that don't truly reflect the reality for Palestinians living under occupation. Such figures matter little to the vast bulk of western leaders, who still talk lovingly of democracy in action in the Middle East. Australian Prime Minister Julia Gillard told a Zionist event in Melbourne in November 2011 that her country and Israel were: "two countries separated by distance but united by values. Liberal democracies that seek freedom and peace."[2]

But mindless Zionist propaganda no longer convinces many young Jews. There is growing fear amongst the older American Jewish leadership that new generations do not venerate Israel as their parents and grandparents have done for decades. A writer in Israel's largest newspaper, *Yediot*, argued in January 2012 that many young Jews were "no longer enamoured with the State of Israel". He went on: "It has become an added headache in trying to explain and understand Israel's prolonged polices in a way that connects to their 'American-Liberal' perspectives."[3] His deluded prognosis could have been written decades ago, although it was less necessary then; better media PR and more money spent on "rapprochement with the disenfranchised American Jewish community".[4]

The article was typical of the tone-deaf attitude amongst the Zionist elites; occupation of Palestine could be justified and better supported if only we used Twitter more cleverly.

I started writing seriously about the Middle East in 2003 and have noted a profound shift in the ways in which the Internet has reframed the debate since then. It is no longer between liberal Zionists (who claim to want a two-state solution) and hard-line Zionists who believe Jews have to right to hang on to "Judea and Samaria" forever. Those voices still exist and dominate the mainstream but fault-lines have emerged that don't rely on the corporate media giving non-Jewish voices legitimacy. Recognition has emerged without the help of the *New York Times*, *Washington Post* or establishment media. Palestinians, Arabs, dissident Jews and interested observers and players now transmit ideas without hoping a mainstream journalist will call to follow up on a press release.

When the Israel Defense Forces (IDF) has a handful of constant tweeters pushing out Israeli government talking points daily about alleged Palestinian terrorism in the West Bank, it's clear the Internet has arrived, even for a nation that prides itself on effective propaganda. Daily press briefings with friendly western journalists, the staple of much Israel-friendly reportage, will no longer suffice to gain favoured coverage.

But the Zionist establishment knows the PR battle is being lost, clearly as a result of internet-speed communication, yet continues to demand Israel simply invest more resources in marketing. The *Australian Jewish News* editorialised in December 2011, stating that the Zionist state was "often less than pro-active in fighting the country's corner when it comes to hasbara ... Having made the desert bloom, the country [Israel] cannot afford to bury its head in that portion of sand that remains."[5]

Israeli Prime Minister Benjamin Netanyahu recognises the power of the web to shape public opinion. In early 2012 the editor of the *Jerusalem Post*, Steve Linde, told a conference in Tel Aviv that the Israeli leader had said the Zionist state faced two leading enemies, the *New York Times* and *Haaretz*. "They set the agenda for an anti-Israel campaign all over the world," Netanyahu stated. "Journalists read them every morning [online] and base their news stories on what they read."

Netanyahu denied the report but readers could not ignore the fact that the cosy days of Exodus-era, soft-lens coverage of plucky little Israel was long gone: reality had snuck in due to the Internet and globalised media.

This breakdown in Israel as a supposed liberal oasis is having profound effects. American Jews simply don't want to move there – a key tenet of Zionism is convincing the global Diaspora that they can only be real Jews in Israel – as they're seemingly happy to stay in a country that doesn't challenge their liberal beliefs; of roughly 5.5 million American Jews, just 3,800, or less than one-tenth of 1 percent, moved in 2011.[6] The director-general of the Jewish Agency for Israel was forced to admit in 2012 that convincing American Jews to move to the Zionist nation had failed, so engaging young people to "experience Israel" through birthright-type propaganda trips was the answer.

Once again, there was no sense by the Zionist establishment that the way young citizens now receive information – not just through dead tree press but by YouTube, Facebook and social media – is without the (once) manageable pro-Israel filter imposed by a persuasive lobby or supportive reporter. Independent minds, with the Holocaust a distant memory, aren't as easily guilt-tripped into backing policies that they would never endorse in their own countries. State-sponsored racial discrimination just isn't cool any more.

But instead of aiming to make Israel a more democratic society, Netanyahu, his Israeli allies and global friends have turned their sights on wielding a censorious weapon. *Electronic Intifada* revealed in January 2012 that Israeli website *Srugim* published an article headlined "[*Haaretz* columnist] Gideon Levy and his friends in the media reinforce anti-Semitism around the world".[7] Its main message, one repeated in Zionist circles in America, Europe and Australia, is that the Internet is breaking down the decades-old message of Israel fighting against nefarious Palestinians. Public opinion in most western nations is far less supportive of Israeli positions than years ago. When in doubt, posits this view, play the anti-Semitic card against critics.

The article explained:

We can blame the anti-Semitism of the Goyim, but we can't say that the fault is only with them ... It is enough to read Gideon Levy in English to understand why we are hated in the world. It is time to make order in the media, as well. The state must see to it that Israel will have reliable, professional, and alternative media to the ones who create weapons material for the war on consciousness, in service of the enemy.

Note the use of emphasis here. The issue isn't anything Israel does inside Israel itself or the Occupied Palestinian Territories. The writer wants complete immunity from criticism alongside continuing global diplomatic, political and military support for the behaviour. All care and no responsibility. But control of the Internet is impossible using the old, tatty tools of Zionist advocates: sympathy for Israel after the Holocaust; Israel lobby pressure on journalists and editors; and little airtime given to coherent Palestinians to make their case. Something is now broken and even the corporate media is catching up. *The Financial Times* headlined a feature in late 2011 "Israel's eroding democracy; A shadow is cast", and wrote that the claim that Israel was a "bastion of liberal values and outpost of the West ... [had] begun to sound hollow"[8] due to successive anti-democratic legislation before the Knesset. "Eventually," Hagai El-Ad, director of the Association for Civil Rights in Israel, told the paper, "if the vast majority of Israelis does not want democracy, they will get what they want." There has been no democracy in the Palestinian territories for more than four decades.

It's important to unpack the collapsing media consensus over Israel. There is still no regular Palestinian or Arab columnist for a major American outlet. There are still no leading American commentators calling for a one-state solution or the dissolution of the Zionist state. Such views must still currently reside on the Internet alone. *New York Times* writers Thomas Friedman and Roger Cohen have both criticised settlements in the West Bank and the power of the Zionist lobby in America, but their mission is to save Israel, not make it more democratic for all its citizens. A *Salon* feature in December 2011 catalogued the litany of mainstream figures in America who now challenge the control of the lobby over Congress but concluded that: "for all the discussion-widening in the chattering classes, official US foreign policy has changed little, if at all."[9]

It is the Internet, however, not the mainstream media, that has led the necessary shift in discussion. The supposed democratic deficit in Israel didn't suddenly appear in the last years; it's been a feature for Israeli Arabs and Palestinians under occupation for years. Why didn't we hear about it more if we relied on mainstream outlets? Media consumers could be forgiven for wondering why they're now discovering more about discrimination inside Israel against, say, non-Orthodox women. While it is true that an extreme minority of Haredi Jews are growing in political power and flexing their muscles against what they see as a secular Zionist state – ironically, many of them thrive by living off Israeli welfare – it would be a revelation for many in the West that the "democratic" tag oft-used by Zionist defenders principally refers to Jewish Israelis. Israeli Arabs have far more rights than Palestinians in the West Bank and Gaza but legally and politically they are isolated and disenfranchised, increasingly seen as a fifth column working against the interests of the nation-state.

But it is the issues faced by Jews that is causing the upsurge in mainstream concern in the West. "Once, Israel's democracy was our calling card around the world," said an Israeli ambassador in Jerusalem in late 2011. "Today, there's a feeling that this is no longer the case."[10] Although the sentiments were correct, the meeting highlighted worries about Jewish religious extremism directed against Jews. Settler violence towards Palestinians was typically ignored, usually featuring in the mainstream media only as an aberration rather than a daily occurrence. Only the Internet, with countless Palestinian bloggers and tweeters and a few Israeli counterparts on the ground, is documenting the occupation that traditional western journalists based in Jerusalem are not.

The web doesn't just allow anybody to see at first hand the situation in the West Bank or Gaza – though it remains a damning indictment of western media that there are no more than a few journalists from foreign outlets permanently based in either place – it forced long-term Zionists to acknowledge what their homeland has become. Whereas once such conversations would be held respectfully at Jewish community events or on the pages of the local Jewish newspaper, today only the most blind refuse to see the direction in which Israel is heading. It is because such truths are revealed online that these writers have had to admit their pain. It is no longer possible, except for the most hard-line, to ignore the depth of the occupation.

Take *The Atlantic's* Jeffrey Goldberg, former IDF prison guard and key propagandist for the 2003 American invasion of Iraq. Although he claims to be a supporter of the two-state solution, he has begun to write on his blog that "a non-democratic Israel will not survive in this world". In agreement with Jewish author of *The Crisis of Zionism* Peter Beinart, he expressed in December 2011 that: "I think we've only a few years away, at most, from a total South-Africanisation of this issue." He chastised Israeli Jews for believing American Jews would "sit idly by and watch Israel permanently disenfranchise a permanently-occupied minority population". But his "only" answer was the two-state solution. "I don't believe a one-state solution is any sort of solution at all; Israel/Palestine will devolve quickly into civil war."[11]

But here's where the reality on the ground in Palestine, largely brought to westerners through an internet that is unavoidably forcing staunch pro-Israel types to respond, brings unsettling revelations.

In 2010 Beinart wrote an influential essay in the *New York Review of Books* on Israel's growing Right-ward shift and American Jewish establishment support for it. In an interview with Goldberg at the *Atlantic*, Beinart admitted his vision for the conflict was shamefully narrow:

> I'm not asking it to allow Palestinians who were forced out (or fled) in 1948 to return to their homes. I'm not even asking it to allow full, equal citizenship to Arab Israelis, since that would require Israel no longer being a Jewish state. I'm actually pretty willing to compromise my liberalism for Israel's security and for its status as a Jewish state.[12]

Despite the massive gains in western awareness of the conflict in the last decade, massively assisted by instant communication brought by the internet, even this kind of rhetoric inflames a Zionist community that barely allows free speech on Israel. Beinart, a former supporter of the Iraq war and conservative, can't even bring himself to supporting democracy for all Palestinians. Welcome to polite Middle East debate in modern America.

Philip Weiss writes on Mondoweiss that because "American Jews are liberal ... they will part ways with Israel out of profound differences."[13] Too many of them are disillusioned with never-ending occupation and racist Knesset legislation. Weiss titled his post "Israel isn't good for the Jews anymore" – and he, alongside co-editor Adam Horowitz, has done more than most Americans to widen public debate online about the Israel/Palestine conflict – but I fear he's exaggerating the change.

Undoubtedly, more American Jews are speaking up for Palestinian rights; either refusing to play along with the conservative leadership or disengaging from the debate entirely. And it's true that Israel couldn't survive without massive American support, largely pushed by an effective Jewish community and lobby. But it remains unclear whether evangelical Christians and Orthodox Jews are as powerful and emotionally connected to replace the reduction of liberal Jews defending Israeli actions.

What supports the Weiss thesis, one that I optimistically support on my better days and which underpins much of this book, is that it's now much harder for Israel and its backers to claim credibly that Israel is a democratic state that upholds the rights of all its citizens. Barely a day goes by without an article in the western media highlighting a racist attack in the West Bank or an outlandish and anti-Arab statement by an Israeli politician. But few in the mainstream make the next logical leap: these aren't aberrations of a society that has lost its bearings but the almost inevitable result of a post-Holocaust world that has indulged Zionist violence, dispossession and occupation for over sixty years. This is what happens when a once oppressed people are allowed to run wild at our expense.

This push to recognise reality over rhetoric has not emerged from the mainstream media or even the mainstream Jewish community. It's an argument that began on the fringes of the Internet years ago and gradually grew during the post-9/11 decade. A small minority of Jews, and many Palestinians and human rights activists, refused to accept the narrative set by the Bush administration (and then the Obama White House) that Israeli exceptionalism, backed by America's exceptionalism, trumped Palestinian rights. It had been possible for decades to maintain the charade of Palestinian intransigence and rejectionism because western audiences barely heard or saw an Arab who wasn't threatening, gun-wielding or unintelligible in English.

In recent years, helped by curiosity about the so-called Arab Spring, the Internet has brought us the post-9/11 question: "Why do they hate us?" Palestinians have started to have a voice, albeit fleeting, and their image has transformed from suicide bombers to people with legitimate grievances. I've lost count of the number of people who've told me they're relieved to be able to read online reports by Palestinians about Palestine on a daily basis. The corporate media filter still exists but it's far easier to bypass.

What is perhaps more difficult to understand is how little effect the sheer volume of human rights breaches in Palestine, information about which is now easily available on the web, has had on our political leaders. Take the example of Israel's Supreme Court finding Israeli companies were legally able to profit from West Bank resources, dismissing the applicability of international law, in late 2011. It's no longer possible to claim they don't know what is going on in our name in Israel and the Occupied Territories.

I am reminded of an early 2012 line by *Haaretz* writer Akiva Eldar, who wondered if in a few years time: "Israel will remain with only a handful of spineless lobbyists who make their living lobbying, along with power-drunk American Jewish billionaires who are ready to fight for Joseph's Tomb to the last drop of our sons' and grandsons' blood."[14] Eldar argued that: "Israel 2012 is forcing more and more Jews overseas to choose between loyalty to the Jewish state and loyalty to their humanistic and universal values." The internet is making those Jews feel less alone and more connected to like-minded individuals around the world, but sadly joining forces with Palestinians in the Diaspora still remains a minority pursuit. This must change, and soon.

Far too often one still sees self-described liberal Jews online defending Israel as a noble attempt at democracy in an ocean of Arab hatred. This is exactly the tactic recommended by leading Zionist think-tank The Reut Institute, members of which have written that "engaging the hearts and minds of liberal progressive elites" is essential to shield Israel from human rights campaigners. But even these liberal Jews know that the old-style debating points no longer work with the general public, given that there is an increasingly narrow space within Israel itself to dissent and debate. The modern language of human rights and equality for all is anathema in Israel and Palestine, excepting a small number of activists, with the Right-ward shift led by Benjamin Netanyahu and Avigdor Lieberman.

When Israeli journalist Shaul Arieli wrote in December 2011 that "in the end, [extremist politician Meir] Kahane won", he was referring to the mainstreaming of Israeli hate:

> When I bumped into far-right politician Baruch Marzel in Hebron recently, he explained the shift in Israeli perception succinctly. "The truth won out," he said, against the backdrop of a Shuhada Street shockingly empty of its Palestinian residents. "The evidence for this is the ever-smaller number of people who attend the memorial for Rabin as opposed to the ever-growing number who attend the memorial for Kahane."[15]

How do liberal Jews try and defend this? They don't: increasingly, they simply turn away.

The reach of the Internet strikes fear into the hearts of Zionist defenders of the Israeli state, because they're no longer as able to pressure editors or journalists to push a certain friendly angle. It should concern these loyalists that the values of a globalised and connected population are increasingly at odds with an occupation-friendly Israel. In early 2011 I was shocked to read of an Israeli poll that found 36 percent of secular Israeli Jews supported settler terror against Palestinians. Although the result didn't receive western media coverage, it ricocheted around the Internet and reached countless eyeballs.[16] It was just another piece in the destruction of once shared values between Israel and its Diaspora supporters; although, in the words of Max Blumenthal, nothing has stopped the Israelification of American domestic security through the use of Israeli-style "counter-terror" techniques.

But something happened in 2011 that forced even the most optimistic two-state adherents to face hard truths. *Haaretz* writer Carlo Strenger said it was the year "the two-state solution died". A. B. Yehoshua, fearing bi-nationalism as a threat to "independent Jewish-Israeli identity", instructed the "peace camp" to imagine such an "emergency". The failure of peace talks led the writer to fear true democracy between Jews and Palestinians, a revealing admission that decades of Zionist privilege may be coming to an end. In November 2011 *Haaretz* publisher Amos Schocken stated that an "Israeli Apartheid regime" was well and truly present, thanks to the relentlessly powerful Gush Eminum settler movement.

None of these views were re-published in the American mainstream media (or in Australia, for that matter) but in many ways it no longer mattered. Interested parties were now sharing this information online on such a scale (Facebook, for example, has more than 800 million global users) that the Zionist narrative had become unsustainable in its old format.

Threats to this established order, real and imagined, are amplified regularly. It was grimly amusing to read in *Ynet* in 2011 that Jewish critics of Israel (including acclaimed historian Tony Judt) "with their words and actions are boosting pernicious Judeophobic propaganda".[17] The writer directed some of his bile at the easy accessibility of such material, an implicit criticism of the scope of the Internet.

However, internet evangelists should not confuse a gradual shift in public debate over Israel/Palestine with the inevitability of a one-state solution. Although I personally believe a democratic state for all its citizens will eventually emerge to solve this conflict, I have seen at first hand the ability of repressive states in places such as Iran and China to both use the tools of the web against activists and counter threats to their existence. Granted, Israel is not an autocratic nation that controls information like the Chinese Communist Party, but it is too easy and indeed wrong to presume that change will come simply because more people use Twitter or YouTube. The Arab revolutions didn't occur because Cairo dissidents used Facebook; they were due principally to years of on-the-ground organising amongst a range of communities. Democratic change must come from within; the web is merely a highly effective conduit through which these sentiments can be spread at lightning speed.

Whereas only ten years ago the outlets for information about the Middle East were myopic and English in the mainstream, today we are overwhelmed with Arabic and English choices. The languages too rarely interact online, however, with the result that there is little discussion between westerners and Arabs who don't speak English. The post-9/11 decade has seen the emergence of an American public conditioned to fear Muslims and Arabs. At the same time, an increasing percentage of society has come to distrust government and mainstream media and looks for alternative information online. This is a robust space, where false accusations of anti-Semitism are hurled frequently but have largely lost their poisonous power.

In late 2011, when a number of young American bloggers associated with the Center for American Progress accused Jewish neo-conservatives of pushing America to invade Iraq in 2003 because of their obsession with Israel, the Simon Wiesenthal Centre responded that the critics were resurrecting a blood libel. It was nothing of the sort and the accusation had little effect on public debate aside from on a handful of interested parties. Years ago, when America's major Jewish organisations piled into an argument, it was likely that the accused person would lose their job. Although this does sometimes still happen, it is now much rarer: this is principally because there are far more players online who both encourage and tolerate freer talk over the Middle East.

If the Internet has achieved anything in the Middle East, it is that once taboo subjects – the one-state solution or the implementation of the Right of Return for Palestinians – are now rightly on the public agenda without the need for western media or official acceptance. Peace with justice is never popular with elites who benefit from inequality. Israel/Palestine is no exception. Relying on an inert and corrupt political system to bring democracy, a paradigm structurally designed to dispossess the occupied, was always a fundamental delusion of the Oslo years. We now have an opportunity to right that wrong, and the web has flourished at a time when new ideas are more important than ever.

Full equality for all the citizens of Israel and Palestine will not be brought by keyboard activists alone but they now have a seat at a table that used to only include *New York Times* columnists, Jewish leaders, the Palestinian Authority and the White House.

We all know how that turned out.

ELEVEN

A Secular Democratic State in Historic Palestine: Self-Determination through Ethical Decolonisation

Omar Barghouti

"Because it is a distortion of being more fully human, sooner or later being less human leads the oppressed to struggle against those who made them so. In order for this struggle to have meaning, the oppressed must not in seeking to regain their humanity (which is a way to create it), become in turn oppressors of the oppressors, but rather restorers of the humanity of both." [1]

PAULO FREIRE

Introduction

The ongoing popular revolutions in the Arab world are ushering in a new phase, one which may break the rusty but still formidable imperial and neoliberal fetters that have consciously, systemically and structurally inhibited human development throughout the Arab region. As well as its anticipated emancipatory impact on people across this region, this process of radical transformation, or what I call a prelude to an Arab renaissance, promises to further the struggle for ethical decolonisation in historic Palestine. This will happen as Arab governments become increasingly representative of their respective peoples' aspirations and opinions, which at their core largely reject Israel's occupation and Apartheid and genuinely support the Palestinian right to self-determination. While still evolving, and facing significant internal and external challenges, the Arab Spring has already made prospects for decolonisation in historic Palestine significantly greater by shaking and considerably undermining the stagnant web of complicit relations that has prevailed between unelected Arab regimes and Israel, mostly dictated by the US and Europe.

Decolonisation should not be understood as a blunt and absolute reversal of colonisation, taking us back to pre-colonial conditions and undoing whatever rights had been acquired to date. Instead, it can be regarded as a negation of the aspects of colonialism that themselves deny the rights of the colonised indigenous population and, as a by-product, dehumanise the colonisers themselves.

This essay argues that a secular, democratic unitary state in historic Palestine (in its British Mandate borders) is the most just and morally coherent solution to this century-old colonial conflict, primarily because it offers the greatest hope for reconciling the ostensibly irreconcilable – the inalienable rights of the indigenous Palestinian people, particularly the right to self-determination, and the acquired rights of the colonial settlers to live in peace and security, individually and collectively, after ridding them of their colonial privileges.

Morality and legality aside, Israel has adopted a strategy of "territorial seizure and Apartheid", as the publisher of the Israeli daily *Haaretz* puts it.[2] That strategy obviates the practical possibility of implementing a two-state solution in line with a minimalist interpretation of relevant UN resolutions. Blinded by the arrogance of power and the ephemeral comfort of impunity afforded to it by the US-led West, Israel, against its own strategic Zionist interests, has failed to control its insatiable appetite for forcibly displacing more of the indigenous people of Palestine and for expanding its colonial control of their lands, thus undermining any real possibility for building a sovereign Palestinian state.

Furthermore, with its siege of Gaza and its latest war of aggression in 2008–9 that killed more than 1,400 Palestinians, the great majority of whom were civilians, Israel has embarked on a new phase in its relentless policy of making life for the indigenous Palestinians so intolerable as to compel them to leave; this phase encompasses acts of slow genocide[3] and the intensification of ethnic cleansing. In the process, Israel has lost all its decades-old masks of democracy and with them its appeal as a "safe haven" for Jews. Former speaker of the Knesset Avraham Burg says:

... the establishment of the State of Israel not only failed to solve the problems for the sake of which it was founded but, on the contrary, made them a great deal worse. Israel is the biggest shtetl in the history of the world. One big town around which walls of segregation and resentment rise higher every day, cutting it off from its surroundings. Few of us know any other existential reality apart from our unrelenting war with everyone, all the time and over all issues.[4]

The fact that the single democratic state is morally and legally superior, however, does not necessarily make establishing it an easy task. It can only result from, among other factors, a long, intricate process of what I call ethical decolonisation, or de-Zionisation, involving two simultaneous, dialectically related processes: reflection and action, or praxis. Ethical decolonisation anchored in international law and universal human rights is a profound process of transformation. Above everything else, it requires a sophisticated, principled and popular Palestinian resistance movement with a clear vision for justice and a democratic, inclusive society. It is also premised on two other pillars: a democratised and free Arab region, which now looks far less imaginary; and an international solidarity movement supporting Palestinian rights and struggling to end all forms of Zionist Apartheid and colonial rule, particularly through boycott, divestment and sanctions (BDS), as called for by the great majority of Palestinian civil society in the historic BDS call of 2005.[5] In parallel, a crucial process of de-dichotomising the identities involved in the colonial conflict should be launched to build the conceptual foundations for ethical coexistence in the decolonised future state.

Moral De-dichotomisation

I define moral de-dichotomisation as a process whereby conceptual as well as concrete dichotomies are undermined so as to overcome resiliently conflicted identities and engender a common identity based on principles of equality, justice and human rights. Such a process can be transformative only when it envisions the relations between the same two subjects, oppressor and oppressed, both in the process of undoing the injustice, and after the causes of injustice have been overcome and a common identity is allowed to evolve.

In this case, the oppressor-oppressed dichotomy itself is viewed not as an abstract concept, but as a transient state of being, and a state of mind. Such a dichotomy is often perceived as a "carved-in-stone" reality that cannot be readily transcended or glossed over. However, if this is true in analysing the history and/or the present of a conflict, it should not necessarily be extended, unchallenged, into the *future*. We cannot change the fact that X has oppressed Y, and has caused her injury, suffering and injustice, which have all become embedded into Y's subjective identity; therefore, we may not be able to challenge the current dichotomy of oppressor vs. oppressed in analysing this conflict. But this does not imply that we cannot envision a process leading to a future which precludes the roots and causes of oppression, and which concurrently is based on a more fluid, hence tolerant, concept of identity.

In other words, in a situation of oppression, changes in perceptions of identity cannot by themselves extinguish the oppression – which is objectively present, irrespective of perceptions – but are necessary in deciding and shaping the outcome of the struggle to end this oppression.

In the process of ending injustice and restoring basic Palestinian rights, and while oppressive relationships are being dismantled and colonial privileges done away with, a conscious and genuine process of challenging the dichotomy between the identity of the oppressed and that of the oppressor must *simultaneously* be nourished. Only then can the end of oppression give birth to a common, post-oppression identity that can truly make the equality between the indigenous Palestinians and the indigenised settlers as sustainable and peaceful as possible.

The Vision: The Ethical De-Zionisation

Among the most discussed paths to resolving the question of Palestine, the civic, democratic state solution lays out the clearest mechanism for ending the three-tiered regime of injustice that Palestinians have suffered since 1948 when Israel was created as a settler-colony on the ruins of Palestinian society. The three tiers are comprised of the occupation and colonisation of the Palestinian – and other Arab – territory occupied by Israel in 1967; the system of institutionalised and legalised racial discrimination,[6] or Apartheid, to which the indigenous Palestinian citizens of Israel are subjected to on account of being "non-Jews"; and the persistent denial of the intrinsic rights of the Palestine refugees, especially the Right to Return, which was affirmed by UN resolution 194. An overwhelming majority of Palestinian civil society has identified[7] these rights as the minimal requirements for the Palestinian people to exercise their inalienable right to self-determination.

A two-state solution cannot adequately, if at all, address the second injustice or the third, the core of the question of Palestine. But what if early Zionists insisted not on a Jewish state, but a bi-national state? Bi-nationalism, initially espoused by liberal Zionist intellectuals,[8] is premised on a Jewish *national* right in Palestine, on a par and to be reconciled with the national right of the indigenous, predominantly Arab population. Bi-nationalism today, despite its many variations, still upholds this ahistorical national right of the colonial-settlers.

A bi-national state solution, of course, cannot accommodate the Right of Return as stipulated in UN General Assembly resolution 194. Furthermore, by definition it infringes the inalienable rights of the indigenous Palestinians to part of their homeland, particularly the right to self-determination. Recognising the *national* rights of Jewish settlers in Palestine or any part of it cannot but imply acceptance of the colonists' right to self-determination. Besides contradicting the very letter, spirit and purpose of the universal principle of self-determination primarily as a means for "peoples under colonial or alien domination or foreign occupation" to realise their rights, such a recognition of national rights for a colonial-settler community could, at one extreme, lead to claims for secession or Jewish "national" sovereignty on part of the land of Palestine, thus undermining Palestinian self-determination.

A Jewish state in Palestine, no matter what shape it takes, cannot help but infringe the basic rights of the land's indigenous Palestinian population and perpetuate a system of racial discrimination that ought to be opposed categorically.

Accepting modern-day Jewish Israelis as equal citizens and full partners in building and developing a new shared society, free from all colonial subjugation and discrimination, as called for in the democratic state model, is the most magnanimous offer any oppressed indigenous population can present to its oppressors. Only by shedding their colonial privileges, dismantling their structures of oppression, and accepting the restoration of the rights of the indigenous people of the land – especially the right of Palestinian refugees to return and to reparations, and the right of all Palestinians to unmitigated equality – can settlers be indigenised and integrated into the emerging nation and therefore become entitled to participating in determining the future of the common state.

The indigenous population, on the other hand, must be ready, once justice has been reached and rights restored, to forgive and to accept the settlers as equal citizens, enjoying normal lives – neither masters nor slaves. The above-explained process of de-dichotomisation at the identity and conceptual level that must proceed in parallel to the realisation of rights is the most important guarantor of avoiding lingering hostility, or worse, a reversal of roles between oppressor and oppressed once justice and equal rights have prevailed. The relatively successful indigenisation of European settlers in some Caribbean states sets an important example that precedes the more recent, still ongoing, process of indigenising whites in democratic South Africa. In the latter case, some South African analysts have argued, the key obstacle delaying or obstructing this process is the prevalence of "economic Apartheid,"[9] or structural economic privileges disproportionately enjoyed by the white minority at the expense of social and economic empowerment programmes for the black majority.

As the One State Declaration,[10] issued by several Palestinian, Israeli and international intellectuals and activists in 2008, states:

> The historic land of Palestine belongs to all who live in it and to those who were expelled or exiled from it since 1948, regardless of religion, ethnicity, national origin or current citizenship status;

Any system of government must be founded on the principle of equality in civil, political, social and cultural rights for all citizens. Power must be exercised with rigorous impartiality on behalf of all people in the diversity of their identities; ...

Feasibility aside, there are several key issues to be scrutinised when raising the slogan of a "Democratic State in Historic Palestine".

The Right to Self-Determination and the Palestinian People

The United Nations has called the right to self-determination a prerequisite to the enjoyment of all other human rights. This right entered international law, formally at least, in the United Nations Charter, Article 1(2), which states: "The purposes of the United Nations are to develop friendly relations among nations based on respect for the principle of equal rights and self-determination of peoples." Note that equal rights of all people precedes the right to self-determination and all other rights as the most fundamental principle in the UN Charter.

By 1960, with the adoption of the "Declaration on the Granting of Independence to Colonial Peoples", GA resolution 1514, the principle of self-determination had been elevated to the position of an unconditional right for peoples under "alien, colonial or oppressive domination", and called for a "speedy and unconditional end to colonialism in all its manifestations". In the following decades, the scope and applicability of the right to self-determination expanded to include indigenous peoples suffering from consequences of past colonial rule, unrepresented peoples, and national minorities oppressed by national majorities within the boundaries of a state.

UNGA resolution 3236, of 22 November 1974, elevates the applicability of the right to self-determination to the people of Palestine to an "inalienable" right. The resolution:

1. Reaffirms the inalienable rights of the Palestinian people in Palestine, including:

a. The right to self-determination without external interference;

b. The right to national independence and sovereignty;

2. Reaffirms the inalienable right of the Palestinians to return to their homes and property from which they have been displaced and uprooted, and calls for their return;

3. Emphasises that full respect for and the realisation of these inalienable rights of the Palestinian people are indispensable for the solution of the question of Palestine.

A morally consistent, rights-based approach to resolving the question of Palestine, therefore, necessitates addressing the three inalienable rights of the indigenous people of Palestine, in harmony with universal human rights and international law.

After Zionism: Reconciling the Inalienable Palestinian Right to Self-Determination with Jewish-Israeli Individual and Collective Rights[11]

Other than the fundamental issue of the inalienable Palestinian right to self-determination, there are several key rights-related questions to be scrutinised. The first is equal and democratic citizenship. This precludes any privileged status for citizens on account of their ethnic, religious or other forms of identity, beyond the initial requirements of justice and reparations for the dispossessed Palestinians. This citizenship should encompass all Palestinians inside historic Palestine as well as in exile and refugee camps; it also encompasses all current Jewish Israelis.

The Right of Return and reparation for Palestinian refugees is arguably the most crucial dimension to consider, particularly given that about 69 percent of the Palestinian population today are refugees.[12] How can repatriation and reparation be implemented in such a state? What should be done with current Jewish–Israeli colonies (settlements) built on Palestinian lands and homes illegally expropriated beginning with and ever since the 1948 *Nakba*? The general rule, as stipulated in international law, is the right of every refugee to return to his or her home of origin and to receive full, retroactive reparations. This must be done while avoiding the infliction of any unnecessary or disproportionate suffering on the Jewish community in Palestine. There is a need, then, to make a distinction between two types of pillaged property: (a) private or collectively owned property; and (b) property that was designated as public or state owned prior to the *Nakba*.

In the first case, private and collectively-owned property should, in accordance with international law, be returned to its rightful owners. When doing so is reasonably expected to cause unjust harm to a large number of citizens, fair criteria need to be developed, inspired by similar ones adopted in Bosnia and elsewhere, to decide what degree of harm and number of those affected is considered unjust. Furthermore, compensation in the form of property of comparable location and worth should be offered to the original owners, or to their heirs if the owners have passed away. In the second case, that of state-owned property, current buildings and structures can remain intact provided they benefit all the democratic state's citizenry without discrimination.

Another question that must be considered is what the Jewish community in a democratic Palestine may look like. Has a "national Jewish–Israeli identity" evolved over the past six decades? If so, who is included in it? Regardless, are Jewish Israelis entitled to the right to self-determination in Palestine as a separate community?

Some researchers, particularly Zionists and those influenced by Zionist assertions, have claimed an inherent or acquired Jewish right to self-determination in Palestine that is equivalent, even morally symmetric, to the Palestinian right to self-determination. By doing so, they blur the essential differences between the inalienable rights of the indigenous population and the acquired rights of the colonial-settler population. Even if we ignore the formidable body of evidence refuting the Zionist historical claim to the land of Palestine, there is no moral parity or legal symmetry between the modern colonisers and the indigenous people who were subjugated to colonialism; something that has been true across the history of colonialism.

The UN-defined and applied right to self-determination was never intended as a tool to perpetuate colonial privileges and reinforce discriminatory regimes of settler-colonial communities. After more than three hundred years of European settler-colonial domination in South Africa, for instance, the settlers never made a credible claim to a right to self-determination as a separate people. Even after political Apartheid was ended and freedom and democracy reigned, whites and Afrikaners were never entitled to self-determination as a *separate* settler community. Only as an equal part of the people of democratic South Africa were they able to share in exercising the right to self-determination.

Somewhat separately, a UNESCO conference of experts on the implementation of the right to self-determination, held in Barcelona in 1998,[13] reaffirmed that the right to self-determination applies to all peoples under contemporary international law. They emphasised its particular applicability to:

> ... peoples under subjugation suffering colonial, racist and occupying regimes, whole populations of states, in terms of the right to determine their political status and their economic, social and cultural development, as well as groups within the population of states, indigenous or otherwise, that are considered "peoples" and suffer under contemporary forms of colonialism, such as settler-colonialism, which do not fit into the traditional and arbitrary concept of "salt water [oversees] colonialism".[14]

In other words, the right to self-determination is an instrument of promoting a just peace and ending oppression, not entrenching it.

Participants in the Barcelona conference further concluded that:

> Self-determination is achieved by fully participatory democratic processes among the people who are seeking the realisation of self-determination, including referenda where appropriate. ... It is imperative to prevent all actions by any relevant actors, which include governments, international and other organisations, individuals and corporations, which may result in the denial of the exercise of the right to self-determination, such as demographic

aggression or manipulation, cultural assimilation and the destruction of the natural environment of importance to the survival of
peoples.[15]

Settler-colonialism aside, do Jewish Israelis constitute a nation or a
people in the sense of entitlement to the right to self-determination?
The widely accepted "Kirby definition", adopted at a UNESCO
International Meeting of Experts on the Implementation of the Right
to Self-Determination as a Contribution to Conflict Prevention in
1989, may suggest an affirmative answer. It identifies a people as "a
group of individual human beings who enjoy some or all of the following common features: history, ethnic identity, culture, language,
territorial connection, etc".

However, according to UNESCO experts, "the group as a whole
must have the will to be identified as a people or the consciousness of
being a people." This subjective element is considered a necessary condition but is lacking in the case of Jewish Israelis, who predominantly
recognise only a "Jewish nation," not an Israeli or even a Jewish–Israeli
nation. This unlikely state of affairs has arisen through deliberate
Israeli government policy.

Today, the Israeli Ministry of Interior recognises more than 130
nationalities, but not an Israeli nationality. Furthermore, as early as
1970 the Israeli Supreme Court ruled that there was no such thing
as Israeli nationality.[16] Avraham Burg writes: "We have done very
little in Israel to develop an internal national-identity model that
is not dependent on the definitions of the external persecutor."[17]
Jewish "nationality", as embodied in the Israeli Law of Return, is an
extra-territorial construct that includes the entire population of Jews
around the world, something that does not accord with international
public law norms pertaining to nationality.[18]

Whatever issues may exist around Israeli nationality,[19] the
question of whether rights can be derived from the consequences of
a wrongful deed ought to be considered. Israel's creation through the
premeditated and systematic destruction of Palestinian society and
the forcible transfer of a majority of the Palestinian people was a war
crime which infringed upon the indigenous Palestinians' right to
self-determination. Moreover, Zionist leaders considered the ethnic

cleansing a necessary condition for establishing a Jewish-majority state. That crime cannot give rise to a right of self-determination for the community of Jewish Israelis, who currently form a majority in the state. This is according to the general international law principle "*ex injuria non oritur jus*": no right or law can be derived from injustice or from the commission of a wrong. This principle prohibits deriving benefits from illegal acts.

Even if the large body of international law cited above were to be ignored, would Jewish Israelis as a group be entitled to the right to a form of completely separate self-determination in Palestine? Among other moral and legal factors, since the right to self-determination entails, at one extreme, the right to separation in an independent state, it cannot apply to a settler-colonial community; this would inherently violate and conflict with the right of the indigenous population to self-determination.

But the realisation of self-determination can assume one of many possibilities in a spectrum. International instruments, in particular the Declaration on Principles of International Law concerning Friendly Relations and Co-operation among States, affirms that the modes of implementation of the right to self-determination extend beyond the right of secession. The Declaration states:[20]

> the establishment of a sovereign and independent State, the free association or integration with an independent State or emergence into any other political status freely determined by a people constitute modes of implementing the right to self-determination by that people ... .

Although there is no universally acceptable distinction between "internal" and "external" self-determination, it may be instructive to investigate the differences between them in the context of the colonial conflict in Palestine. Internal self-determination largely entails participatory democracy: the right of the entire population of a state to decide the form of government and to elect rulers, as well as the right of a population group within the state to participate in decision-making at the state level. Internal self-determination can also mean the right to exercise cultural, linguistic, religious or (territorial) political autonomy within the boundaries of the existing state.

External self-determination (described by some as "full" self-determination), on the other hand, means "the right to decide on the political status of a people and its place in the international community in relation to other states, including the right to separate from the existing state of which the group concerned is a part, and to set up a new independent state", according to Michael van Walt van Praag.

In all cases, since the choice is left to the people entitled to exercise self-determination, one cannot accede to a group's right to self-determination and at the same time restrict that right to exclude the possibility of separation into an independent state. Even if we set aside the extremity of secession, any exercise of self-determination by Jewish Israelis in any part of historic Palestine that excludes the indigenous Palestinians, whether citizens living in that part or refugees uprooted from it, cannot be legal, as it would infringe the inalienable right of that part of the Palestinian people to self-determination; nor can it be moral, as it would deny those Palestinians their basic rights, including the right to equality, the most fundamental of all rights in the UN Charter and human rights conventions.

The Zionist "Law of Return" and the rights of Jewish refugees from Arab and other states also deserve careful consideration. The Law of Return is explicitly racist because it allows one type of person to gain citizenship on the basis of ethnicity while preventing Palestinian refugees from returning – also on the basis of ethnicity. The Law is in contravention of international law and must be abrogated in a democratic state along with all other similarly discriminatory laws. As for Jewish refugees from Arab states, they are entitled, according to international law, to the same rights as refugees everywhere: the right to repatriation and reparation.

Cultural particularity and diverse identities should be nourished, not just tolerated, by society and protected by law. Palestine was for centuries a fertile meeting ground for diverse civilisations and cultures, fostering communication, dialogue and acculturation among them. This heritage, almost forgotten under the cultural hegemony of Zionist colonial rule, must be revived, nourished and celebrated, regardless of any power asymmetry in the new state. We also must keep in mind that half of the Jewish–Israeli population, the Mizrahi/Arab Jews, have their cultural roots in Arab and other Middle Eastern cultures.

The Vehicle: Resistance and Effective Solidarity

Regardless of the above vital components of the vision, perhaps the most nagging question that one-state advocates face is whether our vision is feasible, whether it can be realised and, if so, how. Many commentators and analysts, even among supporters of the one-state solution, seem to be obsessed with one question in this regard: how do you convince Israelis to accept this vision?

There is a basic problem with the assumed premise in this question – that a colonial society can or should be *persuaded* to give up its racist domination and colonial privileges. Throughout the history of colonialism, the colonised were only able to end their oppression through sustained resistance, whether armed, civil, or both – never through begging, appeasing or otherwise persuading colonisers through "dialogue". Only after a common ground based on equality, universal human rights and international law is reached can there be genuine dialogue and reconciliation. The South African experience is an important source of inspiration in that regard, despite its aforementioned flaws in the field of establishing socio-economic justice.

Besides developing and effectively promoting a morally consistent and compelling vision, organising for a secular, democratic state alternative primarily entails developing a corresponding strategy of resistance aimed at ending all forms of Zionist oppression, while creating fertile grounds for future reconciliation and peaceful coexistence based on unmitigated equality, justice and universal human rights. The key constituency to persuade is the Palestinian *shatat*, the refugee and exilic communities, which constitute a majority of Palestinians. This crucial constituency has an inherent interest in endorsing the single democratic state vision as the only one that can realistically address the Right of Return (as well as that of the internally displaced and refugee communities inside historic Palestine). Opposition to a unitary state can also be expected from

Palestinians in the 1967-occupied Palestinian territory, where some might say that "we prefer a state of our own to living with *them*". While a valid opinion, it is based on what I would call a snapshot view of reality.

A snapshot essentially fragments reality, taking certain aspects of it out of context and, as a result, omitting the ever-present interconnections and mutual influences, as well as the never-ending flux that this reality undergoes due to the complex interplay of many human factors. In a still photograph of a ship sailing in the Mediterranean on a nice sunny day, for instance, an image of the ship is captured in some given parameters of time and space . Outside the limited frame or fragment which was captured in the image, anything before or after the specific time of the photograph, or anything around the ship, is not shown and cannot be inferred. So if the ship was wrecked by a sudden and severe storm a moment after the shot, or if it had dumped toxic waste minutes before, these crucial aspects of the journey would elude the snapshot. Similarly, in the context of colonial conflicts, an obsession with snapshots or facts on the ground as if they were irrevocable is detrimental to the understanding of the conflict, not to mention to the pursuit of a just resolution of it.

While many Palestinians living in the Occupied Territories or in exile cannot entertain the idea of ever co-existing with Israelis due to the current harsh reality of Zionist racism, oppression and dispossession, most would agree that in the period that predated the Zionist conquest, when Jews were part of society, co-existence was ordinary. Unlike in most of Europe, the history of Arab and Islamic civilisations does not include massacres or pogroms targeting the indigenous Jewish populations. Indeed, Jewish culture reached a highpoint under Islamic rule in Andalusia. Co-existence after establishing justice, far from being artificial, would connect with deep roots in our own history.

Moral reconciliation between conflicting communities is impossible if the essence of the oppressive relationship between them is sustained. The objectively contradictory identities of the oppressor and oppressed cannot find a moral middle ground. So long as oppression continues to characterise the communities' relationship only coercion, submission and injustice are possible outcomes. Reconciliation and coexistence, then, can result only from ethical decolonisation.

It is fair to assume, however, that the colonisers will use what they have at their disposal to perpetuate their colonial privileges and thwart transformative change towards justice. Some analysts go as far as predicting that Israel would use its nuclear weapons, its "Samson Option", rather than accept the dismantling of its Zionist Apartheid structures. Even without such dramatic predictions, one can surmise that the colonial community in Palestine will not only circle the wagons, as it were, against any common threat to the oppressive order; it will also shed any pretence of democracy or supposed respect for human rights and commit unprecedented egregious crimes against the indigenous Palestinians to maintain the system of oppression.

As the price of resistance rises, so will scepticism, including among some Palestinians, about the very worth of the struggle for emancipation and justice. This practical consideration coupled with ethical principles should therefore guide effective resistance to Zionist Apartheid and inform its adherence at all times to the highest moral standards. Resistance and solidarity forms that adopt a rights-based approach, as in the boycott, divestment and sanctions (BDS) movement, provide a good example. Other than being the right thing to do *per se*, an ethical struggle will encourage Jewish Israelis to join in "co-resistance", which is the most assured path to ethical co-existence.[21]

By emphasising equal humanity as its most fundamental principle, the secular democratic state promises to end the fundamental injustices that have plagued Palestine and, simultaneously, to transcend the national and ethnic dichotomies that now make it nearly impossible to envision ethical coexistence in a decolonised Palestine, based on equality, justice and freedom – a truly *promising* land.

TWELVE

How Feasible is the One-State Solution?

Ghada Karmi

Introduction

Not long ago, the idea of a one-state solution for the conflict in Israel/Palestine was the preserve of a few intellectuals and activists on both sides. Over the last ten years, however, this vision has become an increasingly valid one for discussion and debate. Traditionally, the one-state idea has had its greatest appeal for Palestinians in the Diaspora, but even then amongst a small minority. Various Palestinian scholars and activists have written about the advantages of the one-state solution, as isolated works of interest mainly to similar enthusiasts. But today the situation has changed. A widening and positive debate in print and on the internet about the one-state solution has become commonplace.[1]

Israeli and Jewish scholars have also been converted to the same cause.[2] In the last few years especially, a Jewish/Israeli surge in the debate on the one-state solution has become apparent.[3] Meron Benvenisti's major 5,000-word essay in *Haaretz*'s 22 January 2010 supplement is a striking indication of this surge. In addition, mainstream western publications now regularly carry articles on the one-state solution, unheard of just ten years ago. Examples include the *Los Angeles Times* (Saree Makdisi, "Forget the Two-state Solution," 11 May 2008), *Newsweek* (Sari Nusseibeh "The One-state Solution", 29 August 2008), the *Irish Times* ("Nudge Towards Alternatives in the Middle East", 13 March 2010), *Foreign Policy* (Dmitry Reider, "Who's Afraid of the One-state Solution?", 31 March 2010), and the *Washington Post* (George Bisharat, "Israel and Palestine: A True One-state Solution", 3 September 2010).

Since 2000 several US and European one-state groups have come and gone, but they have constantly been replaced by new ones,[4] and an increasing number of conferences have been held on the one-state solution. In consequence, this solution is no longer seen as a novel or outlandish idea, and the fact that it is now part of the mainstream political discourse is reflected in the alarm expressed by many Israelis who fear it. Ehud Barak's blunt warning to his fellow Israelis – that they either make peace with the Palestinians or face the reality that an Israel which includes the Palestinian territories will be either an Apartheid state or a non-Jewish state – (*Guardian*, 3 February 2010), is a case in point. A commentator in the popular Israeli daily, *Yediot Ahronot* (Gadi Toub, 31 January 2010), notes the increasing western discourse about Israel's transformation into an Apartheid state, for which the best solution should be bi-nationalism. Hence, he concludes, partition of the land into two states is the only way to avoid this undesirable outcome. Another writer uses the failed (in his view) Bosnian bi-national model to warn against a similar arrangement happening in Israel; and yet another describes the two-state solution as "the salvation of Israel", noting that its colonisation of the West Bank is leading to a one-state outcome.[5] A *Haaretz* editorial (5 May 2011) went so far as to welcome the unity agreement between Fatah and Hamas, since it would make possible a Palestinian state and thus enable Israel to have good, neighbourly relations with it, by implication avoiding the possibility of ending up as one state.

At the beginning, one-state solution adherents tended to take that position on grounds of principle, international law and elemental justice. After all, they argued, a major sector of the Palestinian people was living in exile, and would need to be part of any proper solution to the conflict. In 2010 the Palestinian Central Statistical Bureau in Ramallah estimated the number of Palestinians in exile in Arab countries to be five million, with a further 600,000 living in other places.[6] Of the total number of exiles, 4.7 million were UN registered refugees in 2008.[7] All these have a right in international law to return to their homeland – for most, today's Israel. It is self-evident that no just solution to the conflict can exclude the Right of Return of the refugees. As UNRWA's commissioner general pointed out in an interview in 2010, no peace was possible without a just solution for the refugees in line with UN resolutions (*al-Quds al-Arabi,* 2 February, 2010). As if aware of this fact and keen to protect Israel from such an outcome, the US was said to have put forward a plan to solve the refugee problem without offering the Right of Return.[8] This plan proposed a variety of solutions: the patriation of the refugees in their host countries; or moving some of them to a future Palestinian state and others to neighbouring countries, possibly Iraq, with a compensation fund to be set up for them using mainly money from the Gulf States.

There is nothing new here. Variations of these ideas had been circulating in western circles since the late 1990s. But their inherent flouting of international law and the rights of the refugees was a basic aspect of the case for one state amongst its adherents. However, in more recent times, it has been the apparent impossibility of a two-state outcome that has swelled the ranks of the one-staters. A glance at the map of the West Bank's Israeli settlements dotted all over the landscape, with Israeli "security areas", bypass roads and "closed military zones", should convince even the most ardent supporter of the two-state solution of its impossibility.

Nevertheless, the assumption of two states has continued to animate the peace process and to inform the international debate. A poll conducted by Israel's National Institute of Security Studies in 2009 found that 64 percent of Jewish Israelis supported a two-state solution (*Haaretz,* 17 June 2009). Palestinian Prime Minister Salam Fayyad made an address at Israel's tenth major Herzilya conference, affirming the Palestinian aim of creating a Palestinian state beside Israel and outlining a strategy for achieving it.[9]

Most recently, these ideas have culminated in the Palestinian application for statehood submitted to the UN in September 2011. Although it was clear at the time that the application would not get through the UN Security Council – a necessary condition for its adoption by the General Assembly – the Palestinians nevertheless went ahead. No vote had been taken on this issue at the UN at the time of writing, and the project was in abeyance. Nevertheless, this initiative demonstrates the determination in some Palestinian quarters to pursue the two-state solution, irrespective of the facts on the ground – facts which an Israeli geographer, writing in *Haaretz* (6 May 2011), saw as insuperable obstacles to the establishment of a Palestinian state that could include Gaza and the West Bank in one entity. The only result of such an attempt, he felt, would be the creation of two separate Gaza and West Bank states, divided from each other but connected to Egypt on the one hand and Jordan on the other.

Obstacles to the One-State Solution

The previous section discussed the increasing popularity of the one-state idea in recent years, and how it has garnered more supporters than at any time before. Indeed, both common sense and the logic of the situation point to this solution as the best and fairest option. Who could morally argue that a people who had been robbed of its country and made stateless exiles and refugees does not have an absolute right to have those injustices redressed? Or that the perpetrators should have to make reparations for what they had done? Or, on a more practical level, that the victims, if not properly compensated for their wrongs, would continue to seek justice and so perpetuate the conflict?

The fact that something is right and sensible, however, says nothing about its actual feasibility on the ground. And in this case there are formidable obstacles to its realisation.

Not least is the international consensus on the two-state solution. This concept as the only possible way to a resolution of the conflict has acquired an extraordinary hold on the public discourse. Many ordinary people, who wish the Palestinians well, find it easier to sympathise with their struggle for a state than support the dismantling of Israel and its replacement by something new. The Palestinian statehood request to the UN has only served to seal this perception in the public mind. At the same time, there is nowhere near an equivalent body of opinion supporting the one-state alternative which could have challenged this. With a few small exceptions, no major institution or mass movement has adopted any variant of the one-state solution. Indeed, endorsements at any official level have stemmed only from marginal groups or states outside the "western club": in 2004 the US Green Party adopted the one-state solution at its national convention; former Iranian President Hashemi Rafsanjani once called for a united government of Israel and the Palestinian territories; and Libya's former and discredited head of state, Colonel Qaddafi, proposed in 2003 that a unitary Israel/Palestine (which he named "Isratine") be created in place of the current arrangement.

The reality that must be faced is that opponents of the one-state solution far outnumber its supporters, and much of that is based on what they see as the enormous obstacles to its implementation. This has led to the view that the one-state solution is very good in principle but it can never happen, and the dearth of ideas for its implementation has only strengthened this perception. Beyond saying that the endpoint – a situation of equality between the citizens of a unitary state irrespective of religion or race – is "a good thing", no one has come up with a blueprint for the new state, or produced a roadmap of how to get there.

The first problem is that there is no consensus amongst Palestinians, or Israelis, or anyone else that the one-state solution is the best option.[10] Indeed, a 2009 Jerusalem Media and Communication Centre opinion poll found that only 20 percent of West Bank and Gaza Palestinians and just 9 percent of Jewish Israelis favoured a bi-national solution. A 2003 Peace Index poll of Israelis found that 73 percent feared the emergence of a bi-national state, with only 6 percent in favour of one; in 2007, 70 percent still backed a two-state solution.[11] Furthermore, the one-state solution is at odds with the current formal political position of both Israel and the PLO (such as it is), not to speak of the Palestinian Authority. Hamas is likewise on record as having accepted the two-state solution, at least for now. The western support that exists for this solution has led many to believe that it offers the best hope for progress in the Palestinian situation. Hence, according to this view, abandoning the struggle for an independent state with strong international backing for the untried, unplanned one-state option would be pure folly.

It is inescapably the case that both sides identify themselves as national communities with a right to self-determination. The Palestinians under occupation would not willingly abandon their struggle for independence from Israeli rule in order to struggle anew for equality in a joint state where Israel would be likely to have the upper hand. Given the greater development of Israelis, Palestinians would fear becoming a permanent underclass. As for the Israelis, although they do not want Palestinians in their midst, they fear even more the loss of the unfettered exploitation of Palestinian land and resources they have become accustomed to, and would fight to keep these advantages. More generally, the level of distrust, grievance and ill will between the parties is such that the very idea of sharing the land would be anathema to both.

But perhaps more serious than any of this is the way that Israelis and Jews would view the threat a unitary state poses to Zionism, which has become an integral part of the Jewish world view. The state of Israel, which would have to be dismantled in its present form if a unitary state were to be created, has become essential to the identity not just of Jewish Israelis, but of many Jews throughout the world. Its importance as a point of reference for such Jews and as a bulwark against Jewish insecurity, real or imagined, can hardly be overestimated. Keeping a Jewish state in existence is thus a priority, as Alexander Jacobson argues in *Haaretz* (29 January 2010). If a unitary state came into being, bi-national or not, it would rapidly become Arab and Islamic through the implementation of the Palestinian Right of Return, and no Jewish state would exist. Why, he asks, is the right of the Jewish people to national independence any less legitimate than that of other peoples?

Building the Unitary State

The list of obstacles to the one-state solution is daunting, but has not deterred some of its adherents from thinking about its implementation. For example, Israeli academic and activist Jeff Halper advocates a South African-style anti-Apartheid struggle against Zionism.[12] Others endorse the same strategy in the struggle to end the occupation, without explicitly calling for a unitary state.[13] While such a movement could be a way forward, there is nothing comparable at the popular level calling for a one-state solution. The Boycott, Divestment and Sanctions movement against Israel may be one such pathway towards the goal, but it is as yet still too diffuse and ineffective. In any case, as the veteran peace activist, Uri Avnery, points out, the two situations are so different that such an approach is doomed.[14] The South African regime had few international supporters, whereas Israel commands the unstinting support of Jewish communities worldwide and the near unconditional support of the world's only superpower, the United States. It is the Arabs, he says, not the Jews, who are seen as "the world's bogeymen".

An Israeli writer and self-described Zionist, Yoram Avnak has taken a different approach. He has set out his detailed vision of how the single state, however arrived at, would be constituted (*Haaretz*, 7 February 2010). His imagined structure of the "secular state of Israel/Palestine" attempts to put some flesh on a hitherto skeletal concept, "the new Israel/Palestine". To be established by the international community, the proposed state would, in Avnak's view, entail total separation of "church and state", with a ban on religious parties. Education would be strictly secular, and any religious teaching would be funded by parents. In order to maintain the desired demographic balance between Jews and Palestinians (45 percent each), the Israeli law of return would be cancelled, and the Palestinian Right of Return would be restricted to that level. Hebrew, Arabic and English would be the official languages. The state parliament would be made up of 45 percent representation for each side, with 10 percent for others. The Old City of Jerusalem would become a separate body like the Vatican, administered by non-citizen Jews, Muslims, and Christians appointed by the UN. Although Avnak believes his plan represents the last chance to build a healthy society, he provides no strategy to get there.

The broad consensus is that a public education about the one-state concept and the need to understand it in the context of the Palestinian Right of Return and Israel's Zionist ideology is necessary. It is evident that the one-state option needs discussion and promotion in the way that the two-state solution has been promoted. Twenty years ago, the two-state solution was by no means as generally accepted as it is now; that campaign of education and dissemination needs to be replicated for the one-state solution. Those who advocate this course believe that it is a necessary prelude to the implementation of this solution.

The Outlines of a Strategy

Given the range of obstacles in the way of the one-state solution, one could be forgiven for giving up at this point. It is indeed a difficult problem, not least because Israel has attained a position of considerable stability in relation to the Palestinians, whom it controls in their enclaves and can afford to forget. Their leadership is pliant and intimidated, and causes Israel no sleepless nights. This comfortable status quo could continue for a long time. In order to change it, a quite different strategy will be required. Key to this new strategy is the idea of a voluntary annexation of the Occupied Territories to Israel, thus transforming the struggle against occupation into one for equal civil rights within an expanded Israeli state. This is based on recognition that Israel and the Occupied Palestinian Territories form one unit, and in effect make up what is one state. However, the difference between such a state and the one-state solution as advocated is that the former deals unfairly with its Palestinian members and subjects them to an Apartheid regime. The Palestinian demand should therefore be for equal status with Israeli citizens, since they are in effect disenfranchised citizens of the same state.

A call to this effect came from the imprisoned Fatah leader, Marwan Barghouti, in 2004,[15] and is in line with similar calls for the dissolution of the Palestinian Authority (PA) and a direct struggle for equal rights with Israelis.[16] More recently, denials by Palestinian officials that such a possibility has been on the Palestinian agenda have served only to enhance the likelihood that such ideas are being indeed discussed.[17] Palestinian calls for the annexation of the Occupied Territories should not, however, be confused with those of Right-wing Israelis (such as Knesset member Tzipi Hotovely, Knesset speaker Reuben Rivlin, and former Israeli defence minister Moshe Arens), who have been calling for the incorporation of "Judea and Samaria" (the official Israeli administrative term for the West Bank) into a Greater Israel. Though such proposals envisage citizenship for the Palestinian inhabitants, the goal is not to create an egalitarian unity state. Rather, they stem from an assertion of Jewish ownership of the whole of the West Bank, no part of which should be "given away".[18]

If the Palestinians adopted the strategy of a struggle for civic rights, and removed their layer of government, the PA, which currently acts as a buffer between them and Israel, they would be seen for what they are, an occupied people, and the question of the Israeli occupation would return to the political stage. They would have all the rights under the Geneva Conventions which apply to an occupied people, and the game that has gone on since the Oslo Agreement, with a pretend state-in-waiting and a pretend government, would come to an end. Faced with such a situation, it is difficult to see what Israel could do. At one stroke, the Palestinians would call Israel's bluff over the peace process and its unrelenting colonisation, which has benefited so well from the protracted and futile peace talks to date. Their struggle for equal rights would find an echo in the western world, and, as potential citizens of Israel, the Palestinians would explode the demographic argument that has been used to maintain Israel as a Jewish-majority state. This could then be the first building-block of the one-state solution.

It will not be an easy strategy. Its first enemies and possibly its fiercest will be those Palestinian officials who have become accustomed to a different way of running Palestinian affairs, with the two-state solution as an endpoint. And Israel, aware of the potential of this move to change its character and ideology, will try to find ways of defeating it. In addition, there are the practical problems of how international aid, which might be suspended, will reach the Palestinians who are currently so dependent on it. Yet what is the alternative? The two-state solution is defunct and the status quo is not sustainable. As a strategy, if intelligently organised and accompanied by a wide public relations campaign, the citizenship idea will turn the tables on the other side and overthrow the failed assumptions of the past that have so hindered the possibility of a lasting solution.

Conclusion

The one-state solution has seen increasing levels of support in recent years, but there are many obstacles to its implementation. Not least among these has been the dearth of ideas or work on creating a blueprint for the new state and devising a road map for its realisation. The most promising way to attain the single state will be through dissolving the Palestinian Authority and campaigning for equal rights in an expanded Israeli state. That entails recognition of the current reality, that Israel is in fact one state, but one containing an oppressed Palestinian minority. The struggle must be to change that into a situation of equality. In this way, the ground will be laid for the egalitarian one-state solution supported by a growing number of people throughout the world.

THIRTEEN

Zionism After Israel

Jeremiah Haber

The declaration of the State of Israel in 1948 dealt a death blow to what had once been the chief goal of mainstream Zionism: a Jewish autonomous homeland in Palestine. This statement will puzzle readers for three reasons. First, they may assume that the goal of mainstream Zionism was always the establishment of a Jewish ethnic state of the sort established in 1948. Next, they may think that those who argued against statist Zionism consisted only of a handful of inconsequential central European Zionists, who were later proven wrong by history. Finally, they may conclude that the 1948 state, even if not fully predicted by the Zionist ideologues and policy-makers, nonetheless fulfilled the goal of providing for Jewish autonomy in Palestine.

All these assumptions are due to the history of Zionism being written by the victors, the statist Zionists, who all offer roughly the following historical narrative: Herzl founded modern political Zionism with his publication of *The Jewish State*, his efforts to obtain charters for land, and his convening of the first Zionist congress in 1897. Political Zionism proceeded apace through a combination of diplomacy and colonialisation; in the meantime, another strand of Zionism, cultural non-statist Zionism, emphasised the importance of the revival of Hebrew culture. In the end, Herzl's vision of political Zionism, greatly modified by Ben Gurion, vanquished the cultural Zionist opposition, which was led by men like Hans Kohn, Martin Buber and Judah Magnes. Kohn ceased to be a Zionist in 1929; Magnes died shortly after the establishment of the State; Buber accepted the Jewish state and adopted the stance of the moral critic from within.

Yet as Israeli historian Dimitry Shumsky has pointed out recently, this historiography tends "to observe pre-1948 Zionist history through the retrospective lens of the establishment of the State of Israel".[1] Shumsky argues that throughout the 1920s and 1930s, Zionist ideology was not statist but autonomist, and the various mainstream Zionist proposals for Jewish autonomy allowed for Palestinian Arab autonomy as well. The political regime established in Palestine in 1948 was one model for a Jewish homeland, but different models had been advanced earlier by many of the central figures of Zionism, from Herzl to Ben Gurion. Once again, these different models have been dismissed in Zionist historiography as utopian, or born of political weakness or expedience, but they have rarely been viewed as principled. Few non-historians are aware that statehood became an explicit goal of the Zionist movement only in 1942, six years before the establishment of Israel.

While the statist Zionism that found its expression in the 1948 state is, in my view, anachronistic and inherently discriminatory, cultural Zionism is not. Indeed, I wish to argue that the latter should have a place in a future Israeli Jewish / Palestinian Arab political arrangement, one that will look quite different from the present one. The Zionist ethnic state, founded hastily in 1948 and which sixty-three years later still lacks a constitution, much less a bill of rights, has not served the inhabitants of Israel/Palestine and their transnational constituencies well. In the case of the Arabs this is obviously true; in the case of the Jews, it is less obvious, but true none the less (I leave this latter claim to be argued another day). And yet the failure of the State of Israel to deliver on many of the promises of Zionism, in both its political and cultural forms, does not imply a refutation of all forms of Zionism. If we pause here to set the record straight, it is not merely for the sake of historical accuracy, but in order to see what can be salvaged from alternative visions of a Jewish state, once the defects of the ethnic-exclusivist state vision have been revealed.

Just how mainstream was the rejection of ethnic-exclusivist statism? Consider this statement by Berl Katznelson, one of the chief architects of Labour Zionist ideology:

I have no part in concepts of those [....] who regard the realisation of Zionism in the form of a new state of Poland, with the difference being that the Arabs will be in the position of the Jews, and the Jews in the position of the Poles [... The foundations of the National Home should be]: municipal democracy, national autonomy, and the participation of the country's population in influencing the administration of its affairs – participation that will steadily increase – on the basis of parity between the two national divisions.[2]

Far from constituting the bi-national state Katznelson wished for, *on principled grounds*, in 1931, the state of Israel founded in 1948 was precisely the sort of state he had rejected earlier. Moreover, the Israeli Law of Return of 1950 and the Citizenship Law of 1951 not only denaturalised the majority of the natives of Palestine, they created a state that excluded native citizens from the nation represented by the state – and included members who had never lived in the state, as well as those who had become part of the nation through religious conversion. It was as if the Zionist founders of the State wished to replicate Poland in Palestine; without the political recognition, albeit limited, accorded to ethnic minorities in Poland, including Jews, in the interwar period.

Yosef Gorny has written an entire book about the federative and confederative plans proposed by mainstream Zionists in the 1920s and 1930s, plans that looked quite different from the particular political framework adopted by the state of Israel.[3] None other than Vladimir Jabotinsky offered variations on such plans; even when he called for a Jewish state, he insisted on preserving the political rights of the Palestinian Arabs as an ethnic minority. As late as 1940 he wrote:

In every Cabinet where the prime minister is a Jew, the vice-premiership shall be offered as an Arab, and vice-versa. [...] The Jewish and the Arab ethnic communities shall be recognised as an autonomous public bodies of equal status before the law [...] Each ethno-community shall elect its National Diet with the right to issue ordinances and levy taxes within the limit of its autonomy and to appoint a national executive responsible before the Diet.[4]

Jabotinsky did not believe that the Palestinian Arabs had the same national rights to Palestine as did the Jewish people. He, like most mainstream Zionists, insisted on the goal of a Jewish majority and unrestricted immigration. But Jabotinsky was true to his Russian multinationalism throughout his life and on principled ground championed 'the national rights of minorities, whether the Jewish national minority in Russia or the Arab national minority in Palestine.

What happened, then, to the mainstream Zionist vision of bi-nationalism? This is a matter best left to historians, but it seems that several factors transformed Zionism's desire in the late 1930s and the early 1940s for a homeland for the Jewish people in Palestine into the desire for a Jewish ethnic state replacing Palestine. Historical circumstances such the British White Paper restricting Jewish immigration, the fate of European Jewry during World War II, and the absence of any strong Palestinian leadership following the 1936 revolt seemed to make the time ripe for the statists to push. And the Zionist leader who more than any other left his imprint on the formation of the state of Israel, David Ben Gurion, became an enthusiastic convert to statism. The transfer of ethnic populations following World War II appeared to facilitate the moral justification of the involuntary transfer of the native Palestinians and the appropriation of their possessions, to be divided among the Jewish settlers and later immigrants.

Yet what emerged was not an imperfectly liberal "ethnic-nationalist" democracy, but rather an ethnocracy[5] with certain liberal adornments, such as the promise of "full and equal citizenship" for Arab Israelis in the Declaration of Independence. I do not want to minimise statements of this sort: the American Declaration of Independence proclaimed that all men are created equal with certain "unalienable rights"; and yet it was debated for decades whether this was relevant to the question of black men, and later whether "all men" included women as well. Still, such formulations could be used, and in the enfranchisement of blacks were used, to justify the transformation of American society at the appropriate time. But whatever was written in the Israeli Declaration of Independence, it is fair to say that Ben Gurion and the Israeli Knesset, dominated by his Mapai party, proceeded to create institutions that ensured permanent infringement of the rights of the non-Jewish citizens, in many cases severely so. These inequities are not merely *de facto*, as claimed by many supporters, or even *de jure*, as recognised by the more acute of them, but *foundational* to the state of Israel in ways that the inequities described above were not foundational to the United States.

Consider briefly only some of the inequities. The Palestinian Arabs who remained in the newly established state were controlled by a military government until 1966. Their education was handed over to the Zionists, who carefully controlled what they learned and who taught them. The lands of the refugees (including some who were internal refugees) were transferred to state agencies as "absentee property"; and, of course, the refugees were barred from returning to their homes. When Jewish kibbutzim or settlements needed land for growth, the government often sought out ways to transfer Arab land to them. In this way, between 65–75 percent of the land of Arab citizens was allocated for Jewish development. Few if any Jewish lands were allocated for Arab development.[6]

Most important, the political system foundationally discriminated against the Arab citizens of Israel. True, they were courted by Zionist parties for their votes, and their village chieftains could benefit from a certain amount of patronage. But in the parliamentary system of the new state, where political parties are able to provide services for their sectors only if they are members of the government coalition, the Arab sector inevitably lost out. This has become a permanent exclusionary feature of the Israeli political system, one that thwarts the efforts of even the best intentioned Israeli Jews to close the gap between the Arab and Jewish sectors.[7] The gap between the Arab and Jewish sections is sometimes attributed to the hostile relations between Arabs and Jews, but that is putting the cart before the horse – what led to the hostile relations between the two groups was the Zionist demand to establish hegemony in Palestine. They did so through creating an ethnic-exclusivist state that inevitably curtailed the rights of the bulk of the Arab minority.

The hasty establishment of the state of Israel against the will of the majority of Palestine's inhabitants, and the subsequent legislation imposed on them by the nascent state, was both a betrayal of previous Zionist promises to those inhabitants and to the world, and a gross violation of the Balfour Declaration's stipulation that the proposed

Jewish homeland would not prejudice "the civil and religious rights of existing non-Jewish communities in Palestine". But it was also a betrayal of what had been morally defensible about Zionism – not only to strongly bi-national cultural Zionists like Martin Buber and Judah Magnes, but also to mainstream political Zionists like Ben Gurion and Katznelson before their transformation, and even Jabotinsky. This is not to minimise the differences between the two groups, or to suggest that the non-statist Zionism of Buber and Magnes would ultimately have been amenable to Arab nationalists, who were against any power-sharing scheme with the Zionist settlers. Rather it is to point out the often ignored fact that much of Israel's current problems should not be attributed to Zionist ideology *per se*, but to a certain kind of ethnic-exclusivist Zionism ideology that emerged in the 1940s and was crystallised in the 1948 regime, a Zionism that has been drummed into the heads of Israelis and their supporters for over sixty years as *mainstream Zionism*. For those who find much to admire about Zionism, and I am one of them, the question is not "Where is Israel headed after Zionism?" (the post-Zionism question), but: "Where should Zionism be headed? And what role, if any, should Jewish nationalism play in a future Israel/Palestine that emerges from the current imbroglio?"

The Fossilisation of the Israeli National Ethos

Once the goal of statist Zionism was achieved, one would have thought that over time it would cease to be a factor in the psyche of the Jewish state. And to some extent this has been the case:

> The terms "Israelis" and "supporters of Israel" have replaced "Zionist" as the primary ideological label. But while the label "Zionist" has faded to some extent, some of the ideological premises of statist Zionism remain, e.g., the belief that Israel is the state of the Jewish people, almost half of whom live outside Israel, rather than the state of its citizens; the desire for the return of the Jews to Zion through "ascent" (*aliya*), the need to restrict the growth and power of the Palestinian Arab minority (the so-called

"demographic question"), and the necessity for discriminatory legislation and policies, albeit motivated more by preferential treatment for the Jews than by antagonism towards Arabs. The influx
of hundreds of thousands of Jews in the early years of the State had
a direct detrimental impact on the native Palestinians – no longer
considered either "Palestinian Arab" or "native", but now a minority called "Israeli Arabs" or just "minorities".[8]

And waves of immigration have also had a disastrous effect, as new
groups of immigrants (except Ethiopian Jews) take their place at the
government coalition table.

As for the Arab natives of Palestine who had become refugees, the
conventional Israeli historiography was that they had voluntarily left
before and during the War of Independence, and that they should be
resettled among their own brethren in surrounding Arab countries.
In any event, those very countries had forced thousands of Jews from
North Africa and the Middle East to leave, and so things were more or
less balanced. But in those years of state and institution building, few
people outside Israel paid attention to the Arabs inside Israel. They
simply had no positive role to play in the formation of the nationalist
ethos.

The Arabs outside Israel, of course, did. Statist Zionism led almost
inevitably to armed conflict with the Arabs – first the Palestinians,
who were routed, and then the Arab states, whose armies were
outnumbered, poorly motivated, and insufficiently armed.[9] I say
"inevitably", for what people would not resist by force the attempts
of settlers to establish a state, against the will of the majority, in their
land? Much of the Israeli national ethos was built on the notion
of militarism, self-defence and bereavement on the one hand, and
the yearning for peace with Arab neighbours on the other. That
the Arabs of Palestine and the Arab states had resisted what they
viewed to be a colonialist settler-state seemed incomprehensible to
those who had internalised the fundamental principles of Zionism.
After all, had they not offered to *share* the land to which they had
recently immigrated? Zionists reasoned that certainly after the state
was established, recognised by other states, and admitted to the
United Nations, there was no reason for the Arabs not to accept the

legitimacy of Israel's existence as a Jewish state, that is, to accept the claims of statist Zionism. The fact that the Arab states did not accept Israel (and when Egypt and Jordan did, it was at government level and not in accordance with popular sentiment) was perceived by Israelis as indicative of an irrational, deep-seated prejudice against the Jewish state. Israelis inferred that it was necessary to maintain a military and strategic advantage, to erect an "Iron Wall" until the Arabs eventually accepted them.

This narrative does not by any means capture all or even most of the national ethos of Israel in the 1950s and the 1960s; it certainly does not capture the growth and development of the Jewish state, its immigration policies, the socialist political framework led by the Mapai and then the Labour party, cultural achievements, and a host of other developments. My purpose is to remark on the continuity between the statist Zionist ideology of the 1940s during and after the Holocaust, and the nationalist ethos in the early years of the state; an ethos that was little challenged by mainstream Israelis. As we shall see, with the notable exception of the first two years after the Oslo agreement was signed, this ethos has remained in the national psyche until the present.

There seems to be an assumption among western liberals that the period between 1948 and 1967 was a golden age for Israel, an age when its legitimacy in the world was unquestioned, its politics pragmatic, and its decisions, more or less, untrammelled by Zionist ideology. Israel's fall from grace, according to this view, came as a result of the 1967 war, which, although justified as a defensive war, led to the revival of the Greater Israel ideology and the settlements. This narrative forgets many things: the treatment of the Arab Israelis and their lands under the post-1948 military occupation; the attacks on those Arab refugees wishing to return to their homes; the land policy and ideology of settlement that continued unabated from the pre-state years; and the irredentist goals of some players that involved the security control of the West Bank.

As for the Israeli claim that the 1967 war was a defensive one, it is sufficient to recall that on the whole, the border with Jordan had remained quiet from 1956–67 and that Jordan, unlike Egypt and Syria, had not been considered a serious military threat by the Israelis.

If the 1967 push to control Jerusalem and the West Bank was at all motivated by security considerations, the reaction was disproportionate to the threat; indeed, much of the West Bank was occupied after it was known that the Jordanian forces had been ordered to withdraw.[10] The differences of opinion among the Labour and Herut parties in the 1970s and 1980s was not whether to return all of the West Bank, but rather how much of it should be put under direct Palestinian control, given the presence of so many Palestinian Arabs, and how much under the joint control of Israel and Jordan. On Jerusalem there was no disagreement. To this day, no Israeli government and no Zionist political party, Left or Right, has accepted in principle the withdrawal from the West Bank to the 1949 armistice lines. The same applies to acceptance of the right of the Palestinians to a sovereign state, responsible for its own security.

The short-lived period in Israel's history where there seemed to be a shift in the national ethos began with the Madrid Conference (and the revocation of the UN "Zionism is Racism" resolution) and went into high gear with the signing of the Oslo Accords in 1993. That stage began to crumble with the assassination of Prime Minister Rabin in 1995 and ended completely with the second intifada. To be sure, the statist Zionist ethos had already begun to be questioned as a result of the 1980–1 Lebanon War; the work of the "New Historians" like Morris, Pappe and Segev; and the rise of post-Zionism in academic discourse. But the Oslo process for the first time presented to the Israelis the Palestinians as partners, even as aggrieved parties. Palestinians who until recently had been imprisoned as terrorists in Israeli prisons were now appearing on television with their former captors.

Many Israelis were exhilarated, but a large part of the population viewed this normalisation as nothing less than a betrayal of Zionist, even Jewish, principles (similar views existed on the Palestinian side). The idea that Israel could be an accepted member of the Middle East, that there could be normalised relations between Arabs and Jews, was for many too radical a paradigm shift in the national ethos. Opponents of the Oslo process were more than willing to seize upon any counter-evidence (especially terrorism) to suggest that the Palestinian recognition of Israel was an elaborate ruse to weaken and destroy the Jewish state. As an observer of Israeli society during this period, I can report that the prospect of peace was invigorating to many, but nerve-wracking to others, and not just because of territorial concessions or security concerns. Relations with some Arab countries thawed; the Israeli economy boomed; and Palestinians entered the Israeli public sphere. With the breakdown of the Oslo process after the 1996 elections, and finally, with the failure of Camp David II and the horrors of the second intifada, the experience of the early Oslo period was erased and wiped from the collective memory, except, of course the experience of terror, which only reinforced the view that the paradigm should never have shifted.

Indeed, as world criticism of Israel Defense Forces (IDF) military force against civilians in last decade mounted, there was a return to the pre-Oslo period ethos of "All the world is against us". Hamas assumed the role of bugbear once played by the Palestine Liberation Organization (PLO); Ahmadinejad and Nasrallah replaced Arafat; the UN was considered no different from the UN of the 1970s. The quiet negotiations that took place between Ehud Olmert and Mahmoud Abbas in 2008 were totally unlike negotiations during the Oslo period and represented a slight deviation from classic Zionist/Israeli unilateralism. More typical was the disengagement from Gaza in 2005 which, according to Prime Minister Sharon's principal advisor, far from "giving peace a chance", allowed Israeli troops to be redeployed in order to control Gaza better, to relieve pressure on Israel for concessions on the West Bank, and to prevent the establishment of a Palestinian state.[11]

When one combines the feelings of Jewish victimhood inherent in the Zionist national ethos with the most powerful military in the Middle East, it is clear why Israel has become dangerous to anything that it perceives to be a threat. This ethos of victimhood has not weakened its grip on the national psyche, even with its unyielding control of the territories, the end of suicide bombing, the near total exclusion of Palestinians from the Israeli public space, and the enormous asymmetry of power between Israelis and the Palestinians. The general unwillingness today to move past the nationalist pieties and clichés of the founders is striking. Israel's situation may now be very different, but its self-perception has changed but little. The late Tony Judt summed it quite well in 2006 when he characterised Israel as the country that wouldn't grow up, but preferred to remain stuck in its adolescent mindset.

Seen from the outside, Israel still comports itself like an adolescent: consumed by a brittle confidence in its own uniqueness; certain that no one "understands" it and everyone is "against" it; full of wounded self-esteem, quick to take offence and quick to give it. Like many adolescents, Israel is convinced – and makes a point of aggressively and repeatedly asserting – that it can do as it wishes, that its actions carry no consequences and that it is immortal.[12]

Immortal, yet at the same time fearful of its existence.

Although Israel has grown to be a regional superpower, it seems almost Peter Pan-like in its refusal to shed the Zionist statist ethos of its founding years, especially in its relations with the Palestinians. It is willing to seek peace with the Palestinians under occupation, but only if the Palestinians content themselves with something less than a state, a non-militarised entity that will be economically dependent upon Israel, politically toothless, and whose natural resources are shared with Israel – and even this has been rejected out of hand by the Right-wing parties. As for the "Geneva Accord", which has been rejected by the Israeli government and much of the Israeli public as overly accommodating, the Palestinian "state's" security is guaranteed not by its own military but by a multi-national force.[13]

What prevents Israel from normalising its relations with its neighbours and coming to grips with its treatment of the Palestinians is not its security situation, which has never been better, nor its lack of a Palestinian "partner", which it indeed has. It is rather the fact of its being mired in an ethnic-exclusivist nationalist ethos that views its settlement in Palestine as a "return", denies the Palestinian Arabs historical and national rights, and relegates Palestinian natives to an inferior status – those within Israel individually as second- and third-class citizens, and those without Israel collectively, as a "state minus", to use the characterisation favoured by current Prime Minister Netanyahu.

For there to be any significant change, the national ethos must change, at least among a broad segment of the population and its supporters outside its borders. The prospect of that happening is indeed remote at the present, but may become less remote as more people despair of existing solutions, and as the price for maintaining the status quo grows. Abandoning the ethnic-exclusivist vision of statist Zionism will be a bitter pill for many to swallow. But it may be perhaps a little less bitter if one can convince Israelis and their supporters that essential elements of classical Zionism, that is, the preservation and fostering of Hebrew culture, the view of Israel/Palestine as a Jewish homeland, a place which offers some form of self-determination for the Israeli Jewish people (and needless to say, the Palestinian Arab people) – will come about if Israel abandons the 1948 statist ethos.

Statist Zionism decisively rejected and marginalised those Zionist voices that demanded that any political arrangement for a Jewish homeland, indeed even Jewish immigration, be part of a broader political agreement with the native Palestinian Arabs. For statist Zionists, the cultural Zionist "road not taken" was, as one Israeli professor recently put it, "the road to nowhere".[14] Now that Israeli–Palestinian relations have reached a dead end, with one side controlling the lives, liberties and resources of the other for over four decades and counting, some Israeli intellectuals are beginning to examine where Zionism went wrong and how it can get on a road leading to somewhere better. Of course, alternatives to the Israeli state have been proposed by non-Zionists, post-Zionists and anti-Zionists since 1948; one need only point to the "Canaanite" movement of the 1950s, the PLO's "secular democratic state" of the late 1960s, and the various post-Zionist alternatives of the 1980s. What is different about these new proposals is that they reject the ethnic-exclusivist character of Israel without rejecting the possibility, indeed the desirability, of preserving its Jewish character, redefined primarily in cultural rather than in ethnic-exclusivist terms.

The Revival of Cultural Zionism

In the past few years, Israelis have advanced several proposals that reject the ethnic-exclusivist ethos of statist Zionism and replace it with something more in tune with liberal democracies in the twenty-first century. They are contained in books like Bernard Avishai's *The Hebrew Republic* (New York 2008), Chaim Gans's *A Just Zionism*

(Oxford 2008), Moshe Berent's *A Nation like All Nations: Towards the Establishment of an Israeli Republic* (Hebrew; Jerusalem, 2009) and, earlier, Joseph Agassi's *Liberal Nationalism for Israel: Towards an Israeli National Identity* (Jerusalem 1999). These authors may not regard themselves as "cultural Zionists", but they are willing to allow Jewish cultural, heritage, history, calendar and language pride of place in a state that is not a vehicle for Jewish ethnic-exclusivist hegemony.

Of course, there are other authors who reject Zionism altogether, as well as those who deny that Jewish culture and heritage have any place in a future secular, democratic state in Palestine, but they are not my subject here. I merely wish to point out that these four books attest to a growing intellectual willingness on the part of Israeli intellectuals to replace statist Zionism with cultural versions that avoid some of its drawbacks. And this, in itself, is significant.[15] That some of the best political thinkers in Israel have offered proposals to change fundamentally the structure of the Jewish nation-state – and others are compelled to defend that structure – suggests that the Jewish state founded in 1948 is increasingly viewed as problematic among liberal nationalists within Israel. This would be the case even had the state of Israel been founded on some empty expanse in the Arctic. That it was founded by thwarting the self-determination of the Palestinian people through expulsion and expropriation of their lands, and that Israel still thinks that it holds the key to the fulfilment of that self-determination, exacerbate the question of its legitimacy as a modern "ethnic democracy", if indeed it is one.[16]

Cultural Zionism moves the notion of a Jewish state away from the ethnic hegemony of the Jews to the cultural centrality of Israeli Jewish culture. In other words, a Jewish state is one in which Israeli Jewish culture plays a central role in the national ethos. In terms of the outmoded, if convenient, distinction between civic nationalism and ethnic nationalism, the Jewish state I envision would foster a moderate civic nationalism in all its citizens but would accord pride of place, though not exclusively so, to Jewish tradition in the broadest sense and not in its narrowly religious sense. Varieties of religious Judaism will obviously be important in the lives of groups of the Jewish citizenry, and even the non-Jewish citizenry, when there are common concerns. Of course, there will be questions as to how much of a role

Jewish culture would play, and some of these could be settled consti-
tutionally. My own view is that Hebrew language and calendar are
essential; beyond that, the fostering of Jewish culture, as a function of
what is important in the large segment of the citizenry, is an important priority of a state I understand as Jewish.

The justification for Jewish cultural centrality is simple: there are
over five and a half million Jews in Israel/Palestine, and Jewish culture,
again in the broadest sense, including the Hebrew language, is central
to their identity and well-being. From the standpoint of liberal nationalism (and I am clearly adopting that standpoint), the state does not
have to adopt a strictly neutral stance with regard to what are central
components in the identities of its citizens, or to shy away from them
in the public sphere. Again, the degree of state support would have
to be negotiated with the various elements of society. There is a large
traditional religious population in Israel/Palestine, and while I am
personally in favour of the separation of church and state, the role of
religion would also have to be negotiated. It is critical to remove the
religious affiliation of the citizens from the question of their nationality. The most illiberal element of the state of Israel today is its identi-
fication of the nation with a certain religion, or, more accurately, its
definition of the Jewish nation in sufficiently religious terms so as to
exclude Israelis who have other religions from being Jewish.

Jewish cultural centrality can be feature of a state whose population is overwhelmingly Israeli Jewish, but it can also be a feature
of one "Abrahamic" state from the Jordan to the Mediterranean.
Clearly in the latter state, Palestinian Arab culture would also play
an equally central role. I would still call that bi-national state a *Jewish*
state, indeed, *the* Jewish state, though not the *exclusively* Jewish state,
because of the centrality of Jewish culture. Yet whatever the configu-
ration of the Jewish state, a civic national cultural identity of all its
citizens would also be fostered. Once again, one's ethnicity or religion
would not be an integral notion of the state's nationalism. It is not
likely, for example, that Palestinian Arab Muslims will feel comfortable with adopting a Jewish national identity, because of the religious
dissonance, but there is no reasons why they cannot adopt an Israeli or
"Abrahamic" nationalism. And, indeed, despite the absence of official
Israeli recognition of an Israeli national identity, it very much exists

today among the 600,000 Palestinian Arab Israelis.

Statist Zionists often argue that a Jewish state is necessary not only to foster Jewish culture and enrich the identity of many of its Jewish citizens, but to ensure the physical survival of Jews. After two thousand years of precarious existence, only a Jewish ethnic state can do that. Moreover, as a nation, Jews should have the right to determine their own destiny, and this can only be done through ethnic hegemony. If a Jewish state is not a haven for persecuted Jews, it has lost an important *raison d'être*.

My own opinion is that these views had a certain purchase in the aftermath of World War II, although even then their validity was questionable, but now they are much less convincing. For one thing, the most dangerous place for Jews to live qua Jews over the past sixty-plus years has been the state of Israel, where thousands of Jews have died as a result of Israel's wars. If one is to believe the alarmists, the existence of the five and a half million Jews in Israel is perpetually in danger. I know many Jews who believe that Iranian President Ahmadinejad is planning to annihilate the Jewish state, and that even if he doesn't succeed, thousands or hundreds of thousands may die. Moreover, anti-Semitic attacks against Jews outside of Israel have a direct correlation to Israel's actions, even if those actions are defensible. So while some Jews may feel more secure within Israel than outside it (and during periods of increased Israel-related anti-Semitism, they may be right) that seems more the result of their Zionist indoctrination.

For another, the self-determination of a people does not have to be achieved through the vehicle of an ethnic-exclusivist nation-state; in fact for most of the world, it is not. Again, as long as Jewish nationalism has an irreducible religious element to it that excludes people of other religious faiths from being part of the Jewish nation, there is good reason not to view the self-determination of the Jewish people along those lines. What is needed now for there to be a Jewish state that is not a post-Zionist Israel, but rather a post-Israel Zionism. Maybe that sort of Zionism can find expression in a liberal nationalism that is both "Jewish and democratic".

About the Contributors

OMAR BARGHOUTI is an independent Palestinian researcher, commentator and human rights activist committed to upholding international law and universal human rights. He is a founding member of the Palestinian Campaign for the Academic and Cultural Boycott of Israel (PACBI) and the Palestinian Civil Society Boycott, Divestment and Sanctions (BDS) campaign against Israel. He holds bachelor's and master's degrees in electrical engineering from Columbia University, NY, and a master's in philosophy from Tel Aviv University. He is the author of *BDS: The Global Struggle for Palestinian Rights*. His commentaries and interviews have been featured on CNN, BBC, and in the *Guardian*, *Al Jazeera*, *Huffington Post*, *Russia Today*, *Al-Ahram*, and *Democracy Now!*.

JONATHAN COOK is a journalist and writer based in Nazareth, Israel, since 2001. He is the author of three books on the Israel/Palestine conflict: *Blood and Religion*, *Israel and the Clash of Civilisations* and *Disappearing Palestine*. In 2011 he won the Martha Gellhorn Special Prize for Journalism. An archive of his writings can be found at www.jkcook.net.

JOSEPH DANA is a journalist based in the Middle East and Africa. He has written for *Le Monde Diplomatique*, *The Nation*, *GQ* (Germany) and the *Mail & Guardian* among other publications. Using the radio platform, he files reports on topics ranging from gentrification in Cape Town, South Africa to West Bank green energy projects for *Monocle 24*. Spending half the year in Africa and half in the Middle East, he is currently working on a memoir about identity politics and family history in Israel/Palestine.

JEREMIAH HABER writes the Magnes Zionist blog, which the Leiter Reports has recently called "a refreshing repository of humane sensibility and intellectual integrity ... in the poisonous morass of American discussion about Israel". "Jeremiah Haber" is the pen name of Charles H. Manekin, a professor of philosophy at the University of Maryland, who specialises in medieval Jewish and Muslim philosophy. An American-Israeli and an Orthodox Jew, he divides his time between Jerusalem and Washington, DC.

JEFF HALPER is an Israeli anthropologist and the Coordinator of the Israeli Committee Against House Demolitions (ICAHD). He is the author of *Between Redemption and Revival: The Jewish Yishuv in Jerusalem in the Nineteenth Century*, *Obstacles to Peace* and *An Israeli in Palestine*. His latest book is on Israel's involvement in the global arms and security industry. He participated in the Free Gaza Movement, serves on the Bertrand Russell Tribunal on Palestine and was nominated for the 2006 Nobel Peace Prize.

GHADA KARMI is a research fellow at the Institute of Arab and Islamic Studies at the University of Exeter, where she teaches conflict resolution in the Israeli–Palestinian conflict. Her major area of work has been on the Israel/Palestine conflict and she has published widely on this subject. Her books include a widely acclaimed memoir, *In Search of Fatima; a Palestinian story*, and *Married to Another Man: Israel's Dilemma in Palestine* which deals with the one-state solution in Israel/Palestine.

SAREE MAKDISI is professor of English and Comparative Literature at UCLA and the author of *Palestine Inside Out: An Everyday Occupation*, among other books.

JOHN J. MEARSHEIMER is the R. Wendell Harrison Distinguished Service Professor of Political Science and the co-director of the Program on International Security Policy at the University of Chicago, where he has taught since 1982. He has published five books, among them *The Tragedy of Great Power Politics* and *The Israel Lobby and U.S. Foreign Policy* with Stephen M. Walt, which has been translated into twenty-one languages.

ILAN PAPPE is the director of the European Centre for Palestine Studies at the University of Exeter and a fellow of the Institute of Arab and Islamic Studies at the University of Exeter. He is the author of several books, among them *The Ethnic Cleansing of Palestine, A Modern History of Palestine; One Land, Two Peoples* and *Gaza in Crisis* with Noam Chomsky.

SARA ROY is a senior research scholar at the Center for Middle Eastern Studies, Harvard University. She has written extensively on the Israeli–Palestinian conflict with a focus on the political economy of the Gaza Strip. Her most recent book is *Hamas and Civil Society in Gaza: Engaging the Islamist Social Sector.*

PHILIP WEISS is a long-time New York writer. He is the author of the political novel *Cock-A-Doodle-Doo*, and *American Taboo: A Murder in the Peace Corps*, an investigation into a murder in the Peace Corps. He is founder and co-editor of Mondoweiss.net, a website about the Israel/Palestine conflict.

Notes

Preface AHMED MOOR *and* ANTONY LOEWENSTEIN

1. 'Understanding the True Nature of the Hamas-Israel War' by Thomas L. Friedman, *New York Times*, 28 November 2023.
2. 'Palestinians Lack Faith in Biden, Two-State Solution' by Jay Loschky, Gallup, www.gallup.com, 18 October 2023.
3. 'Israelis have grown more skeptical of a two-state solution' by Sarah Austin and Jonathan Evans, Pew Research Center, www.pewresearch.org, 26 September 2023.
4. 'Democrats' Sympathies in Middle East Shift to Palestinians' by Lydia Saad, Gallup, www.gallup.com, 16 March 2023.

Introduction AHMED MOOR *and* ANTONY LOEWENSTEIN

5. http://www.haaretz.com/print-edition/news/
top-pm-aide-gaza-plan-aims-to-freeze-the-peace-process-1.136686

Presence, Memory, and Denial AHMED MOOR

1. See http://www.guardian.co.uk/world/2011/dec/10/palestinians-invented-
people-newt-gingrich
2. Golda Meir, quoted in the *Sunday Times*, 15 June 1969; and in the *Washington Post*, 16 June 1969.
3. See http://www.washingtonpost.com/blogs/fact-checker/post/rick-santo-
rums-claim-that-no-palestinian-lives-on-the-west-bank/2012/01/04/gIQAcx-
sIbP_blog.html
4. See http://www.nybooks.com/articles/archives/2003/oct/23/israel-the-
alternative/?pagination=false

The State of Denial ILAN PAPPE

1. See for instance a recent collection Alon Kadish (ed.), *Israel's War of Independence, 1948–1949*, 2 vols., Tel-Aviv 2004 (Hebrew).
2. Edward W. Said, *Culture and Imperialism*, New York 1994.
3. See Ilan Pappe, *The Forgotten Palestinians, A History of the Palestinians in Israel*, New Haven and London 2010, pp. 46–94.
4. The scope of the tragedy is well described in a collection of articles: Ghada Karmi and Eugene Cotran (eds.), *The Palestinian Exodus, 1948–1988*, London

and Ithaca 1999.

5.   See Walid Khalidi, "Revisiting the UNGA Partition Resolution", in *Journal of Palestine Studies*, 27 (1), autumn 1997, pp. 5–21.

6.   Ilan Pappe, *The Making of the Arab–Israeli Conflict, 1948–1951*, London and New York, 1992, pp. 124–43.

7.   See Ilan Pappe, *The Ethnic Cleansing of Palestine*, London and New York, 2006.

8.   See Meron Benvenisti, *Sacred Landscape: The Buried History of the Holy Land since 1948*, Berkeley 2002, pp. 11–55.

9.   See Pappe, *The Ethnic Cleansing*, pp. 91–103.

10. See an intriguing analysis in David Landy, *Jewish Identity and Palestinian Rights; Diaspora Jewish Opposition to Israel*, London 2011.

11. See Ilan Pappe, "Post Zionist Critique: Part I: the Academic Debate", in *Journal of Palestine Studies*, 26 (2), Winter 1997, pp. 20–41.

12. See Ilan Pappe, "Israel: Between Civic Democracy and Zealotocracy", in *Journal of Palestine Studies*, 29 (3), Spring 2000, pp. 33–45.

13. See Pappe, *The Ethnic Cleansing*, Ibid.

14. See these quotes and others in Ilan Pappe, "The Tantura Case in Israel: The Katz Research and Trial", in *Journal of Palestine Studies*, 30 (3), Spring 2001, pp. 19–39.

15. See Nur Masalha, *The Expulsion of the Palestinians: The Concept of "Transfer" in Zionist Political Thought, 1882–1948*, Washington 1992.

16. Entry for 12 June 1895, where Herzl discusses his proposal to shift from building a Jewish society in Palestine to forming a state for Jews, as translated by Michael Prior from the original German: see Michael Prior, "Zionism and the Challenge to Historical Truth and Morality", in Prior (ed.), *Speaking the Truth about Zionism and Israel*, London 2004, p. 27 .

17. Ben Gurion Archives, correspondence section, letter to Amos, 12 July 1937.

18. Central Zionist Archives, Protocols meeting with the executive of the party, 12 July 1938.

19. I have discussed this issue at length in Ilan Pappe, "De-Terrorising the Palestinian National Struggle; the Roadmap to Peace", in *Critical Studies on Terrorism*, 2 (2), August 2009, pp. 127–46.

20. See Pappe, *The Academic Debate*

21. Ben Kaspit, "Two Years to the Intifada", in *Maariv*, 13 September 2002.

22. See the appeal to the Supreme Court by Adalah and the Adalah Annual Report 2011, 4 May 2011.

23. This was already noted in 1999: see Ramis Kahmayseh, "Demography, Engineering Demography and Demographobic Discourse", in *The Book of the Arab Society*, Volume 4, Jerusalem 1999, pp. 13–25 (Hebrew).

24. A summary of the Herzliya report appeared in *Haaretz* on 27 March 2001.

25. Benny Morris, "Survival of the Fittest" interview in *Haaretz* reproduced in the *Journal of Palestine Studies*, 33 (3), Spring 2004, p. 168.

26. Benny Morris, 1948, London and New Haven 2010.

27. Ilan Pappe, "The Vicissitudes of the 1948 Historiography of Israel", in *Journal of Palestine Studies*, 39 (1), Autumn 2009, pp. 6–23.

28. A recent PhD has looked thoroughly at this struggle; see Annie Pfingst, "Erasure, enclosure, excision: framing Palestinian return", PhD, University of Technology Sydney 2011. See also Ronit Lentin, *Co-memory and Melancholia: Israelis Memorialising the Palestinian Nakba*, Manchester: 2010.

29. See the Adalah Annual Report for 2011.

Reconfiguring Palestine SARA ROY

1.   An abbreviated version of this chapter can be found in Sara Roy, "U.S. Foreign Policy and the Israeli–Palestinian Conflict: A View from Palestine", Institut Francais des Relations Internationale (IFRI), http://www.ifri.org/downloads/notesararoy.pdf.

2.   Dr Husam Zomlot, "A Paradigm Shift: The Arab-Israeli Conflict and Regional Transformation," Lecture, Center for Middle Eastern Studies, Harvard University, 23 March 2011, Cambridge, MA.

3.   Ibid.

4.   Noura Erakat, "Can the Palestinian Leadership Pave the Way from Statehood to Independence", on *Jadaliyya*, http://www.jadaliyya.com/pages/index/2245/can-the-palestinian-leadership-pave-the-way-from-s, 28 July 2011.

5.   Mouin Rabbani, "Palestine at the UN: An alternative strategy,", on *The Hill's Congress Blog*, http://thehill.com/blogs/congress-blog/foreignpolicy/130145-palestine-at-the-un-an-alternative-strategy, 19 November 2010.

6.   Ethan Bronner and Isabel Kershner, "Fatah and Hamas Announce Outline of Deal", in *New York Times*, 27 April 2011.

7.   Josh Ruebner, "The two speeches of Barack Obama," *The Hill's Congress Blog*, 20 May 2011, http://thehill.com/blogs/congress-blog/foreignpolicy/16238.

8.   Ibid.

9.   Adam Shatz, "Is Palestine Next?", in *London Review of Books*, Volume 33, Number 4, 14 July 2011.

10. 10 Joel Beinin, "The Israeli–Palestinian Conflict and the Arab Awakening," *Middle East Research and Information Project*, www.merip.org/mero/mero080111, 1 August 2011.

11. Mahmoud Abbas, "The Long Overdue Palestinian State", in *New York Times*, 16 May 2011. Also see Camille Mansour, "Palestinian Options at the United Nations," Institute for Palestine Studies, http://palestine-studies.org/column-details.aspx?t=2&id=34; Akiva Eldar, "The battle for September", in *Ha'aretz*, 5 June 2011; and Lamis Andoni, "Palestinian Statehood and bypassing Israel", on *AlJazeera.net*, 16 June 2011.

12. The document is titled: "The political situation in the light of the continued suspension of the negotiations and the success of Palestinian options."

13. Ahmad Khalidi, "A West Bank Anachronism", in *The Guardian*, 19 April 2011.

14. Abbas (16 May 2011).

15. Al-Haq, *Al-Haq's Questions & Answers on Palestine's September Initiatives at the United Nations*, Ref. no. 249/2011, 20 July 2011.

16. Dr Husam Zomlot, Lecture, Massachusetts Institute of Technology (MIT), Cambridge, MA, 12 September 2011.

17. Shatz (14 July 2011).

18. See, for example, Michael Sfard, "The Legal Tsunami is on its way," *Ha'aretz*, 29 April 2011; Victor Kattan, "The case of UN recognition of Palestine," *The Electronic Intifada*, 14 June 2011; Martin Waehlisch, "Palestine, the UN, and international law," Al Jazeera, 25 July 2011; John Whitbeck, "America's Dangerous Game at the UN," Al Jazeera, http://english.aljazeera.net/indepth/opinion/2011/09/2011928153635754605.html, 29 September 2011; Ami Isseroff, "Unilateral Palestinian state declaration – More important than settlement freeze," 14 September 2009, http://www.zionism-israel.com/log/archives/00000713.html; Ali Abunimah, *Recognising Palestine? The efforts of the Palestinian Authority to push for statehood are nothing more than an elaborate farce*, 13 April 2011; Dr. Salman Abu Sitta, "The PLO is to 'liberate' not to legalise partition," http://australiansforpalestine.com, July 2011; Sam Bahour, "Palestinians will soon come full circle," *The Guardian*, 4 August 2011; Joel Beinin, *Fatah-Hamas Reconciliation and Palestinian–Israeli Peace*, 11 May 2011, http://jewishvoiceforpeace.org; Abdel Razzaq Takriti, "Analysis: Implications of Palestinian statehood," Ma'an News Agency, http://maannews.net/eng/ViewDetails.aspx?ID=416887, 29 August 2011; Darryl Li, "Occupation Law and the One-State Reality," *Jadaliyya*, http://www.jadaliyya.com/pages/index/2295/occupation-law-and-the-one-state-reality, 2 August 2011; and "The Legal Opinion of Dr. Francis Boyle Regarding Palestinian Statehood," *Salem-News.com*, 28 August 2011.

19. Ethan Bronner, "In Seeking Statehood, Palestinians Stir Concern", in *New York Times*, 10 September 2011.

20. Kattan (14 June 2011). A justifiable concern among many critics of the UN bid is the failure of the Palestinian leadership to follow through and implement the new legal options available to them.

21. Some of these obstacles include: internal Fatah disputes, particularly between the elite and the rank and file within Gaza and within the West Bank; a strengthening security apparatus in the West Bank; the continued isolation and marginalisation of Hamas; and divisions between the West Bank and Gaza at the popular level, with Gazans cast as culturally, socially and politically inferior.

22. More specifically, this includes a technocratic government representing all factions, security arrangements, reconstitution and revitalisation of the PLO to allow Hamas membership, a tribunal for general elections, and a date for elections within a year of the signing of the final agreement.

23. Analyst, Gaza, email communication, 28 April 2011.

24. Political official, Ramallah, telephone communication, 18 May 2011.
25. Beinin (1 August 2011).
26. Analyst, Gaza, email communication, 17 May 2011.
27. Political official, Ramallah, telephone communication, 18 May 2011.
28. The Middle East Media and Research Institute, "Reflecting Possible Change in Hamas Stance, Movements' Columnists Attack Assad: You Will Meet Same Fate as Ousted Tyrants," http://www.memri.org/report/en/0/0/0/0/0/0/5602.htm, 29 August 2011.
29. Analyst, Gaza, email communication, 17 May 2011.
30. Fares Akram and Ethan Bronner, "A Nervous Hamas Voices Its Issues With a Palestinian Bid for UN Membership," *New York Times*, 19 September 2011. Also see "Hamas: Abbas relinquishing Palestinian rights with UN bid," *Ha'aretz*, 23 September 2011.
31. Ibid, *New York Times*.
32. International Crisis Group, *Radical Islam in Gaza*, Middle East Report No. 104, March 2011, p. i.
33. Ibid, p. 5. Also see Benedetta Berti, *Salafi-Jihadi Activism in Gaza*, Terrorism Center at West Point, 3 May 2010, http://www.ctc.usma.edu/posts/salafi-jihadi-activism-in-gaza-mapping-the-threat.
34. Mushtaq H. Khan, "Learning the Lessons of Oslo: State Building and Freedoms in Palestine," Paper presented at a closed meeting, Jerusalem, December 2010; and Zomlot (23 March 2011).
35. Ibid.
36. See, for example, "Palestinian Freedom Riders on Their Way to Jerusalem Violently Arrested on Israeli Settler Bus," in *Press Release*, Jewish Voice for Peace, 15 November 2011.
37. Jamil Hilal, "Palestinian Answers in the Arab Spring", in *Al Shabaka Policy Brief*, May 2011. See also Jeff Halper, *The Palestinian Authority's Historic Mistake—and Opportunity*, 24 June 2011, http://icahdusa.org/2011/06/the-palestinian-authority's-historic-mistake-and-opportunity; and Khalidi (19 April 2011). In this regard also see Nathan J. Brown, "The Palestinians' Receding Dream of Statehood", in *Current History*, December 2011, pp. 345–51.
38. Noura Erakat, "Palestinian Youth: New Movement, New Borders", on Al Jazeera, May 4, 2011, http://english.aljazeera.net/indepth/features/2011/05/201153101231834961.html.
39. Shatz (July 14, 2011).
40. Nadia Hijab, "Just as well that Obama had no details about Middle East peace", on *The Hill's Congress Blog*, May 2011, http://thehill.com/blogs/congress-blog/foreignpolicy/162395.
41. Erakat (4 May 2011).
42. Ibid.
43. Khalidi (19 April 2011).

44. Shatz (14 July 2011).

45. Ibid.

46. A critical factor is the Boycott, Divestment and Sanctions (BDS) movement launched in 2005 by a broad coalition of Palestinian NGOs.

47. Karl Vick, "Palestinian Border Protests: The Arab Spring Model for Confronting Israel", in *Time Magazine*, 16 May 2011. See also "Here comes your non-violent resistance", in *The Economist*, 17 May 2011; and Rami G. Khouri, "A New Palestinian Strategy Unfolds", in *Agence Global*, 29 June 2011.

48. Zomlot (12 September 2011).

49. Darryl Li, "Occupation Law and the One-State Reality", on *Jadaliyya*, http://www.jadaliyya.com/pages/index/2295/occupation-law-and-the-one-state-reality, 2 August 2011.

50. "BBC World Service poll reveals public narrowly backs UN recognition of Palestine", *Press Release*, 18 September 2011, http://www.bbc.co.uk/pressoffice/pressreleases/stories/2011/09_september/18/poll.shtml.

51. Geoffrey Aronson, "Back to Square One –The Obama Administration Resets U.S. Policy", in *Report on Israeli Settlement in the Occupied Territories*, Volume 20, No. 6, November–December 2010, p. 1.

52. Ibid., p. 4.

53. Ibid.

54. Interview with Professor Shibley Telhami and Robert Malley, National Public Radio, 19 May 2011.

55. See Norman Finkelstein and Jamie Stern-Weiner, "How to End the Israeli–Palestinian Conflict: An Interview with Norman Finkelstein", on *New Left Project*, 14 November 2011. Also see Bradley Klapper, "US to work with Arab Spring's Islamist Parties", in *Bloomberg Businessweek*, 8 November 2011.

56. See Josh Ruebner, "Straining Every Nerve against UN Membership for Palestine", http://palestinechronicle.com/view_article>details.php?id=17032.

57. Interview, telephone communication, May 2011.

58. NPR Interview with Telhami and Malley, May 2011.

59. Netanyahu described his foreign policy position as follows: "The demand that Palestinians recognize Israel as the national homeland of the Jewish people; a commitment to end the conflict; a solution to the Palestinian refugee issue that did not require absorption within Israel's borders; the establishment of a Palestinian state only in accordance with a peace deal that did not infringe on Israel's security; that said Palestinian state be demilitarized; the preservation of large settlement blocs within the West Bank; and the insistence that Jerusalem remain the undivided capital of Israel." See "Netanyahu: Israel willing to 'cede parts of our homeland' for true peace", in *Ha'aretz*, 16 May 2011.

60. J. J. Goldberg, "Israel's Security Elite Joins the Opposition", in *The Forward*, 11 May 2011 (issue of 20 May 2011), http://forward.com/articles/137697.

61. Ibid.

62. Jeff Halper, "The Tent Protests in Israel: Can They Break Out of the Zionist/Security/Neo-Liberal Box?", on www.ichadusa.org, 10 August 2011. Also see Matan Kaminer, "On the Current Conjuncture in Israel", on *Jadaliyya*, http://www.jadaliyya.com/pages/index/2379/on-the-current-conjuncture-in-israel, 15 August 2011; and Attila Somfalvi, "Ben-Eliezer: Israel headed for disaster," http://www.ynetnews.com/articles/0,7340,L-4102967,00.html, 1 August 2011.

63. Analyst, Gaza, email communication, 13 April 2011.

64. Ibid, 11 May 2011.

65. David Kirkpatrick and Ethan Bronner, "Israelis Flee Cairo Embassy as Protesters Invade Offices", in *New York Times*, 10 September 2011.

66. Anthony Shadid, "Turkey Predicts Alliance with Egypt as Regional Anchors", in *New York Times*, 18 September 2011.

67. Finkelstein and Stern-Weiner (14 November 2011).

The Power of Narrative SAREE MAKDISI

1. See http://www.maannews.net/eng/ViewDetails.aspx?ID=415804

2. See http://www.guardian.co.uk/world/palestine-papers

3. See http://www.guardian.co.uk/world/2011/oct/01/us-congress-blocks-aid-palestinians

4. See http://www.prc.org.uk/newsite/en/palestinian-refugee-news-resource/articles-palestine/1624-Virtual-statehood-or-the-Right-of-Return.html

5. See http://electronicintifada.net/content/palestinian-bedouins-al-araqib-we-wont-leave/9268

6. See http://www.reuters.com/article/2011/11/23/us-israel-bedouin-idUSTRE7AM2EZ20111123

7. See http://www.lrb.co.uk/blog/2011/09/27/mouin-rabbani/abbas's-next-move/

8. See http://www.haaretz.com/general/maximum-jews-minimum-palestinians-1.105562

The Future of Palestine JOHN J. MEARSHEIMER

1. This chapter is a modified version of the Hisham Sharabi Memorial Lecture delivered at The Palestine Center in Washington, DC, on April 29, 2010.

Israel's Liberal Myths JONATHAN COOK

1. "No neighbourly welcome for Israeli Arabs in Rakefet", in *Haaretz*, 15 September 2011.

2. "Israel's High Court orders Jewish Galilee town to accept Arab couple", in *Haaretz*, 14 September 2011.

3. At a hearing in early 2011, the president of the Supreme Court, Dorit Beinisch, asked state officials: "What is the personal flaw in these people [the Zbeidats]? ... Unless you are saying that an Arab couple is unsuitable for such a community.

Is that what you're saying?" "Beinish criticizes town's reception committee", in *Ynet*, 1 February 2011.

4.   "Olmert decries 'deliberate and insufferable' discrimination against Arabs", in *Haaretz*, 12 November 2008.

5.   "For Israel's Arab Citizens, Isolation and Exclusion", in *Washington Post*, 20 December 2007.

6.   "High Court rules Arab couple can live in Jewish town", in *Ynet*, 14 September 2011.

7.   There are more than forty unrecognised Bedouin villages in the Negev, and more than a dozen more in the Galilee. All are denied access to public services, including electricity, water, sewerage, roads and telephone lines. All homes in the villages are under constant threat of demolition.

8.   Some of these pretexts are well known, such as the 1950 Absentee Property Law, which confiscated land from refugees, including those internally displaced, and the 1953 Land Acquisition Law, which allowed the state to expropriate land with minimal compensation. However, there were also many other less visible techniques used by officials, including retroactively changing the qualifying cultivation period for claiming ownership of a plot of land; misusing aerial photographs from the British Mandate period; enforcing a new "50 percent rule", which required cultivation of at least half a parcel of land even if most of the land was not actually cultivable; restricting the traditional area outside villages that was considered cultivable; and de-recognising cultivated land belonging to communities built after 1858. In such cases, the state was able to nationalise the land. Geremy Forman, "Israeli Supreme Court Doctrine and the Battle over Arab Land in Galilee: A Vertical Assessment", in *Journal of Palestine Studies*, Vol. 40, No 4 (Summer 2011).

9.   "Arabs shouldn't live with Jews, Shas minister says", in *Jerusalem Post*, 3 July 2009.

10. "'Israeli Arabs have no choice but to build illegally'", in *Haaretz*, 29 July 2010.

11. "New housing for Arab villages stonewalled", in *Haaretz*, 2 January 2012.

12. According to Kais Nasser, a lecturer at Hebrew University in Jerusalem, seventy-seven Arab communities were without a valid master plan, and most of the rest had outdated master plans approved in the 1980s, making legal building almost impossible. See "Policy wonks and public present ideas to Trajtenberg committee", in *Haaretz*, 24 August 2011. A study by the Arab think-tank Dirasat found that only 6 percent of Arab local authorities had a local planning committee to submit a master plan to, compared with 55 percent of Jewish communities. See "Israeli Arabs have no choice but to build illegally".

13. *Adalah Newsletter*, Vol 42, November 2007.

14. "Israel's legislation could eventually serve its enemies", in *Haaretz*, 1 November 2010.

15. The term "Judaisation" is a less commonly used today, with other euphemisms

preferred, such as "development of state lands" or "attracting stronger populations". But the sentiment behind it has remained undiminished. In 2009 the government announced a programme to attract 600,000 Israeli Jews to the Galilee and Negev, using tax benefits, discounted land and incentives for businesses to relocate. "Shalom aims to attract 600,000 to periphery by 2020", in *Jerusalem Post*, 14 September 2009.

16. Quoted in a brochure produced by the Tel Amal tower and stockade museum.

17. A Jewish Agency official set out the goals of the *mitzpim* as "to prevent Arabs from 'taking over' government lands, keep Arab villages from attaining territorial continuity and attract a 'strong' population to the Galilee." See "The view from the hilltops", in *Haaretz*, 14 October 2010.

18. See Ilan Pappe, *The Forgotten Palestinians*, Yale, 2011, pp. 129–32. The day is commemorated annually by Palestinians as Land Day.

19. Ian Lustick, *Arabs in the Jewish State*, Cambridge, 1984, pp. 317–8n.

20. "Jewish town won't let Arab build home on his own land", in *Haaretz*, 14 December 2009.

21. This role is well explained in Susan Nathan, *The Other Side of Israel*, London, 2006, chapter 4.

22. One study revealed that most government ministries allocated no more than 7 percent of their municipal budgets to Arab local authorities, even though these authorities were the most deprived in the country. Ibn Khaldun, *Civic Developments Among the Palestinian Arab Minority in Israel*, Tamra 2004, pp. 35–7.

23. "A decade of dreams down the drain", in *Haaretz*, 29 September 2011.

24. "Of little people and landmark decisions", in *Haaretz*, 27 November 2008.

25. In a response in late 2004 to two legal petitions against its land policies, the JNF stated: "The JNF, as the owner of the JNF land, does not have a duty to practise equality towards all citizens of the state." www.adalah.org/eng/pressreleases/pr.php?file=07_07_29

26. "Mazuz: ILA must sell JNF land to Arabs, too", in *Globes*, 27 January 2005.

27. "In Watershed, Israel Deems Land-use Rules of Zionist Icon 'Discriminatory'", in *Forward*, 4 February 2005.

28. "Bill allocating JNF land to Jews only passes preliminary reading", in *Haaretz*, 19 July 2007.

29. "Poll: 81% of Israelis want JNF land for Jews only", in *Ynet*, 10 November 2007.

30. "Adalah to Israeli Government: Proposed Exchange of Land Between the State and JNF will Exacerbate Discrimination against Arab Citizens of Israel and Violate their Basic Rights", in *Adalah Newsletter*, Vol. 14, June 2005.

31. "Galilee community admits only supporters of Zionism", in *Haaretz*, 1 June 2009

32. "Second Galilee town considering 'Zionist values' bylaws", in *Haaretz*, 2 June 2009.

33. Ibid.

34. Similar calculations were behind a move by Britain's Prime Minister Margaret Thatcher in the 1980s when she sold off much of the country's council housing stock to first-time buyers, in part to win them over to her Conservative Party.

35. "Israel sells off refugees' hopes", in *The National*, 14 August 2009.

36. Those opposed were drawn from all the main Zionist political parties. "Petition: Land privatization law negates Zionist ethos", in *Jerusalem Post*, 9 February 2010.

37. "Israel sells off refugees' hopes". See also "Foreign nationals limited from purchasing ownership of land", in *Jerusalem Post*, 29 March 2011.

38. "'Loyalty oath' to keep Arabs out of Galilee town", in *The National*, 8 June 2009.

39. According to figures from Adalah, 68 percent of all communities in Israel would be covered by the law. "Knesset panel okays bill letting small communities bar Arabs", in *Haaretz*, 28 October 2010.

40. When the bill's initiators were accused of racism, one joked: "That isn't true. Every Jewish community needs one Arab resident. Otherwise, who will repair the refrigerator that breaks down on Shabbat?" See "C'tee okays bill that lets communities reject newcomers", in *Jerusalem Post*, 27 October 2010.

41. "Bill allowing towns to reject residents gains ground", in *Ynet*, 27 October 2010.

42. The text of the law can be read here: www.adalah.org/upfiles/2011/discriminatory_laws_2011/Admissions_Committees_Law_2011_English.pdf

43. "Knesset passes 'Nakba bill'", in *Ynet*, 23 March 2011.

44. "Israel's legislation could eventually serve its enemies", in *Haaretz*, 1 November 2010.

45. "South Africa is already here", in *Haaretz*, 31 October 2010. The Act led to more than three million blacks being forced out of their homes.

46. "Segregation of Jews and Arabs in 2010 Israel is almost absolute", in *Haaretz*, 29 October 2010.

47. "High Court Issues Order Nisi against Acceptance to Communities Law", in Acri press release, 20 June 2011.

48. "Equitable housing plans for Jews and Arabs", in *Jerusalem Post*, 28 October 2010.

49. "South Africa is already here".

Zionist Media Myths Unveiling ANTONY LOEWENSTEIN

1.   Chaim Levinson, "Israel has 101 different types of permits governing Palestinian movement", in *Haaretz*, 23 December 2011.

2.   Adam Kamien, "PM: secure Israel vital", in *The Australian Jewish News*, 2 December 2011.

3.   Steve Rubin, "Is Israel losing the battle?", in *Ynet*, 5 January 2012.

4.   Ibid.

5.   "Israel's uneasy silence", in *The Australian Jewish News*, 23 December 2011.

6.   Alan Hoffman, "A better approach to aliyah", in *Haaretz*, 20 January 2012.

7. Ali Abuminah, "Despite Netanyahu denial, campaign to smear *Haaretz* as 'enemy' already underway", in *Electronic Intifada*, 19 January 2012.

8. Tobias Buck, "Israel's eroding democracy: A shadow is cast", in the *Financial Times*, 8 December 2011.

9. Jordan Michael Smith, "The media consensus on Israel is collapsing", on *Salon*, 21 December 2011.

10. Barak Ravid, "Envoys worldwide feel brunt of Israel's worsening image", in *Haaretz*, 29 December 2011.

11. Jeffrey Goldberg, "Peter Beinart is right – or a one-state solution is now inevitable if settlements continue", in *The Atlantic*, 8 December 2011.

12. "Goldblog vs Peter Beinart Part II", in *The Atlantic*, 18 May 2010.

13. Philip Weiss, "Israel isn't good for the Jews anymore", on *Mondoweiss*, 7 December 2011.

14. Akiva Eldar, "Israel is shaming Australian Jews", in *Haaretz*, 23 January 2012.

15. Shaul Arieli, "In the end, Kahane won", in *Haaretz*, 25 December 2011.

16. Max Blumenthal, "46% of Israelis support settler 'price tag' terror, Congress blames Palestinians for incitement", on www.maxblumenthal.com, on 22 March 2011.

17. Giulio Meotti, "The anti-Israel Jews", on *Ynet*, 5 April 2011.

A Secular Democratic State in Historic Palestine OMAR BARGHOUTI

1. Paulo Freire, *Pedagogy of the Oppressed*. New York 1993.

2. Amos Schocken, "The necessary elimination of Israeli democracy", in *Haaretz*, 25 November 2011.

3. An independent fact-finding committee, commissioned by the League of Arab States and composed of prominent international law experts led by the South African former UN Rapporteur John Dugard, reached the following conclusion: "The Committee found Israel's actions met the requirements for the *actus reus* of the crime of genocide contained in the [UN's 1948] Genocide Convention, in that the IDF was responsible for killing, exterminating and causing serious bodily harm to members of a group – the Palestinians of Gaza. However, the Committee had difficulty in determining whether the acts in question had been committed with a special intent to destroy in whole or in part a national, ethnical or religious group, as required by the Genocide Convention."

4. Avraham Burg, "When the walls come tumbling down", in *Haaretz*, 1 April 2011.

5. www.BDSmovement.net

6. In its most recent session in Cape Town, South Africa, the Russell Tribunal on Palestine concluded that: "Israel's rule over the Palestinian people, wherever they reside, collectively amounts to a single integrated regime of apartheid." http://www.russelltribunalonpalestine.com/en/sessions/south-africa.   Even human rights reports issued by the US State Department have condemned Israel's "institutional, legal and societal discrimination" against the indigenous

Palestinians. For example, see the 2010 report: http://www.state.gov/g/drl/rls/hrrpt/2010/nea/154463.htm

7. Almost the entire spectrum of Palestinian civil society has endorsed these three basic rights in the historic call for boycott, divestment and sanctions (BDS), issued in July 2005. http://www.bdsmovement.net/call#.Ts-hF2O8jVY

8. See, for instance, M. Reiner, Lord Samuel, E. Simon, M. Smilansky, Judah Leon Magnes, *Palestine – Divided or United? The Case for a Bi-National Palestine before the United Nations*, Connecticut, 1983.

9. See, for example: Joseph Edozien, "Ending Economic Apartheid", in *South African New Economics Network*, Vol.8 No.4, 13 October 2008. http://www.sane.org.za/docs/views/showviews.asp?ID=253

10. http://electronicintifada.net/v2/article9134.shtml

11. As argued earlier, these collective rights exclude national rights.

12. Palestinian Central Bureau of Statistics, Palestinians at the end of 2011. http://www.pcbs.gov.ps/Portals/_pcbs/PressRelease/palestineEnd2011E.pdf

13. http://www.unpo.org/content/view/446/83/

14. Amy Maguire, "Law Protecting Rights: Restoring the law of self-determination in the neo-colonial world", in *Law Text Culture*, Volume 12, Issue 1. 2008.

15. UNESCO conference of experts, ibid.

16. Moshe Gorali, "So this Jew, Arab, Georgian and Samaritan go to court", in *Haaretz*, 28 December 2003.

17. Avraham Burg, ibid.

18. BDS National Committee Strategic Position Paper, United Against Apartheid, Colonialism and Occupation, 2009. http://www.bdsmovement.net/files/2011/02/English-BNC_Position_Paper-Durban_Review1.pdf

19. For more on this see: *United against Apartheid, Colonialism and Occupation – Dignity and Justice for the Palestinian People*, Palestinian Civil Society Strategic Position Paper. October 2008. http://bdsmovement.net/files/English-BNC_Position_Paper-Durban_Review.pdf

20. http://www.whatconvention.org/en/conv/0703.htm

21. Maath Musleh, "Co-Resistance vs. Co-Existence", in *Maan News*, 14 July 2011.

How feasible is the one-state solution? GHADA KARMI

1. See for example, Mazin Qumsiyeh, *Sharing the Land of Canaan: Human Rights and the Israeli–Palestinian Struggle*, London 2004; Ali Abunimah, *One Country: a Bold Proposal to End the Israeli–Palestinian Impasse*, New York 2006; Ghada Karmi, *Married to Another Man: Israel's Dilemma in Palestine*, London 2007, Chapters 6 and 7.

2. Daniel Gavron, *The Other Side of Despair: Jews and Arabs in the Promised Land*, Lanham, 2003; Peter Hirschberg, "One-state awakening", in *Haaretz*, 12 December 2003; Daniel Lazare, "The One-state solution", in *Nation*, 11 October 2004.

3. For example, Abraham Burg's new political party of Jewish and Arab Israelis

aimed at transforming Israel (within its 1948 boundaries) into a "state for all its citizens"; see Ari Shavit, *Haaretz,* 23 July 2010.

4.   For example, the "One State in Palestine" group, established in Britain in 2011 by a number of Palestinian and Israeli scholars and activists. See http://web. me.com/haimbresheeth/One_State_in_Palestine/Welcome.html

5.   Nir Arieli, *Haaretz,* 9 February 2010; Talia Sasson, *Yediot Ahronot,* 14 September 2010.

6.   Report in *Al-Quds al-Arabi,* 31 December 2010.

7.   "Palestinian refugees, PLO Negotiations Affairs Department, November, 2010.

8.   "The US administration presents a plan approved by Arab states and under international auspices to end the Palestinian refugee problem", *al-Quds al-Arabi,* 16 April, 2010.

9.   Zuhair Andraos, *al-Quds al-Arabi,* 11 February, 2010.

10.   Salim Tamari, "The Dubious Lure of Binationalism", in Mahdi Abdul Hadi, ed., *Palestinian–Israeli Impasse: Exploring Alternative Solutions to the Palestine–Israel Conflict* (Jerusalem: PASSIA, 2005), pp. 67–73; Jeff Halper, "A Middle Eastern Confederation: A Regional 'Two-stage' Approach to the Israeli–Palestinian Conflict" on *Arab Media Internet Network,* 15 December 2002; "Abed Rabbo Rules out Bi-national State", on Palestine Media Centre official Web site, January 2004; Alexander Jacobson, "A Bi-national State Here?", in *Haaretz,* 29 January 2010.

11.   *The Peace Index,* October 2003, published by the Tami Steinmetz Center for Peace Research, Tel Aviv University; "Peace Index—Demographic Fears Favor Unilateral Separation", in *Haaretz,* 7 December 2003. The 2007 poll is reported in *Haaretz,* 3 July 2007

12.   Jeff Halper, "One State: Preparing for a Post Road Map Struggle Against Apartheid," a 2003 paper given at the UN International Conference on Civil Society in Support of the Palestinian People, New York, 5 September 2003, http://www.fromoccupiedpalestine.org/node/772.

13.   See John Mearsheimer's lecture at the Palestine Center, Washington, D.C., 29 April 2010, http://www.thejerusalemfund.org/ht/d/ContentDetails/i/10418

14.   Uri Avnery and Azmi Bishara "A Binational State? God Forbid!" *Journal of Palestine Studies* 28, no.4 (Summer 1999), pp. 55–60.

15.   "Palestinians Ready to Push for One State", in *Associated Press,* 9 January 2004.

16.   A number of those people calling for the dissolution of the PA have done so for tactical reasons rather than in support of a one-state solution. Ali Jarbawi, a PA minister in Salam Fayyad's government and former Birzeit University academic, was the first to call for the dissolution of the PA in 1999; see his "Remaining Palestinian Options", in *The Arab World Geographer* 8, no.3 (2005), http://arab-worldgeographer.socsci.uva.nl/content.htm#awg8182. Also see Rami Khoury, "Dissolve the Palestinian Authority", in *Daily Star,* 20 February 2008.

17.   Zuhair Andaros, *Al-Quds al-Arabi,* 16 August 2010.

18.   Moshe Arens, "Is There Another Option?", in *Haaretz,* 2 June 2010; Moshe Arens,

"Give Palestinians Israeli Citizenship", in *Jewish Chronicle*, 5 March 2010.

Zionism After Israel JEREMIAH HABER

1. Dimitry Shumsky, "Brith Shalom's Uniqueness Reconsidered: Hans Kohn and Autonomist Zionism", in *Jewish History* 25 (2011): pp. 339–53, esp. p. 339.

2. B. Katznelson, "On Issues of the Political Regime in Palestine," *Writings*, vol. 2, Tel Aviv 1946, pp. 150–67 (Hebrew). Translated in Shumsky, p. 345.

3. Y. Gorny, *From Binational Society to Jewish State: Federal Concepts in Zionist Political Thought, 1920–1990, and the Jewish People*, Leiden/Boston 2006.

4. V. Jabotinsky, *The Jewish War Front*, London 1940, pp. 216–8. Translated in Shumsky, p. 346.

5. O. Yiftachel, *Ethnocracy: Land and Identity Politics in Israel/Palestine*, Philadelphia 2006. (In this essay I use the expressions "Arab Israeli" and "Palestinian Israeli" interchangeably.)

6. I. Lustick, *Arabs in the Jewish State: Israel's Control of a National Minority*, Austin, 1980, p. 276, n. 26. Cited in B. White's useful synthesis, *Palestinians in Israel: Segregation, Discrimination, and Democracy*, London 2012, p. 26.

7. In 1996, for example, Arabs voted almost unanimously for Ehud Barak, who later formed a government without even bothering to meet with representatives of the Arab parties. Unlike anti-Zionist ultra-orthodox parties, Arab parties have never been offered a place in the ruling coalitions, and rarely, if ever, are they even invited to talks. In the 1992 elections, the Rabin government received the support of two Arab political parties, *outside of the coalition*, in exchange for increased allocations to the Arab sector. See D. Elazar and S. Sandler, *Israel at the Polls, 1992*, Lanham 1995, p. 37.

8. I. Peleg and D. Waxman, *Israel's Palestinians: The Conflict Within*, New York 2011, pp. 21–2.

9. A. Shlaim, *The Iron Wall: Israel and the Arab World*, New York, 2000, p. 35.

10. Ibid., p. 245.

11. Interview with Dov Weisglas, in *Haaretz*, 6 Oct 2011 https://www.haaretz.com/2004-10-06/ty-article/top-pm-aide-gaza-plan-aims-to-freeze-the-peace-process/0000017f-e56c-dea7-adff-f5ff1fc40000

12. http://www.haaretz.com/hasen/spages/711997.html

13. http://www.geneva-accord.org/mainmenu/english

14. For other non-statist Zionist options, see N. Pianko, *Zionism and the Roads Not Taken: Rawidowicz, Kaplan, Kohn*, Bloomington, 2010.

15. See A. Yakobson and A. Rubenstein, *Israel and the Family of Nations: the Jewish Nation-state and Human Rights*, London, 2009; and various publications of R. Gavison.

16. See M. Berent, "The Ethnic Democracy Debate: How Unique Is Israel?", in *Nations and Nationalism*. 16 (2010): pp. 657–74.

Acknowledgements

This collection is the culmination of a long journey. Initially conceived years ago with Phil Weiss and Adam Horowitz, from the invaluable Mondoweiss website, it developed organically into an idea that we both nurtured.

Saqi Books with Lynn Gaspard have been stellar publishers who both support and understand the material. Thank you for seeing our vision from the beginning. Alice Waugh has been a savvy copy-editor.

Thank you to all the contributors, from many corners of the globe, who remain dedicated to peace in the Middle East and are unafraid to publicly challenge accepted truths. This book would never have materialised without your thoughtful commitment to justice. Your vision permeates *After Zionism*.

To the myriad of friends, colleagues, bloggers, dissidents and activists who dedicate their lives to imagining a better, one-state tomorrow for Palestine and Israel, we hope this book will be a useful guide in bringing justice to the occupied and peace to the oppressed.

Index

References to notes are indicated by n.